Sewing
for Fashion Designers

Sewing
for Fashion Designers

Anette Fischer

Laurence King Publishing

First published in Great Britain by

Laurence King Student & Professional
An imprint of Quercus Editions Ltd
Carmelite House
50 Victoria Embankment
London EC4Y 0DZ

An Hachette UK company

A CIP catalogue record for this book is available
from the British Library

UK HB ISBN 978-1-78067-230-4
US HB ISBN 978-1-78067-231-1

10 9 8 7 6

Book design by The Urban Ant
Photography for step by steps by James Stevens Sample makers Valentina Elizabeth
and Sue Turoff Line drawings by Gary Kaye
Picture research Evi Peroulaki

Printed and bound in China by C&C Offset Printing Co., Ltd.

Papers used by Quercus are from well-managed forests and other responsible sources.

Contents

6 Introduction

8 Chapter 1
Getting Started
10 The Studio
11 Pins and Needles
14 Cutting Equipment
16 Marking Tools
18 Measuring Tapes and Rulers
20 The Right Sewing Machine
   for the Job
23 Four Main Machine Stitches
24 Machines for Special Tasks
26 What to Watch out for when
   Stitching Seams
28 Pressing Equipment
30 Taking Body Measurements
34 How to Work With Patterns
36 Understanding Symbols
   on Patterns
39 Seam Allowance
40 Hem Allowance
42 Understanding the Fabric
44 How to Use the Grain Line
46 Preparing the Fabric
48 Pattern Layout on the Fabric
52 How to Mark the Pattern onto
   the Fabric
55 Cutting Out
56 Industry Production Methods

58 Chapter 2
Materials and Sewing Supplies
59 Fabrics
62 Cotton
64 Wool
66 Silk
68 Linen
70 Man-made and Synthetic Fibres
72 Textured Fabrics
74 Knitted and Jersey Fabrics
76 Lining Fabrics
78 Lace
80 Haberdashery
91 Supporting Materials
103 Corsetry and Underpinnings

110 Chapter 3
The Basic Stitches
111 Hand-Sewing Techniques
119 Machine Seams and Seam Finishes

144 Chapter 4
Sewing Techniques
145 Garment Construction
146 Gathers, Pleats, Tucks and Darts
156 The Neckline
165 The Waistline
177 Pockets

192 The Sleeve
204 Hemlines
212 Lining
224 Fastenings
245 The Finishing Touch

246 Chapter 5
Fabric- and Cut-Specific
Techniques
247 Working with Fabrics
248 Denim
254 Knitted and Stretch-Woven Fabrics
262 Transparent and Semi-Transparent
   Fabrics
270 Lace, Sequined and Beaded Fabrics
276 Napped and Pile Fabrics
282 Leather and Fur
290 Felted and Non-Woven Fabrics
294 Latex, Neoprene and Plastic
   Materials
300 Patterned Fabrics
306 Mixing Fabrics
310 Bias-Cut Fabrics

312 Glossary
315 Further Reading
316 Index
319 Picture Credits
320 Acknowledgements

Introduction

Sewing for Fashion Designers is a comprehensive guide to garment construction related closely to contemporary fashion and combined with up-to-date manufacturing methods. The book provides essential skills for basic construction methods and explores techniques used within the fashion industry, showing how basic sewing methods are applied at a designer level. Once the basic methods are mastered, the sewer can explore more advanced techniques, which can be challenged to achieve individual design ideas.

The book offers instructions, images and illustrations to assist fashion educators, students and professionals working within the fashion industry. It will also be invaluable to the sewer with an interest in fashion. To support each topic, photographs of designer garments highlight garment construction techniques and the materials used.

A pinboard is useful for keeping pattern pieces organized and easily accessible.

Chapter 1 will introduce you to the sewing and pressing equipment used in fashion studios and the fashion industry. A guide on taking body measurements leads into working with paper patterns and understanding their symbols. A guide to seam and hem allowances will assist you when drafting patterns. Basic cutting-out techniques, the use of the grain line and how to prepare the fabric for cutting are all covered, plus pattern layouts and how to mark the pattern pieces.

Chapter 2 introduces textiles, including natural and man-made fibres, blends and fabric finishing. It covers haberdashery, explaining different types and where they are placed on garments. The reader is encouraged to explore other possibilities and materials for decoration and fastening. Also discussed in this chapter are supporting materials and where and how to apply them, quilting and padding techniques and corsetry and underpinnings, including a guide to constructing a corset.

The basic stitches are explored in **Chapter 3**, with hand sewing followed by machine seams and seam finishes. This chapter prepares the reader for sewing, with a section on how to match up seams, with examples of reducing seam bulk, and how to construct shaped seams. A section on taping seams leads to facings, exploring the different shapes to help you make the right choice when using a facing as an edge finish.

Chapter 4 covers sewing techniques. *Gathers, Pleats, Tucks and Darts* shows how fullness can be controlled to shape a garment onto the body. *The Neckline* introduces basic collar shapes from step-by-step instructions for a shirt collar to finishing necklines with a facing. A range of waistband finishes are shown in *The Waistline* including fastening options. *Pockets* are presented with step-by-step sewing instructions, while *The Sleeve* covers how to insert a sleeve, cuff openings and constructions. Various hemming methods, each related to garment hem shapes and fabric types, are demonstrated in *Hemlines*.

Lining gives a good overview of how and when to use a lining, full and partial lining, what to look out for and how to line a jacket. The placement and use of all types of *Fastenings* are presented with step-by-step illustrations in the next section. Chapter 4 ends with *The Finishing Touch* stressing the importance of final pressing.

Chapter 5 explores *Fabric- and Cut-Specific Techniques*. The specific materials discussed are: denim; knitted and stretch-woven fabrics; transparent and semi-transparent fabrics; lace, sequined and beaded fabrics; napped and pile fabrics; leather and fur; felted and non-woven fabrics; latex, neoprene and plastic materials; and patterned fabrics. Mixing fabrics within a garment and bias cutting are also discussed.

This chapter covers the specific construction of each material and what to watch out for when buying, and guides the reader through the relevant pattern-cutting, cutting-out and construction techniques, including fabric-specific seams, hems and edge finishes and a guide to fastening ideas.

The sewing techniques in this book will provide a solid base for a career in fashion design. With them, the sewer is free to begin experimenting, breaking the rules and exploring new and more advanced sewing. This is the key to innovative garment design.

Getting Started

1

The Studio

The studio area, also called the fashion atelier, is the heart of all fashion businesses. This is the place where everything comes together. Depending on the size of the company this space is shared mostly between the pattern cutter, sample machinist, studio manager and sometimes the designer.

The skill base found in a studio ranges from translating fashion drawings into patterns to sample making. The studio has all the materials and tools to translate creative ideas into the finished piece.

A fashion studio usually has a cutting table big enough to cut out a floor-length garment. Most designers have industrial sewing machines and an overlocker, as well as a pressing table with a steam iron. A well-stocked studio area provides basic fabrics for sampling, linings and a range of fusible materials. Drawers contain an array of fastenings such as buttons, zips and closures, as well as tapes and threads for all purposes.

Whether sewing in a professional studio or at home it is always a good idea to organize the space. Make sure the sewing machine and iron station are set up next to each other and that there is enough table space for cutting. The floor is not suitable for a good cutting result. Also make sure there is good-quality lighting. If possible choose a daylight lamp or any high-intensity light.

This chapter will introduce the reader to the equipment necessary for constructing garments. It will explain its usage and place within a production line. Sewing essentials, tools for measuring and marking, machinery and pressing equipment are also introduced.

Fashion students working in a studio. The large table is essential both for cutting out and as a general work surface.

Pins and Needles

Pins and needles come in different shapes and sizes to suit all kinds of sewing tasks. Pins are used to attach pieces of material together temporarily. The job of a needle is to bring a thread through material for either temporary or permanent attachment.

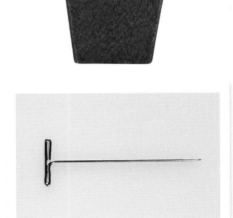

Pins

Consider the following when choosing a pin:
- Fabric weight.
- Texture of fabric.
- The job in hand – modelling on the stand, temporarily attaching layers of fabric.

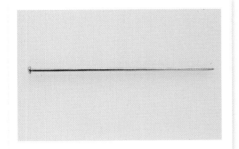

Steel Pins are used to pin all kinds of materials together, as well as fixing fabric onto a mannequin when working with design ideas on the stand. They come in different sizes for different tasks. A long pin, for example, is used to pass through several layers of fabric.

A **Brass Lace Pin** is very fine and will avoid creating holes in lightweight materials such as chiffon.

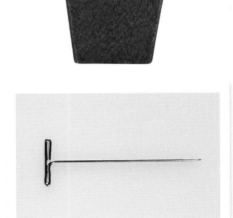

T-Head Pins can be used for loose or open weave fabrics as well as loose-knitted materials. The T-head will make sure that the pin stays in place.

A **Safety Pin** will not get lost in loose-woven fabric or knitted material, unlike a straight pin.

Leather, PVC and plastic materials should not be temporarily pinned together as the pin can leave a mark. Instead use **Paperclips** or **Bulldog Clips** to hold these materials together.

Pins are hard to keep in one place. Use a pincushion for easy access and to keep the sewing space safe and tidy. A **Magnet** is handy to pick up pins and needles.

Needles

Consider the following points when choosing a hand-sewing needle:
• Weight of fabric.
• Structure of fabric.
• Type of thread – size and weight.
• Design intention.

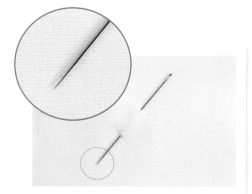

The **Sharps Hand-Sewing Needle** is a general needle used for a wide range of hand sewing tasks.

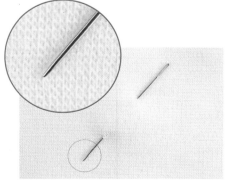

The difference between a **Ballpoint Needle** and a sharps needle is that the point is rounded instead of sharp. The ballpoint slides between the yarns instead of piercing, and potentially damaging or breaking, the yarn. Ballpoint needles are used for knitted fabrics and loose-woven materials.

Betweens are short needles that produce short stitches. This needle is used in detailed handwork such as quilting and tailoring.

Beading Hand-Sewing Needles have a sharp point and are very fine and long. The needle eye is very narrow enabling it to fit through the hole of a bead. The needle is long so that a number of beads can be strung at the same time.

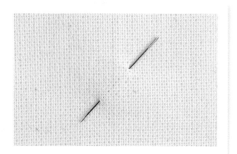

Embroidery Needles are medium-sized and designed with a long oval eye to carry multiple strands of thread and thicker yarns.

Chenille Needles are thick, short and sharp-pointed with a large oval eye to work with thick yarns, embroidery floss and several strands of thread. The sharp point helps to penetrate closely woven fabrics.

The **Tapestry Needle** is short, with a blunt end so it can pass through loose-woven materials without tearing or catching. It has a long oval eye for using multiple strands of thread. Tapestry needles are also used to join sections of wool or knitted garments together.

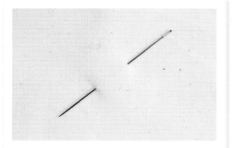

Straws, also called **Milliners Needles**, are traditionally used for hat making. Straws are long and ideal for smocking, gathering, basting and tacking.

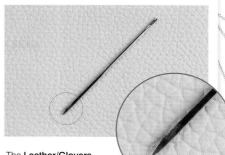

The **Leather/Glovers Needle** is medium length with a triangular point. The three-faced point is designed to pierce leather without tearing it. The needle can also be used on plastic or imitation leather.

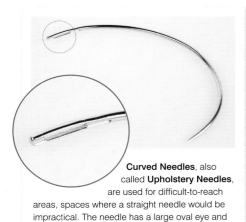

Curved Needles, also called **Upholstery Needles**, are used for difficult-to-reach areas, spaces where a straight needle would be impractical. The needle has a large oval eye and a sharp point at the other end.

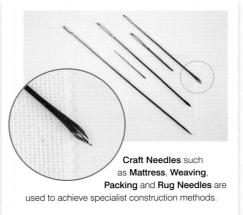

Craft Needles such as **Mattress**, **Weaving**, **Packing** and **Rug Needles** are used to achieve specialist construction methods.

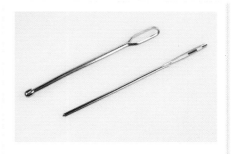

Bodkins are large needles with a big eye for threading elastics and ribbon through channels, casings and open weaves, as well as knitted materials.

To make threading needles easier, especially fine-eyed needles, use a **Needle Threader**.

A **Thimble/Tailor's Thimble** is a metal cap with an indented surface that fits on the tip of the middle finger. Always use a thimble when hand sewing, as it will protect the finger when pushing the needle through the fabric. The dents in the thimble prevent the needle from slipping off.

Cutting Equipment

A good-quality cutting tool makes the job in hand trouble-free. Always consider the blade needed for the type of material to be cut. Blades come with serrated, zigzag, waved or straight edges. Make sure that the blades are sharp, as dull blades can damage the material and slow the process down. Never use fabric shears on paper, as it will blunt the blades.

Paper Scissors are for paper and card only.

Shears come in two sizes, medium and heavy; the choice of size depends on the weight of the fabric. Bent-handled shears allow the blade to lie flat on the cutting surface; they are more comfortable to use and allow better control.

Serrated Shears are used on fine fabrics. The serrated blade grips slippery, fine fabric. The serrated edge must never be sharpened.

A **Utility Knife** or **Craft Knife** is used to cut leather. A **Leather Shear** can also be used to cut leather, suede and plastics.

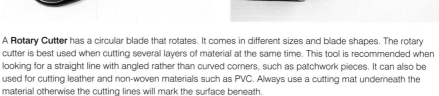

A **Rotary Cutter** has a circular blade that rotates. It comes in different sizes and blade shapes. The rotary cutter is best used when cutting several layers of material at the same time. This tool is recommended when looking for a straight line with angled rather than curved corners, such as patchwork pieces. It can also be used for cutting leather and non-woven materials such as PVC. Always use a cutting mat underneath the material otherwise the cutting lines will mark the surface beneath.

Pinking Shears have two zigzag blades for finishing raw seams and seam allowances. The zigzag edge will help prevent some fabrics from fraying (see Pinked Finish, page 123).

Embroidery Scissors are small in size with a sharp-pointed blade, for needlework.

A **Thread Clipper** is useful for thread cutting and handy to have next to the sewing machine. The clipper has two pointed blades with a self-opening spring.

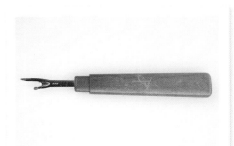

A **Seam Ripper** is a small tool with a bladed hook on one side used to unpick stitches. The seam ripper is also used to open machine buttonholes.

The **Cutting Mat** is used in combination with the rotary cutter and craft knife to protect the cutting surface and the blade.

A **Revolving Hole-Punch** is perfect for punching round holes into material. It has a rotating head with different-sized holes.

Marking Tools

Marking equipment is used to identify information such as placement points and positioning marks on paper patterns and is also used to transfer all the requirements onto the fabric to ensure a good fit. Different tools are used for marking paper patterns and fabric.

Marking tools for the paper pattern

The **Pattern Notcher** is used for making marking points on paper patterns. It takes small cuts out of the paper's edge to indicate balance points, for example, such as at the position of the waist or to show seam allowance. The balance points identify where seams match together to ensure a good fit.

A **Pattern Drill** is for punching holes through the paper pattern. It is used for a variety of markings, including the position of pockets.

The **Pattern Punch** is used to cut a hole into pattern pieces to facilitate hanging.

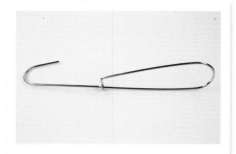

A set of pattern pieces can be collected and hung on a **Pattern Hook**.

Marking tools for fabric

Tailor's Chalk is used to apply temporary markings onto fabric. Although the chalk does brush off, it can sometimes remain. Tailor's chalk should, therefore, be used primarily on the wrong side of the fabric to avoid permanent staining. It comes in several colours and forms.

Chalk Pencils come in a range of different colours. These are good for marking placement points.

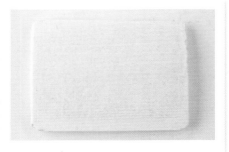

The advantage of using a **Vanishing Chalk** is that the marking will disappear by itself over time, or immediately upon ironing. Vanishing chalk can be used on the right or wrong side of the fabric, but should always be tested to ensure that the chalk can be removed without leaving any marks.

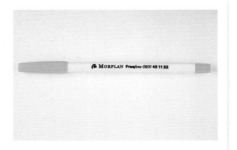

The same considerations for using vanishing chalk also apply to a **Disappearing-Ink Pen**. The marks will disappear by themselves over a couple of days. The marks from some pens will react to water and disappear immediately.

Tracing Paper, also known as **Carbon Copy Paper**, is used in combination with a tracing wheel. It is used to transfer markings from one piece of fabric to another (see Marking with carbon copy paper and a tracing wheel, page 54).

A **Tracing Wheel** is used with carbon paper to transfer markings from paper to paper, or from paper to fabric.

An **Awl** can be used for marking points on paper and materials. It is usually used to mark positioning points by punching through the paper pattern onto the fabric to indicate, for example, the end of a dart. The awl will slip between the threads of the fabric to leave a small hole.

Measuring Tapes and Rulers

A range of measuring tools and rulers is available to ensure correct measurements as well as balanced curves and straight lines. As purchasing all of these could be very costly a combination of two or three rulers should be enough to cover most purposes.

The **Tape Measure** is a flexible tool for measuring both straight and curved lines. A **Dressmaker's Tape** has a small metal cap on both ends.

The **Tailor's Tape Measure** has a metal piece on one end about 5cm (2in) long; this is used for taking the measurement of the inside leg up to the crotch.

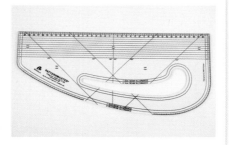

The **Pattern Master** is a ruler that has both a true right angle and a curved edge. It is mostly used for pattern drafting, but can also be useful in garment construction for tasks such as marking hemlines.

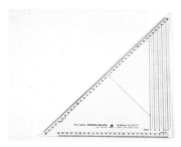

A **Set Square** is used to draw lines at 45- and 90-degree angles to each other. This ruler is very handy when cutting bias binding strips.

French Curves have a range of curved edges. These little rulers can be used to correct the run of a curve, such as a neckline or a collar shape.

A **Metre Stick** is a long ruler. It comes in handy when establishing the length of a garment from the floor, and for working out the correct grain line when placing patterns onto fabric. It is also a good tool to measure a length of fabric from the roll. The metre stick is mainly used for pattern drafting, for drawing the grain line and for long straight lines such as trouser legs.

An **L-Square Ruler** is used when a set square is too small for the job. This ruler is a tailor's favourite and is found in all tailoring studios.

The **Sewing Gauge** is a short metal or acrylic ruler, with a sliding tab that can be set at any point along the ruler. This small ruler is used to measure hemlines or the distance between buttonholes. It can also be used for measuring space for quilting, gathering or smocking lines.

The **Skirt Marker** is an adjustable tool used to measure hemlines. The skirt marker has a puffer attached, which puffs a chalk line onto the garment to help create even hems.

WHAT TO PUT IN YOUR SEWING BOX

It is not necessary to purchase all the equipment and tools described here at once; your sewing box can be built up over time. The items below would make a good starter kit.

- Steel pins and magnet.
- Sharps hand-sewing needle and thimble.
- Paper scissors and fabric shears.
- Thread clipper and embroidery scissors.
- Seam ripper.
- Tailor's chalk and disappearing pen.
- Tracing wheel.
- Awl.
- Tape measure.
- Pattern master.
- Metre stick.

The Right Sewing Machine for the Job

Sewing machines and overlockers are essential in today's garment production. A domestic sewing machine or overlocker is good enough for producing sample garments. However, when going into mass-production an industrial sewing machine and overlocker are required, as they are more efficient. A wide range is available to cover all kinds of sewing tasks. The machines usually come with basic attachments, and, if required, specific attachments such as a binding foot or a special stitch needle can be purchased separately (check the attachment will be compatible with your machine).

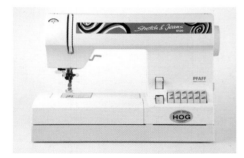

Domestic Sewing Machines are perfect for the beginner (left). The sewing speed is not as fast as an industrial sewing machine, and is therefore easier to control. Most domestic machines produce a lock stitch, with adjustable stitch length, which can form a straight or zigzag stitch. Some can perform different kinds of embroidery stitches, as well as making buttonholes.

The domestic sewing machine is used for:
- Joining garment seams together.
- Sewing all woven and semi-stretch materials.
- Stitching on one, two or more layers of material.
- Decorating material with embroidery stitching.
- Any part of garment construction, not only the edges.

Industrial Sewing Machines, also called *Flatbed Machines*, are sturdy machines for mass-production with a high sewing speed (right). This machine is set into a table, whereas the domestic sewing machine is easily portable. On a flatbed machine the sewing foot can be lifted by pushing the leg against a pedal brake, located underneath the machine table. This is a time-saving device, allowing the practitioner to have both hands free to manoeuvre the fabric into different positions. By contrast, on the domestic machine the foot presser has to be lifted by hand. The flatbed also has a bobbin system that winds a bobbin while sewing. This machine is designed to save time and increase productivity.

The flatbed machine is used for:
- Joining garment seams together.
- Sewing all woven and semi-stretch materials.
- Stitching on one, two or more layers of material, with adjustable stitch length.
- Any part of garment construction, not only the edges.

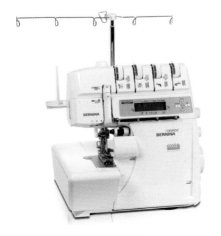

The *Overlocker* or *Serger* is mostly used for finishing edges and to join seams on knitted garments (left). It has a two-blade cutting system that works like a pair of scissors, trimming fabric and overhanging threads while sewing. The overlocker can be set up as a 3-thread, 4-thread, or 5-thread overlocker. This depends on the material and garment use, as well as design.

The overlocker is used for:
- Sewing all kinds of knitted materials as well as woven fabrics.
- Overcasting the fabric edge to prevent it from fraying (with a 3-thread overlocker).
- Stitching a seam allowance together, as well as overcasting it at the same time (with a 4-thread overlocker).
- Chain stitching a seam, overcast stitches, or to create a roll hem effect (with a 5-thread machine).

Sewing machine needles

Sewing machine needles are designed to suit different kinds of materials. They come in different sizes ranging from 60/8 for fine and sheer materials to 100/16 for heavyweight material. The size and point of the needle should correspond to the weight and type of material, as well as the thickness of the thread. The sharp, ballpoint and wedge point needles are available both for domestic and industrial sewing machines and overlockers.

Universal needles are a general-purpose needle and have a slightly blunter point than a sharp needle. They can be used to sew most woven and stretch fabrics.

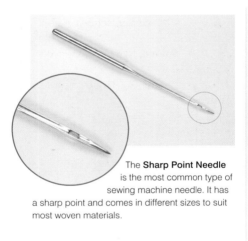

The **Sharp Point Needle** is the most common type of sewing machine needle. It has a sharp point and comes in different sizes to suit most woven materials.

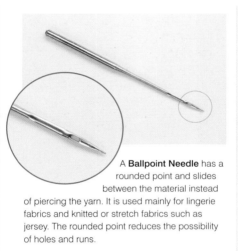

A **Ballpoint Needle** has a rounded point and slides between the material instead of piercing the yarn. It is used mainly for lingerie fabrics and knitted or stretch fabrics such as jersey. The rounded point reduces the possibility of holes and runs.

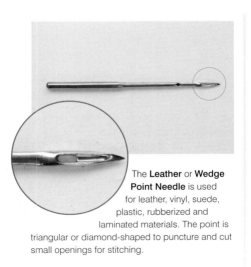

The **Leather** or **Wedge Point Needle** is used for leather, vinyl, suede, plastic, rubberized and laminated materials. The point is triangular or diamond-shaped to puncture and cut small openings for stitching.

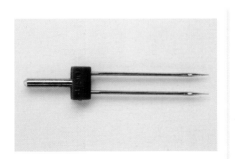

The **Twin Needle** is available with a sharp point or ballpoint and consists of two single needles inserted into an attachment to create a double stitch line. Both industrial and domestic machines use this needle. The twin needle is used mostly for topstitching.

TIP

Depending on the sewing machine, the needle eye can face different directions. However, irrespective of the direction, always thread a machine needle from the long groove to the short scarf (see below). If a machine is not threaded correctly problems can arise with thread snapping, or the top thread skipping stitches.

Always ensure that the tip of the needle is not blunt, bent or dull, as this can lead to fabric being damaged, skipped stitches and thread snapping.

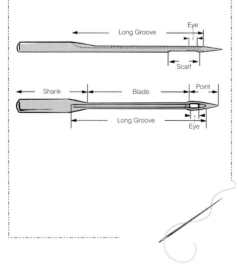

Specific machine feet

The choice of foot depends on the sewing task and design required. Teflon-coated feet facilitate the smooth movement of the material; others create a particular type of stitch, and, if required, can duplicate the appearance and technique of a hand stitch.

A **One-Sided Zipper Foot** is available as either a right- or left-sided attachment. It allows stitches to be sewn close to the raised edge of the zipper teeth. The one-sided zipper foot is used for sewing centred, lapped, open-ended and fly-front zips. This foot can also be used for any sewing close to a raised edge. For more on zips, see page 238.

The **Invisible Zip Foot**, also called the **Concealed Zip Foot**, is used to insert invisible zips. The teeth of the zip slide through the grooves underneath the foot and unroll the zipper in front of the needle, enabling the needle to stitch closely under the teeth (see also page 244).

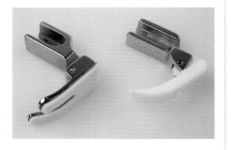

The **Teflon Foot** is a fabric-specific tool, used on materials that stick, such as synthetic leather. Its non-stick coating eliminates any drag of the foot moving over the surface.

A **Binding Attachment** has a long cone that guides and folds a bias strip in different sizes. This tool makes it easy to apply a binding to a fabric edge or hemline. See page 122 for more on bias binding.

The **Compensation Foot** has different levels on the bottom of the foot, with one side shorter than the other to compensate for an uneven surface. Use this foot when sewing a sink stitch, for example, on a waistband finish (see also page 251).

The **Pin Hem Foot**, also called a **Roll Hem Foot**, is used for lightweight fabric edge finishing. The foot double-folds the fabric; the raw edge is fed through the foot attachment, which then completes the folding and stitching.

The **Piping Foot** has a groove on the bottom of the foot to allow the piping cord to be fed through while attaching it to the material.

A **Gathering Foot** creates soft gathers. The underside of the foot is raised behind the needle to allow for the gathered fabric. The amount of gathering is regulated by the stitch length.

Four Main Machine Stitches

Machine stitches can be functional or decorative. They can be seen on the face of a garment or concealed within. There are four principal plain stitches: chain stitch, overlock stitch, lockstitch and cover stitch. See Chapter 3 for more stitch types.

The size and type of stitch depends on:
- The design and style of the garment.
- The function and use of the garment.
- Fabric weight and character.
- Care, lifespan and quality of the garment.
- Construction technique.
- Production budget.
- Availability of machine attachments.

Chain stitch

Chain stitch is formed from a single thread interlocking with itself on the opposite side of the fabric.
- A flexible stitch, suited for use on loosely woven fabrics and knits.
- Not very secure and can be removed by pulling on the thread end.
- Found on domestic and industrial sewing machines.

Lockstitch

Two threads form the lockstitch, one passing through the needle and the other coming up from the bobbin, interlocking midway between the surfaces of the material.
- Looks the same on the top and bottom.
- Much more stable than the chain stitch and is, therefore, the most widely used in the industry.
- Can be used for all woven fabrics, skins and semi-stretch materials.
- Not ideal for stretch and knitted materials as it has very little give.

Overlock stitch

The overlock stitch can be formed with three to five threads. A 3-thread overlock stitch has two loops and one needle thread, and a 4-thread has two loops and two needle threads. The 5-thread overlock stitch has three loops and two needle threads.
- Used to finish raw edges.
- Its stitch formation produces a flexible stitch for joining seams of knitted and stretch materials.
- Found on domestic and industrial overlockers.

Cover stitch

Cover stitch is created by two or more needles and one or two loopers interlocking, with one looper forming a bottom cover stitch against the needle thread.
- Mostly used in sports and leisurewear to attach trims, finish hems and join seams together.
- Used to join all kinds of knitted and stretch materials.

BOBBIN AND BOBBIN CASE

The bobbin and bobbin case sit under the machine needle. The bobbin has thread spooled onto it and can either be placed into a fixed bobbin case in the machine or, more commonly, inserted into a removable bobbin case.

Machines for Special Tasks

A wide range of specialized machinery is available to cover all the design eventualities of garment construction. These machines are mainly used in the fashion industry on mass-production lines. They cover specific areas and, having powerful motors, are faster and more durable.

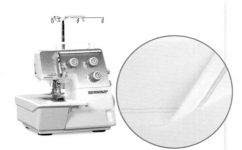

A **Cover Stitch Machine** is mainly used to sew garment seams together and, at the same time, prevent seam allowance and hemlines from unravelling, rolling or fraying.
The cover stitch machine is used:
• To join seams of stretch fabric and knitted materials together.
• To finish hemlines and raw edges.
• To join exposed seams on the right side of the garment for design or decorative purposes.

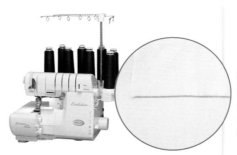

The **Superlock**, sometimes called the **Baby Lock**, creates an unturned edge finish. Any overlocking machine can also be set up as a superlock; the difference is in the density of the stitch formation. The superlock has a very tight stitch formation and a narrow stitch length.
The superlock is used:
• For finishing knitted fabric edges or hemlines, creating a frilly, unturned finish.
• To reduce production costs when using fine and sheer fabrics such as chiffon, avoiding the need for hand finishing.
• To create a certain look on a garment finish, matching the style.

A **Leather Machine** has a stronger motor than a flatbed machine, which ensures that the sewing needle can penetrate several layers of leather. It also provides a larger stitch size, up to 1cm (⅜in).
The leather machine is used:
• To work leather, vinyl, suede, plastic, rubberized and laminated materials.
• For joining garment seams together.
• For finishing hemlines and topstitching.
• For stitching one, two or more layers together, on any part of the garment construction and not only on the edge.
• For shoe and bag construction.

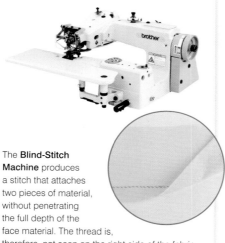

The **Blind-Stitch Machine** produces a stitch that attaches two pieces of material, without penetrating the full depth of the face material. The thread is, therefore, not seen on the right side of the fabric.
The blind-stitch machine is used:
• For turning up hemlines.
• To apply non-fusible interfacing to a collar, lapel or any jacket or coat front.

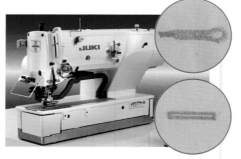

A **Buttonhole and Keyhole Machine** produces a wide range of buttonholes in different sizes and stitch densities. The machine can also be set up to cut the buttonhole open.
A buttonhole machine produces:
• Fly-bar end buttonholes.
• Keyhole buttonholes with or without a bar-tack finish.
• Buttonholes with gimp or cord filler, with or without a bar-tack finish.
• Open-end buttonholes.

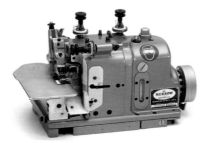

The **Purl Merrow** machine produces a decorative edge finish by sewing a narrow rolled hem on light- to medium-weight fabrics. The finish has a very tight stitch and can also be ruffled to create a 'lettuce edge' look.
The Purl Merrow machine is used:
• For finishing knitted fabric and woven fabric edges or hemlines.
• To reduce production costs when using fine and sheer fabrics such as chiffon, avoiding the need for hand finishing.
• To create a ruffled edge on a garment.

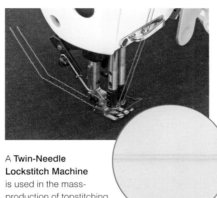

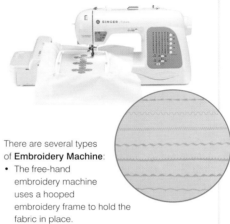

The **Button Sewing Machine** is used in mass-production, such as on a shirt production line. The machine-attached buttons have one drawback; they are not as secure as hand sewn buttons. The button sewing machine is used:

* To attach flat buttons onto garments.

A **Twin-Needle Lockstitch Machine** is used in the mass-production of topstitching effects.
A twin-needle lockstitch machine is used:

* For all woven and semi-stretch materials.
* For joining garment seams together and, at the same time, sewing two parallel rows a fixed distance apart simultaneously.
* To reinforce seams by topstitching
* To create a flat fell seam.

There are several types of **Embroidery Machine**:

* The free-hand embroidery machine uses a hooped embroidery frame to hold the fabric in place.
* A digital embroidery machine uses specialized computer software to recreate photographs or picture designs.
* Pre-programmed decorative stitches can be found on both domestic and industrial machines.

What to Watch out for when Stitching Seams

When sewing fabrics together problems can occur when the thread tension is not correct, the needle or bobbin is not inserted properly, or the machine is not threaded correctly. Threading instructions for sewing machines and overlockers are included in the machine's manual and should be consulted before you start sewing.

Always stitch a sample first:
- Use a sample piece of the material you are about to sew.
- Check you have chosen the right needle size and thread to suit the fabric type and weight.

- Always place two layers of fabric together when producing a sewing sample to check thread tension, needle type and stitch length.

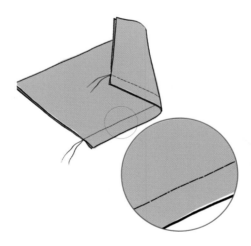

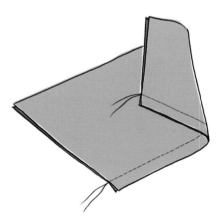

Correct thread tension
A correct thread tension looks smooth and flat on both sides of the seam. The needle and bobbin threads interlock midway between the surfaces of the material.

Needle thread tension is too loose
The needle thread needs to be tightened if the stitching thread shows loops on the underside. On the other hand if the needle thread is too tight, it will pull up the bobbin thread and also show it on the topside. If this is the case, then loosen the needle thread tension, but avoid adjusting both needle and bobbin tension.

Bobbin thread tension is too tight
When loops form on the topside of the seam the bobbin thread needs loosening.

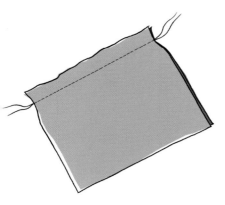

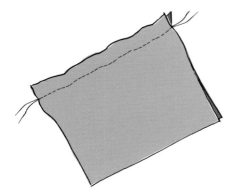

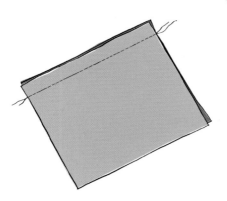

Seam puckering

If seams on lighter weight fabrics are prone to puckering, loosen the thread tension a little and adjust to a larger stitch length.

Fabric stretching

This can happen when sewing fabrics cut on the bias or with some stretch. Make sure you only lead the fabric through the sewing process and gently push the fabric towards the foot; avoid excessive pulling and pushing. It might also occur if the pressure on the foot is too tight, in which case loosen the foot pressure.

Skipping stitches

Many factors can lead to skipped stitches. Check if the needle has been inserted in the right direction, is the right size and type, that the point is not dull or bent and the machine is threaded correctly.

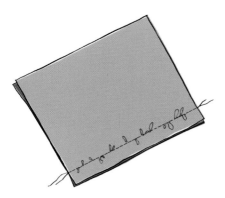

Random loops

If the machine is not threaded correctly, or the thread has not been placed properly inside the tension disks, a series of loops can appear.

Loose seam

This indicates that the tension is too loose on both the bobbin and needle thread, the machine has not been threaded correctly, or the thread has not been placed properly between the tension mechanism.

A stitch regulator on an industrial flatbed sewing machine. On this machine the stitch length can vary from 0–4mm.

Pressing Equipment

Pressing equipment works with heat, pressure and, sometimes, a vacuum. These tools are essential for an effective garment finish. It is important to use the right temperature on an iron as this, combined with the knowledge of how and when to apply pressure can, for example, assist in the shaping of sleeves, curved seams and dart areas. Once you know how to press a garment properly, you can rectify small sewing errors and achieve a much more professional look.

For home use a **Domestic Ironing Board** and a good steam iron with temperature regulation are sufficient. The ironing board should have a soft surface with a narrow end, and should be covered with a material that can tolerate high temperatures and is colour true.

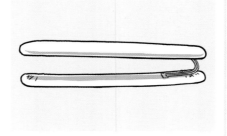

A **Sleeve Board** is useful when pressing a sleeve, any tube-like piece, or small part of a garment. Sliding the sleeve through this small ironing board prevents the impression of an unwanted crease when pressing seams.

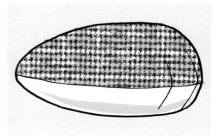

The **Tailor's Ham** is a small, firmly padded, oval cushion, with a cotton fabric on one side and wool on the other. The cotton side can be used for pressing most fabrics; the wool side is only for woollen materials. It is used for shaping collars, lapels, darts and sleeve cups, and to shrink fullness and press rounded areas.

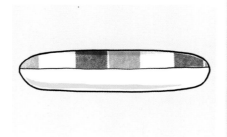

A **Sleeve Roll** is a firm padded, cylindrical cushion, used to press hard-to-reach areas such as seams in sleeves. It helps avoid wrinkling the rest of the garment as the sleeve roll can be held up and away from the table.

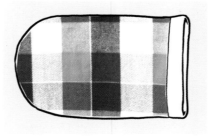

A **Pressing Mitt** is hollow so the hand can be slid inside and is ideal for pressing sleeve cups and any other areas that should not be laid flat onto an ironing board.

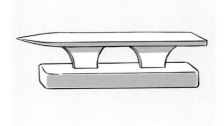

The **Point Presser and Pounding Block** is a two-part wooden board. The narrow top with a tapered point is used for pressing sharp corners, such as collar corners. The flat base can be used as a clapper to pound creases into materials after steaming, such as trouser creases and pleats.

A **Steam Iron** comes with a temperature regulator that can be adjusted according to the material being ironed. A **Steam Iron with a Pressure Tank** will give a professional finish.

Most **Industrial Ironing Tables** have a vacuum facility, which sucks steam from the iron through the fabric and into the table. The fabric is cooled enough to give a sharper pressing effect. Some industrial ironing tables have a **Canvas Shelf**, a hammock-like sling underneath the board. This prevents fabric from touching the floor and stops knitted material from stretching during ironing.

The **Fusing Machine** or **Fusing Press** is used to attach interfacing to material. It includes a temperature and pressure regulator and a timer.

A **Velvet Board**, also called a **Needle Board**, is covered with wire needles and is used to prevent fabric pile from matting and crushing. The fabric, such as velvet, is placed face down against the wire needles during pressing.

A **Clothes Brush** is handy when working with woollen fabrics or materials with a nap. It helps to raise the nap and correct over-pressing. It can also be used to remove threads and unwanted fluff.

A **Pressing Cloth** is a piece of either cotton or woollen loose-woven fabric. Place it between the fabric and the iron to prevent shine and protect the surface of the fabric. A **Strip of Paper** can be slipped between darts and seam allowance, on the wrong side of the fabric, to prevent an impression from appearing on the right side of the fabric.

Spearmint Water or **Crisped Mint Water** (*Aqua menthae crispae*) is used to eliminate strong folds, such as unwanted trouser creases and break lines. It also gets rid of shine created by over-pressing. Apply with a lint-free cloth or brush and then steam, or add spearmint water to the water in the iron. See also The Finishing Touch, page 245.

PRESSING TIPS

- Wait until the steam iron has reached the correct temperature, as the iron could start to spit water if not hot enough.
- Before beginning to iron, test the temperature on the edge of the fabric. This helps determine whether to use steam or not, and the best pressing method to employ.
- Always press the fabric before cutting out to allow for eventual shrinkage.
- As a rule always press on the wrong side of the fabric. If this is not possible, use a piece of the same material to cover or use a pressing cloth.

- It is best to press in the direction of the grain line.
- Avoid pulling, or holding down the edges of the fabric when pressing, as this can result in the fabric becoming overstretched.
- Never iron over pins as they can leave marks in the fabric.
- Only apply permanent pleats and creases once the garment is fitted and correct. Once formed they are hard to remove.
- Press as you go when constructing a garment.

Taking Body Measurements

Before starting any garment construction a pattern needs to be developed either from a design idea, or copied from an existing garment. When starting to sew you can also use sewing patterns from companies such as Vogue, McCall's, Simplicity or Burda.

To create a pattern, body measurements need to be established. If working on a personalized garment, individual body measurements are necessary to ensure a good fit. However, if you are working on a sample collection for the fashion industry the measurements can be taken from a size chart. These differ between regions, companies and from designer to designer.

How to take individual body measurements

For a made-to-measure fit, individual body measurements need to be taken with a tape measure. Ask the client to wear suitable underwear or body-conscious clothing, to take the measurements as close to the body as possible. Make sure your client is standing in a relaxed posture and ask the client to move away from the mirror, as there is a big temptation to hold in the stomach and stand up straight. This would give you the wrong impression of the client's body shape and lead to an incorrect set of measurements.

Measurements for different blocks

Skirt block	Bodice block	Trouser block
Waist	Body height	Waist
Hip	Bust/chest	Hip
Waist to hip	Waist	Waist to hip
Skirt length	Hip	Waist to floor
	Waist to hip	Inside leg
	Back waist length	Crotch depth
	Arm length	

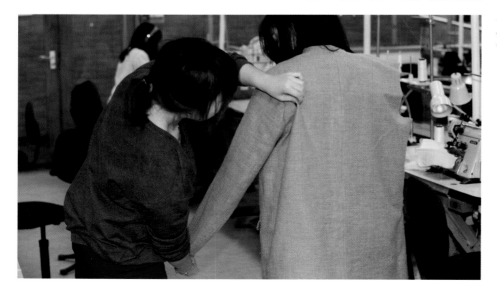

Students checking the fit of a jacket. When working on a sample garment it is important to check the fit and overall look throughout the construction process.

Taking measurements

Body height

Measure the body height first. Stand the model flat against the wall, without shoes, and measure from the top of the head to the floor.

Waist

Women: Place a tape around the natural waistline and take the measurement from behind.

Men: Place the tape around the natural waist starting at the navel.

Bust/Chest

Women: Place the tape around the fullest part of the bust. Make sure the tape is placed horizontally across the back and under the arms. Take this measurement from the back.

Men: Make sure the tape is over the fullest part of the chest and measure around the body under the arms, with a slightly expanded chest or two fingers under the tape.

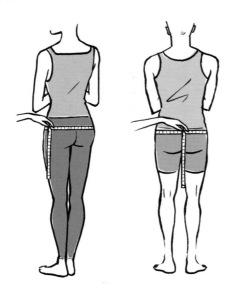

Hip

Women: Measure the fullest part of the hips from behind. Make sure that the tape is placed horizontally around the body and does not drop down on one side. Stand to the side when taking this measurement.

Men: Make sure the model has his feet close together. Take the measurement comfortably at the widest part of the hip and the midpoint of the pelvic bone.

Back waist length

Take the measurement from the prominent bone at the neck, in line with the centre back, to the natural waistline. Press the tape against the waist point to get an accurate measurement.

Waist to hip

You need two tapes to take this measurement. Place one tape around the natural waistline and with the second tape measure from the waistline down the side to the fullest part of the hip.

Inside leg

Women: Measure from the crotch to the floor of the inside leg using a tailor's tape measure. Use the metal piece of the tape at the crotch area so that the metal piece and not the hand reaches to the top of the inside leg.

Men: Take the measurement in the same way as for women, also using a tailor's tape measure. In menswear tailoring a difference is made between the right and left side of the inside leg. A tailor would ask his client which side he 'dresses' on. This is to make allowance for a client who wears loose fitting underwear by adding extra fabric to the inside leg to accommodate the genitals.

Skirt length

The skirt length depends on the design and can be taken from the waist along the side of the body to the knee, or full length to the floor.

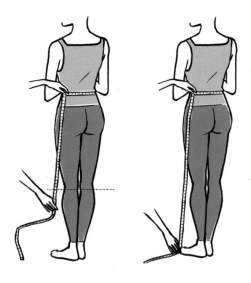

Waist to floor

Take this measurement from the waist to the floor, over the hip on the outer leg.

Crotch depth

You need two tapes to take this measurement. Ask your model to sit on a chair with a hard seat and place one tape around the natural waist. Using the second tape, measure from the waist to the seat.

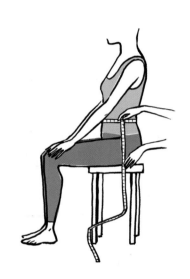

Required ease	cm	in
Full bust	8–13	3–5
Front waist length	1–3	⅜–1⅛
Back waist length	0.5–1	³⁄₁₆–⅜
Back shoulder width	1	⅜
Upper arm circumference	5–8	2–3⅛
Wrist circumference	1–3	⅜–1⅛
Hand circumference	1	⅜
Waist	2–3	¾–1⅛
Hips	5–8	2–3⅛

Arm length

Measure from the shoulder tip along the outer arm across the elbow to the wrist bone, with the arm relaxed and slightly bent.

ALLOWING FOR EASE

Make sure you do not measure too tightly or too loosely when taking individual measurements. Also remember the measurements taken are without any allowance for comfort. An allowance for comfort, also known as ease, is added when drafting the pattern block. See table of suggested measurements above.

How to Work with Patterns

It is essential to have a good understanding of garment construction in order to understand pattern cutting and how a two-dimensional template – the block or pattern – corresponds to a body shape. The job of a designer or creative pattern cutter is to cut a pattern that records all the information of a design.

Once created, the pattern is then cut out in a sample fabric for a first fitting and made into a toile. A toile is a garment cut out of cheaper fabric, such as muslin or calico, close to the final fabric weight and structure. The first toile is to check the overall shape, proportion and fit of the garment. At this stage the seams are not tidied up and the toile has no facings, fastenings or lining. The toile can be fitted on a mannequin or on a live model. However, it is best to fit on a live model as you can see the garment in movement. If necessary, the pattern is altered after the fitting and attention then turns to the details, such as pockets and facings.

Sometimes a second fitting in toiling is required; if not, the garment can be cut out in the final fabric.

Most designers include a shell fitting, which shows the garment made up in the final fabric in its raw state, without fastenings and lining. This enables the designer to make minor changes. Once seen in shell, and if you are happy with the result, the garment can be completed.

Blocks and patterns are found hanging on the wall of most design studios.

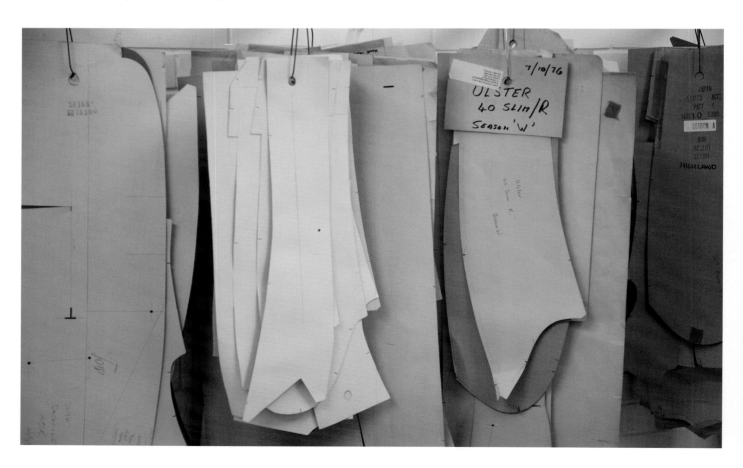

What is the difference between a block and a pattern?

A block (made of card or plastic) includes all the information necessary to fit a basic shape, such as a bodice for the upper part of the body. The block includes an allowance for comfort, as well as shaping through darts if required.

The block can then be modified into a pattern to develop a design idea. The pattern (cut out of pattern paper) includes all design information such as style lines, pocket ideas and collar design. Seam allowance will only be added when the block has been made into a pattern.

Step by step adapting a basic block to make a pattern

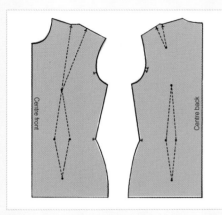

Step 1
A basic block such as this can be adapted into a design through dart manipulation.

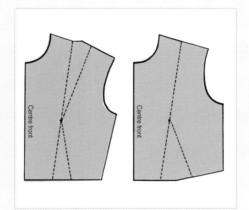

Step 2
Here the shoulder dart of a basic bodice block is closed up and opened into the waist.

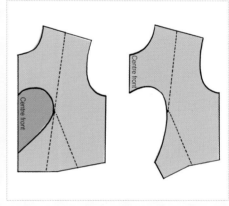

Step 3
A heart shape is added to the centre front. The waist dart is closed and opened into the heart shape.

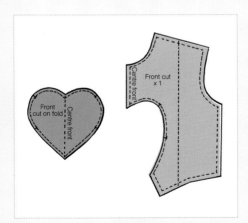

Step 4
The new pattern with seam allowance added.

Step 5
A toile of the new design.

Understanding Symbols on Patterns

Whether you are working on a pattern for yourself or a company, it is essential to mark your patterns correctly so that they can be easily understood by anyone who uses them. A pattern cutter uses a set of symbols and technical terms that is understood by everyone in the industry. This way anyone can carry out further work on the pattern, such as a cutter cutting out the pattern in fabric or a manufacturer abroad, without the pattern cutter being present. The same symbols are also used on the block, but usually fewer are needed.

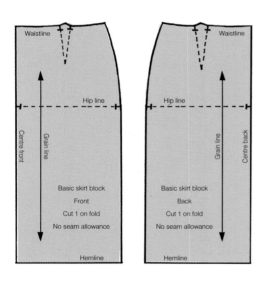

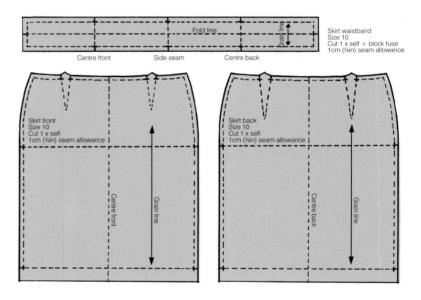

A basic skirt block has to indicate front and back, grain line, waist and hip line, size and how many times it needs to be cut out. Placement-marking symbols such as notches and hole punches give further information to the person constructing the garment.

When a block is taken for pattern modification it might be divided into further pieces. The information on the block needs to be transferred to the modified pattern and additional information is then often added to each piece. Seam allowance is added to the finished pattern piece at this stage.

Purpose	Example
To tell the cutter to place the pattern onto the right side of the fabric with the pattern information facing upwards. Used when a pattern is not reversible, such as an asymmetrical design. ***Shown on pattern:*** RSU (right side up)	 Centre front RSU RSU Centre front Centre front
To tell the cutter to use the pattern wrong side up. ***Shown on pattern:*** WSU (wrong side up)	WSU WSU
To indicate balance points showing where seams fit together. ***Shown on pattern:*** Notches (small cut-outs in the paper pattern). For sleeves, use one notch for the front of the armhole and two for the back.	Shoulder notch Centre front Sleeve Centre back

Purpose	Example
To indicate the beginning and end of a pleat. ***Shown on pattern:*** Notches To show the direction in which to fold a pleat. ***Shown on pattern:*** Arrow	Pleat Pleat Pleat Pleat Centre front
To indicate gathers. ***Shown on pattern:*** A wavy line with a notch at the beginning and end of the area to be gathered. Also indicate the amount to be gathered.	Gathering Grain line
To mark the position of a pattern piece, such as a pocket. ***Shown on pattern:*** Small holes punched into the pattern. Place the holes 5mm (³⁄₁₆in) inside the shape so the mark is covered when the pocket is attached.	Centre front
To indicate dart endings. ***Shown on pattern:*** A hole punched in the pattern. Either mark at the end of the dart or 5mm (³⁄₁₆in) from the end so it is covered when sewn.	Centre front Centre front

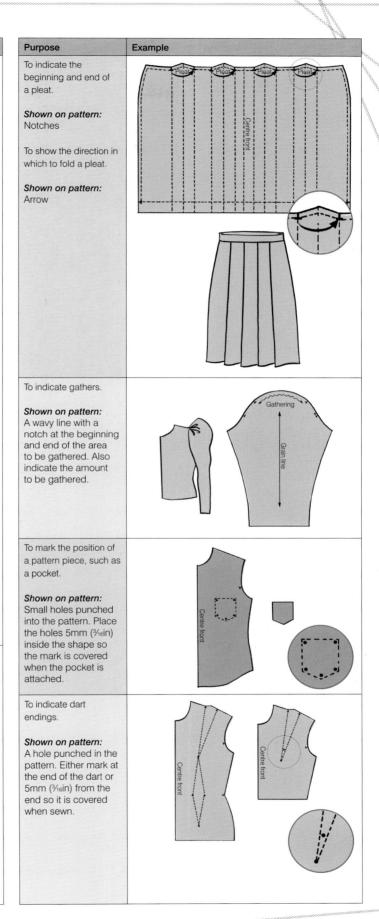

Purpose	Example
To indicate cutting lines. ***Shown on pattern:*** A pair of scissors. Use a hole punch to mark the end of the line.	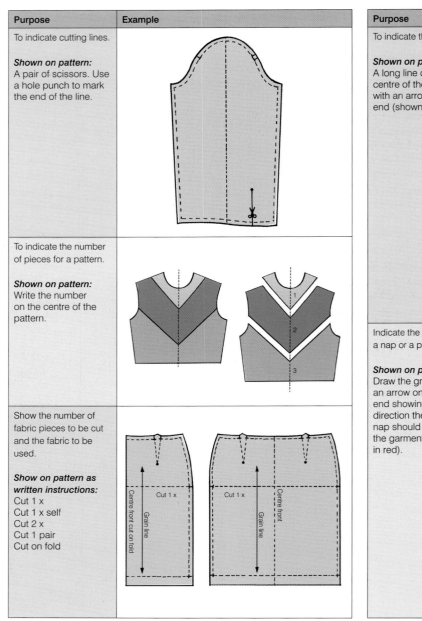
To indicate the number of pieces for a pattern. ***Shown on pattern:*** Write the number on the centre of the pattern.	
Show the number of fabric pieces to be cut and the fabric to be used. ***Show on pattern as written instructions:*** Cut 1 x Cut 1 x self Cut 2 x Cut 1 pair Cut on fold	

Purpose	Example
To indicate the grainline. ***Shown on pattern:*** A long line down the centre of the pattern with an arrow on each end (shown in red).	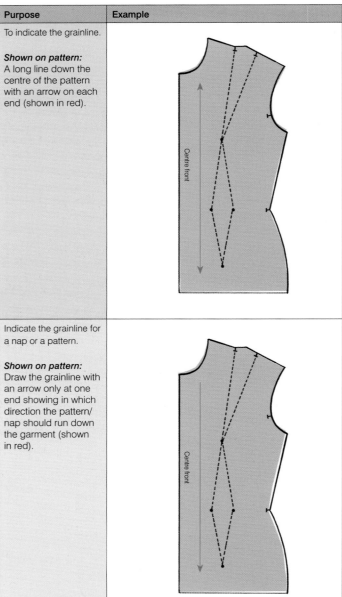
Indicate the grainline for a nap or a pattern. ***Shown on pattern:*** Draw the grainline with an arrow only at one end showing in which direction the pattern/nap should run down the garment (shown in red).	

Seam Allowance

Seam allowance enables you to sew the garment pieces together and to attach other garment parts, such as closures, trimmings, facings and collars. Seam allowances are added to the sewing edge and preferably included on a pattern piece before the pattern is cut out. The allowance can vary from 0.5 to 3.5cm (³⁄₁₆–1⁵⁄₁₆in) depending on the material structure, fabric weight, the intended seam finish and garment design.

Seam allowances affect the way the seam and the entire garment hang. Smaller seam allowances are easier to handle as they are less bulky and the sewing result will be more accurate than with a large seam allowance.

Type of seam or fabric	Seam allowance	
Most garment seams	1cm (⅜in)	This is the most widely used seam allowance in the industry.
Shaped seams	0.5cm (³⁄₁₆in)	Such seams include necklines and enclosed seams, such as facings or collar pieces. This is to avoid having to clip or trim the seam. Also used for less stressed seams.
Textured materials Loose-woven fabrics Fabrics that fray easily, such as chiffon Heavyweight fabrics	1.5–2cm (⅝–¾in)	A wider seam allowance not only allows for fraying but will ensure a heavyweight fabric lies flat after pressing.
Toiles – first fitting	2–2.5cm (¾–1⁵⁄₁₆in)	A wider seam can be let out if necessary for the second fitting.
Centre back and crotch seam of trousers, especially for men's tailoring	2.5–3.5cm (1⁵⁄₁₆–1⁵⁄₁₆in)	A wide seam offers more support and can be let out over time if necessary. You can also use a wider side seam to prolong the life of a garment.
Bias binding or a raw-edged finish	No allowance needed	
Specific seam finishes	French seam: 1cm (⅜in) Flat fell seam: 2cm (¾in)	
Overlocked seams	0.5–1cm (³⁄₁₆–⅜in)	Do a test sample on the overlocker before adding seam allowance.

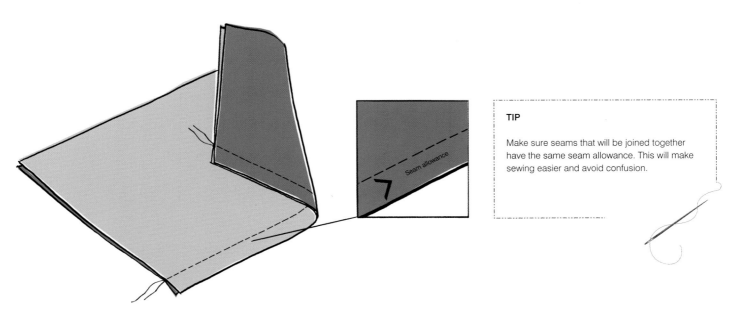

Seam allowance is added to all pattern pieces before sewing.

> **TIP**
>
> Make sure seams that will be joined together have the same seam allowance. This will make sewing easier and avoid confusion.

Hem Allowance

The hemline is the lower edge of a garment and the hem allowance is the width between the hemline and the hem's edge. The hemline is usually folded under towards the wrong side of the fabric to tidy up the edge. Hem allowance is determined by the garment silhouette, design and fabric weight. The measurement can vary between 0.5 and 5cm (³⁄₁₆ and 2in). As a general rule, the wider and fuller a skirt, the smaller the hem allowance. The hem allowance can be added to a garment or, alternatively, the hemline can be finished with a facing, bias binding or trimming.

Jacket and coat hem allowances

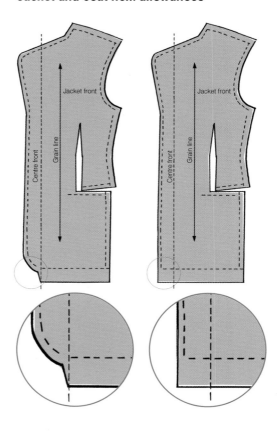

Hem allowance: 3–5cm (1⅛–2in)
Finishing: In general, be generous with jacket and coat hems. Add to the hem edge or cut as a separate facing.

Sleeve hem allowances

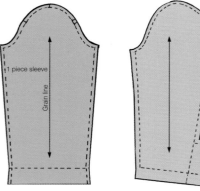 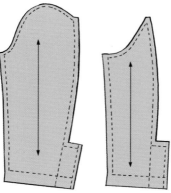

Type of sleeve: Jacket or coat
Hem allowance: 3–5cm (1⅛–2in)

Finishing: Add to the hem edge or cut separately as a facing.

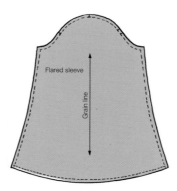

Type of sleeve: Flared to the hemline
Hem allowance: Up to 1cm (⅜in) or a facing cut in the shape of the hemline.

Finishing: Depends on the design and fabric weight.

Trouser hem allowances

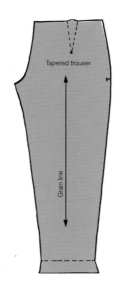

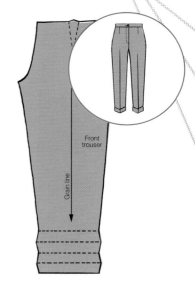

Type of trouser: Flared leg
Hem allowance: Up to 1cm (⅜in) or a facing cut in the shape of the hemline.
Finishing: Depends on the design and fabric weight.

Type of trouser: Tapered leg
Hem allowance: 3–5cm (1⅛–2in)
Finishing: Once the hem allowance is added, fold it up before cutting the sides off the pattern in order to get the correct angle.

Type of trouser: Straight leg
Hem allowance: 3–5cm (1⅛–2in)
Finishing: Fold up the hem allowance and either hand or machine finish.

Type of trouser: Trouser with cuff or turn-up
Hem allowance: Depends on the design. Add twice the depth of the cuff to the hemline plus the hem allowance.
Finishing: Fold up the allowance into the right position before cutting the sides off the pattern in order to get the correct shape.

Skirt hem allowances

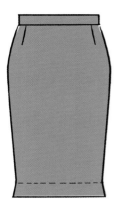

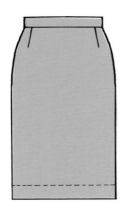

Type of skirt: Pencil skirt
Hem allowance: 3–5cm (1⅛–2in)
Finishing: Once the hem allowance is added, fold it up before cutting the sides on the pattern in order to get the correct angle for this tapered skirt.

Type of skirt: Straight skirt
Hem allowance: 3–5cm (1⅛–2in)
Finishing: Fold up the hem allowance and either hand or machine finish.

Type of skirt: A-line skirt
Hem allowance: 1–3cm (⅜–1⅛in)
Finishing: When adding this hem allowance, consider the shaped sides of the skirt. An A-line skirt can also be finished with a separate facing cut in the shape of the hemline.

Type of skirt: Flared skirt and full circle skirt
Hem allowance: Up to 1cm (⅜in) or a facing cut in the shape of the hemline.
Finishing: Depends on the weight and type of fabric; a chiffon skirt would be finished with a pin hem, whereas a full circle silk satin duchesse skirt would have a facing as a hem finish.

Understanding the Fabric

A major part of garment construction is being familiar with the fabric before cutting out. Cutting out can be time-consuming and the more care you take to understand the fabric before cutting out, the better the outcome will be when you start construction.

Fabric structure

Fabric structure falls into two categories, woven and knitted. A woven fabric is created by a vertical yarn, the 'warp', interlacing with a horizontal yarn, the 'weft', at right angles to each other. The edges of the fabric, the selvedge, are woven more tightly and run along the length of the fabric in the direction of the warp, which is the lengthwise grain. The warp yarn is held in tension on a loom and the weft yarn creates the crosswise grain, weaving over and under the warp yarn; the warp is, therefore, the stronger of the two. There are four main weave structures: plain weave, also known as linen weave; basket weave; twill weave; and satin weave.

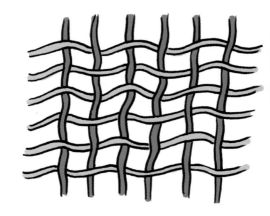

The warp runs the length of the fabric, while the weft runs crosswise.

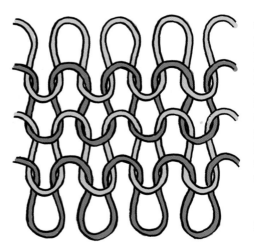

Unlike weaving, a knitted fabric can be made with as little as a single yarn. Knitted fabrics are made by interweaving yarns to form a series of connected loops. The variety of knitted fabrics available is much wider than woven, as a greater selection of yarns can be used. Fabric made by machine knitting can be warp knitted or weft knitted and makes use of the four basic stitches: plain, rib, purl and warp. Weft knitting uses one continuous yarn looping stitches in the crosswise grain, producing two main knitting types, single knit and double knit. The warp knit is formed by looping stitches in the lengthwise grain, utilizing many yarns and producing a tricot or raschel knit.

The main difference between a woven and a knitted fabric is that in general knitted fabric has greater stretch in both directions than woven fabric.

Knitting is formed from interlocked loops.

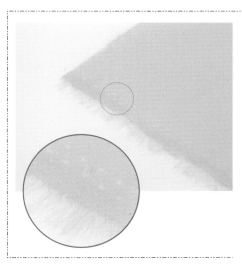

HOW TO TELL THE RIGHT FROM THE WRONG SIDE OF THE FABRIC

The selvedge of a fabric usually has little perforations or holes where the fabric has been attached to a loom or frame. If the perforation of the hole is facing you, essentially where the needle comes out of the fabric, this is the right side of the fabric.

The selvedge on a chiffon fabric with the right side up.

Cutting out. The fabric is laid out on a large cutting table with the pattern pieces pinned on, ready to be cut out.

How to Use the Grain Line

The grain indicates the yarn direction. A pattern piece can be cut out lengthwise, crosswise or on the bias.

Lengthwise or straight grain

Most garments are cut on the straight grain in line with the warp yarn. This grain line runs parallel to the selvedge. On a pattern piece the grain line runs down the body length, lining up with the centre front and centre back. The weft provides a bit more give in the fabric, which allows the garment to fit comfortably around the body, whereas the warp runs down the body length and provides stability.

Crosswise or horizontal grain

The crosswise grain runs at a 90-degree angle to the selvedge. Most pieces cut on the cross are decorative, or help with the construction and support the stability of a garment – such as the cuffs and yoke on a shirt – because the straight, stable grain would run horizontally across the pattern piece.

Bias grain

A 'true' bias grain line runs at a 45-degree angle to the selvedge. The bias cut works beautifully on draped designs. It provides more stretch and clings to the body, unlike a garment cut on the straight grain. You will, however, need to use more fabric. Bias seams are difficult to sew, but do not be put off; the outcome will be worth it.

Knitted fabrics

Knitted fabrics also have a grain line or direction in which the garment needs to be cut. The horizontal rows correspond with the crosswise grain and are called courses, while the vertical rows correspond with the lengthwise grain and are called wales. Most knitted fabrics show an obvious rib pattern. Examine the vertical ribs before cutting. Following the wales, with the courses at 90 degrees, is the same as cutting a woven fabric on the straight grain.

Napped or patterned fabrics

Fabrics with a nap or pattern need to be cut in a specific direction so that the pattern runs down the garment in the direction in which it was designed. This should be indicated on the pattern pieces by the grain line (see Napped and Pile Fabrics, page 276).

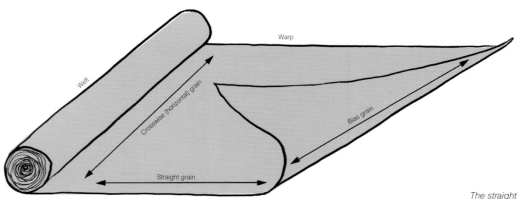

The straight, crosswise (horizontal) and bias grain on a roll of fabric.

Finding the crosswise grain line

Before you put a pattern onto fabric, find the crosswise grain and use it to ensure that the ends of the fabric pieces are straight.

- You can tear the fabric across the crosswise grain. Lightweight fabrics, cotton, some man-made fabrics and silks tear well. If the fabric is loosely or coarsely woven, has a texture or is knitted, however, it cannot be torn. Many heavier woven fabrics may also distort if torn. Always test the fabric before tearing completely. If it shows signs of pulled threads on the lengthwise grain, stop. Cut the selvedge first, as it is difficult to tear.
- If the fabric cannot be torn, cut into the selvedge and pull gently on one weft thread. The pulled thread will show you the crosswise grain line, which you can then cut along to get a straight edge.

- On knitted fabrics follow a row of looped stitches (courses) or take a right angle from the length grain (wales) and mark a line to cut along.
- If the fabric has a check or stripe as part of the woven pattern, follow a line of the pattern to straighten the edge. If the check or stripe is printed, then use one of the methods above.
- If the fabric is coarse or loosely woven you might be able to see the weave pattern and straighten the edge by judging it by eye, cutting carefully across the crosswise grain.

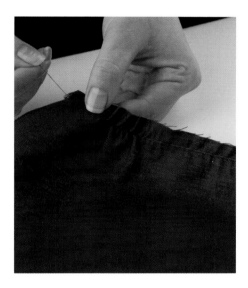

> **TIP**
>
> Always cut your toile or sample garment in the same grain line as the proposed final garment. Each grain direction behaves differently and will affect how the fabric drapes on the body.

A fashion student adding the grain line to a paper pattern piece. To place a pattern correctly onto fabric, a grain line needs to be established and drawn on each pattern piece.

Preparing the Fabric

Remember the saying, 'A little preparation goes a long way'. This also applies to preparing the fabric before cutting out. Check if the fabric requires pre-shrinking and straightening out. Make sure you examine the fabric carefully and watch out for the following points:

- Check the fabric for a nap; some fabrics, like velvet or corduroy, look different from one direction to the other. The direction of the nap is your own choice. Once the direction is decided on, make sure your pattern pieces have been labelled with a grain line running in one direction only.
- Establish if the fabric has a one-way design or a pattern repeat, and mark your pattern pieces accordingly.
- Examine the fabric for flaws or snags. You will need to avoid these when cutting out.
- Check for the right or wrong side of the fabric. There is no rule about which you should use. If you prefer the wrong side then go ahead; just make sure you stick only to that side.

TIP

To find out if the fabric has a nap, a one-way design or an uneven stripe or check, hold the fabric in the centre of the length and check if the colour or pattern matches on both sides.

Pre-shrinking

Once you have established how you will use the fabric, the next step is to press or pre-shrink. Many fabrics shrink when dry-cleaned or laundered; the most common of these are 100% wool, cotton and linen materials. Always check the label for instructions. Some fabrics indicate that they are 'needle ready', which means that the fabric is ready for cutting and sewing, as it has been treated and will not shrink after washing or dry-cleaning.

- If the fabric needs steaming or washing, check the label for fibre content and yarn structure, as well as for any manufacturer's recommendations and further information about dry-cleaning or washing instructions.
- If the fabric is machine-washable use the washing machine on the rinse cycle, which uses the minimum amount of water. For a hand-wash use a cold water bath to pre-shrink the material. Once the fabric has dried, press it before cutting out the pattern.
- Most woollen fabrics are not washable, but a good steaming is usually enough to pre-shrink the fabric. Use a steam iron with temperature control to steam the fabric. If you do not have one to hand ask a dry-cleaner to steam and press it for you; no cleaning is required.
- Some fabrics, such as synthetic blended fabrics, do not need pre-shrinking. They require only a good press to remove any existing creases or break lines.
- As a general rule, always press before you cut.

Straightening the fabric

After the fabric has been pre-shrunk and pressed, check the fabric grain is aligned correctly with the lengthwise and crosswise grain at right angles. Fold the fabric in half and bring the selvedges together. If the fabric is hard to level and looks twisted, it is distorted and needs alignment. There are several methods to re-align the grain line.

- If it is only distorted a little, fold the fabric on the bias, hold it at both ends, then pull and stretch the fabric in the opposite direction to correct the distortion. Repeat this process until the fabric is lying flat with the selvedges aligned.
- If the fabric distortion cannot be pulled into the right alignment, fold the fabric in half lengthwise and, with the wrong side up, pin the crosswise edge and selvedges together,

smoothing the fabric out as you pin. Next, use an iron to press the fabric into the correct grain by moving the iron from the centre towards the outside edges, then repeat the ironing process as necessary.
- If it is very distorted and the fabric is washable, dampen the fabric and pull it on the diagonal from each side over the whole of the fabric width, repeating until the fabric grain is corrected. Press the fabric before cutting out.

Above: The pre-shrinking process may have caused the fabric to distort.
Right: Fold the fabric on the bias and pull it back into alignment.

USING A STEAM IRON

To press, apply pressure with the iron in one place.

To steam, let the iron hover over the fabric without touching it and release the steam jets onto the material.

To iron, glide the iron with some pressure over the material.

To finger press, steam the seam by holding the iron a couple of centimetres above the surface, remove the iron, then press the seam flat with your fingers.

Pattern Layout on the Fabric

The layout of the pattern pieces depends on the fabric type and pattern design. Choose a flat and firm cutting surface, large enough to fit the length of material required, as you want to pin all the pattern pieces onto the fabric before cutting out. Pattern pieces can be laid out in a one-way or two-way direction and on single or double fabric layers.

How to lay the pattern pieces onto the correct grain line

Each pattern piece should have a grain line, which also indicates the direction in which the pattern needs to be laid onto the fabric. All grain lines should be placed parallel to the selvedge on the fabric, whether the grain lines are marked horizontally, vertically or at a 45-degree angle on the pattern pieces themselves. To ensure that the pieces are placed correctly onto the grain, measure from the selvedge to the grain line at both ends of the pattern piece.

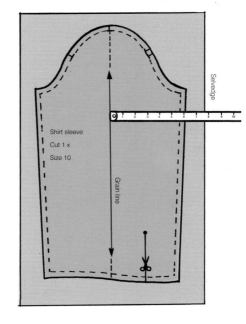

Place the pattern pieces with the grain line parallel to the selvedge and use a tape measure to check they are level.

TIP

It is advisable to do a practice layout plan using all the pattern pieces before cutting the fabric. This is to make sure that you do not omit any pattern pieces and also to check that they are laid out in an efficient way to avoid wastage. Pieces should be placed close together and arranged to avoid too many awkward-shaped pieces of fabric being left over. Once you are happy with the layout, secure the pattern pieces to the material, either by weighing the pattern pieces down or pinning them to the fabric. Use long fine pins, which make it easier to attach pattern and fabric together. Short pins can allow movement, and subsequent pinning can move the pattern off the grain. Avoid moving the fabric once you have secured all the pattern pieces, as they can easily be moved off the grain.

You can use pins or weights to hold the pattern in place ready for marking.

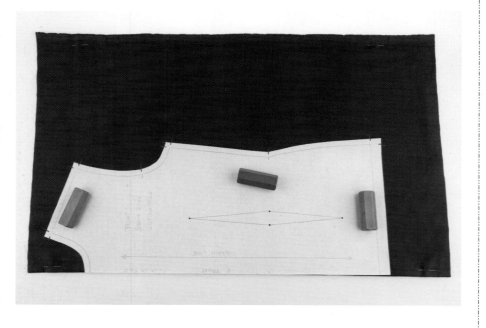

Cutting and layout plans

There are different options for laying the pattern onto the material. First you need to determine the cutting plan, which will depend on the type of fabric you are using, the direction of the grain you wish to use for your garment, and whether you need to cut out your pattern pieces in a single layer or can double your fabric to cut two pieces. Once you have selected your cutting plan, decide on the best way to place your pattern pieces on the fabric to avoid wastage. This is the layout plan.

Start with the larger pieces and lay the smaller pieces, such as pockets, in any gaps. Usually you would place the pattern pieces onto the wrong side of the fabric; this makes it possible to mark the pattern onto the fabric.

One-way pattern layout

This method would be used for a fabric with a nap or pile, for knitted fabrics, or for a fabric with a design worked in one direction only. In this layout, all pattern pieces face in one direction so that all fabric shading and design features will face the same way.

Two-way pattern layout (below)

This layout is more cost-effective as the pattern pieces can be laid in both directions. The two-way layout is used on all plain fabrics without any shading, and patterned fabrics where the design has no direction.

Double layout

Fold the fabric on the lengthwise grain and align the selvedges together to achieve a double layout. This cutting plan is used to cut out pairs of pattern pieces with the cutting instruction 'cut 2 x' or 'cut 1 pair'. It is also possible to cut a piece on the fold, marked as 'cut on fold'. Cut on fold is used on symmetrical pattern pieces; lay the marked pattern edge in line with the folded fabric edge. Always place the pattern pieces that need to be cut on the fold first and then place the rest of the pieces around them.

Single layout

The single layout is mostly used to cut out fine, stretchy or bias-cut pattern pieces and for fabrics with a pattern design or direction. This layout is ideal to cut asymmetric pattern styles as only one piece is cut out at a time on a single layer of fabric. The pattern pieces for this layout will be marked as 'cut 1 x' or 'cut 1 x self'.

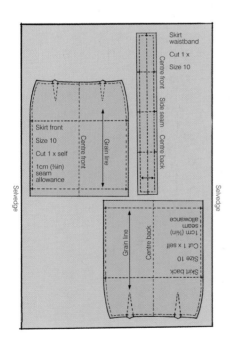

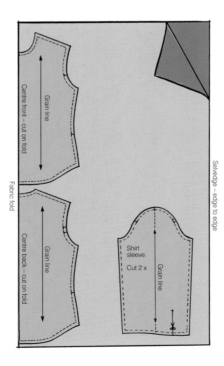

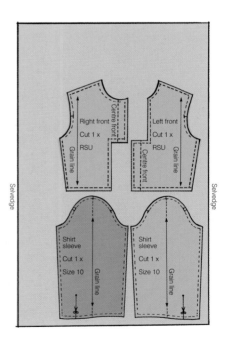

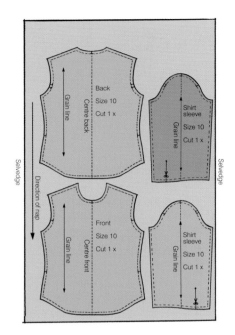

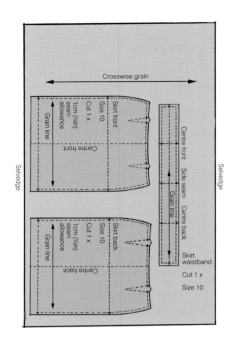

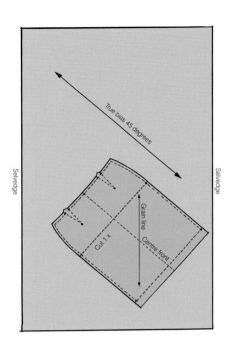

Layout for fabrics with a nap or pile and one-way pattern design

Fabric with a direction can be cut out on a single or double layer. Decide on the direction of the nap or fabric design and mark the grain line accordingly on the pattern. The pattern pieces need to face in one direction using a one-way pattern layout. (Find more information in Napped and Pile Fabrics, page 276.)

Crosswise layout

Pattern pieces placed so that the crosswise grain runs down their length (from neckline to hem) will have the more stable lengthwise grain running horizontally across them. Pattern pieces cut in this way, therefore, are usually those that help with stability and construction, such as a waistband. You can also lay pieces across the crosswise grain if you want the pattern of the fabric to run around, rather than down, the garment. Remember that the crosswise grain has more give and will affect the hang of the garment. The crosswise layout is also used for more complex and bigger pattern pieces that do not fit on the lengthwise grain.

Bias layout

The best layout for a bias cut is a single layout plan, as most bias-cut pattern pieces are big and sometimes asymmetric. Another reason for cutting out on a single layer of fabric is that most fabrics used for bias-cut garments are fine or lightweight. Take extra care when placing the pattern pieces onto the fabric at a 45-degree angle to the selvedge, as a 'true' bias-cut garment will always hang better. (Find more information in Bias-Cut Fabrics, page 310.)

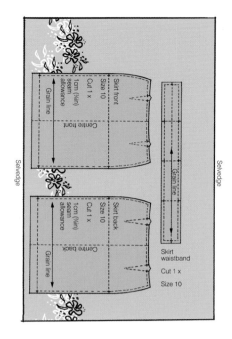

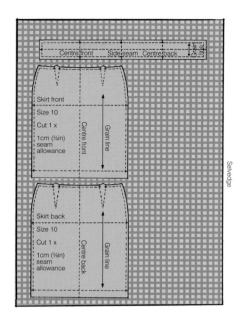

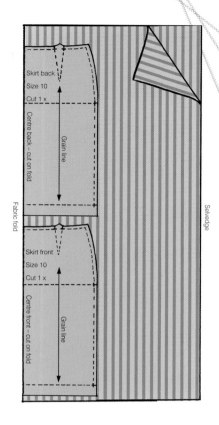

Design placement layout

Some fabrics have a large pattern that you will want to position carefully on the finished garment. Take time to examine your fabric design and to mark the design placement onto your pattern pieces. Make sure the placement is aesthetically pleasing and avoid placing patterns such as circles on a bust point or around the crotch area of the garment. (Find more information in Patterned Fabrics, page 300.)

Checks and stripes

First establish if the check or stripe pattern is regular, meaning it can be matched in either direction, or if it is irregular. Use a one-way layout for an irregular pattern and either a one-way or two-way layout on a regular check or stripe. Both can be cut on a single or double layout.

Match up the check or stripe on adjoining pieces in obvious places such as the centre front and centre back, the hemline, pockets and parts of the armhole and sleeve.

Mark essential matching points onto the pattern pieces before placing the pieces onto the fabric. When using a double layout, before placing the pattern pieces down match the checks and stripes of the fabric together and place a pin every 5–10cm (2–3⅞in), depending on the size of the fabric pattern. (Find more information in Patterned Fabrics, page 300.)

How to Mark the Pattern onto the Fabric

Different marking tools and methods can be used to mark placement points and pattern pieces onto fabric. Once the layout plan has been made and the pattern is securely in place, the marking process can begin. It is best practice to mark all the information onto the fabric and lift the pattern off before cutting out. This will ensure that none of the pattern pieces are accidentally cut into or, even worse, cut off.

Pinning the pattern pieces to the fabric

If the material is suitable for pinning, secure the pattern to the wrong side of the fabric by putting a pin into each corner of the pattern first, then secure the rest of the pattern with pins a couple of centimetres apart. Try and pin along the fabric edge and stay away from the cutting line; avoid over-pinning as it will distort the fabric.

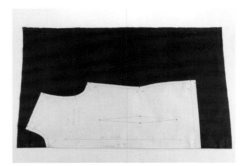

Place pins at each corner of the pattern first.

> **TIP**
>
> Sometimes the selvedge is too tightly woven, with the result that the fabric cannot lie flat on the cutting surface. If this is the case, snip into the selvedge every couple of centimetres to release the tension. If this is still not sufficient, carefully cut the selvedge off in a straight line.

Chalk marking the pattern onto fabric

Most fabrics can be chalk marked except for very fine and lightweight materials, as the markings will show through to the right side of the fabric. Always check that the chalk does not show through.

When the pattern has been pinned or weighed down on the wrong side of the fabric, begin tracing around the pieces with tailor's chalk. Make sure the notches, matching and placement points, are all marked before lifting the pattern off. Use a sharp tailor's chalk to keep the lines narrow. If you use a blunt chalk the line could become too wide and a couple of millimetres added on when cutting out will result in an inaccurate piece.

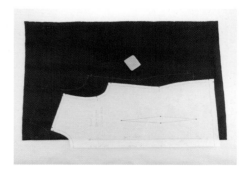

Draw around the pattern piece with tailor's chalk and transfer all marks onto the fabric.

Darts, placement points and notches

A dart point shows where the dart needs to be stitched. Dart points are usually indicated by holes punched in the pattern. Different techniques can be used to mark through the hole onto the fabric. You can use tailor's chalk or a chalk pencil to mark the hole's position. Then lift the pattern off and place either a pin or an awl through both layers of fabric at the position of the dart point. You can then use chalk to mark the position on the second layer. Remember, when using an awl you end up with a small hole in the fabric, so mark the dart point 1cm (⅜in) inside the end of the dart.

Use the same technique for placement points, such as pocket positions. Most materials can be marked with chalk or an awl but if the fabric is delicate, transparent or lightweight use thread marking instead. Avoid marking knitted fabrics with an awl as the knit could start to run.

Notches can indicate where seams fit together or be used as marking points to show the centre front or centre back. The notch is marked on the pattern with a small cut-out and should be marked onto the fabric with a chalk line. Once the pattern is removed, the chalk mark can be snipped with scissors. Be careful when snipping into the fabric as it might fray if the notch is cut too deep, resulting in the seam becoming unstable. Notches should not be any longer than 3mm (⅛in). Notching is the quickest way to mark and can be used on most woven and knitted fabrics.

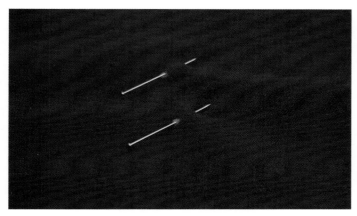

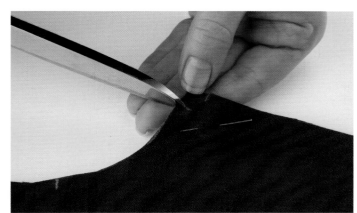

Top left: Use a pin to mark the dart point.

Top right: Chalk the position at the point of entry before turning the fabric over and chalking the second side.

Above left: Mark a dart point with an awl up to 1cm (⅜in) inside the end of the dart.

Above right: Do not cut too deeply into the seam allowance when cutting a notch.

Thread marking

Some lightweight fabrics, or areas on a pattern piece, cannot be chalk marked as the chalk might show through or not show up. In this case thread mark all the marking points on the pattern pieces, including dart positions and any placement points. This technique is also called tailor's tacking. Use a basting, cotton or silk thread and a hand-sewing needle, double threaded. Sew a stitch with entry and exit points a couple of millimetres apart, creating loops on both sides. Ensure that the stitches are loose as loops pulled too tight could distort the fabric. If you have marked a double layer, carefully separate the fabric layers and clip the thread between them leaving thread marks on each side of the fabric piece.

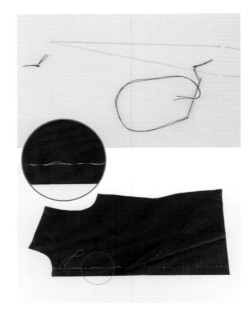

Thread marks are also used to show positioning and placement points on the right side of the fabric. This is a good method to use when marking a centre front or lapel break line on both sides, for example. This method, used in tailoring, is called tacking. Using a single or double thread and a hand-sewing needle, sew long running stitches through both layers of fabric, along the line that needs to be marked. Keep the thread loose when sewing. Carefully separate the fabric layers and clip the thread between them, leaving thread marks on each side of the fabric piece.

Above: Transfer marks for features such as a dart using thread marking or a tailor's tack.

Left: Tacking can be used to mark a centre front.

Marking with carbon copy paper and a tracing wheel

This method can be used on most woven fabrics to transfer marks from one marked side to the second layer. Place the carbon paper on the wrong side of the unmarked piece of fabric. The marked piece of fabric is then placed on top with the wrong side facing. Then, using a tracing wheel, trace along the lines of the marked fabric. Take extra care when using this method as the fabric and copy paper can easily slip in the process. Always test it first on a spare piece of fabric as the marks can show through to the right side of the fabric.

Use carbon paper and a tracing wheel to transfer marks between different layers of fabric.

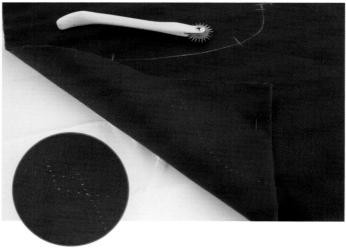

Cutting Out

Start cutting out after the pattern has been marked and lifted off the fabric.

Watch out for the following when cutting out:

- Choose a flat and firm cutting surface, large enough to fit the length of material required and tall enough for the cutter to stand up straight.
- Use the right cutting tool.
- Make sure the cutting blade is sharp.
- When cutting two or more layers at the same time, secure the fabric layers together with pins around the cutting area after lifting off the pattern pieces.
- Cut with the garment shape on the left-hand side of the scissors.
- While cutting, rest the scissors on the cutting surface so that the fabric is slightly raised but not lifted off the surface.
- Move your body into a good cutting position, not the fabric.
- Place one hand lightly on top of the fabric, close to the cutting area.
- Use the whole of the blade when cutting by closing the scissors right up to the tip.
- If possible, cut the small pieces first and then move to the bigger ones.
- Only snip in the notches after all the pattern pieces have been cut out.
- Make sure the fabric is slack or relaxed when laid out ready for cutting; if cut when taut the fabric will bounce back when the tightness is released.
- Transfer marking and placement points after all the pieces have been cut out.

THE TEN-POINT CUTTING GUIDE

1. Analyse the fabric.
2. Pre-shrink and press the fabric.
3. Align the fabric grain.
4. Decide on the cutting plan.
5. Decide on the pattern layout.
6. Place and secure the pattern pieces onto the fabric using the correct grain line.
7. Mark all pattern pieces onto the fabric.
8. Cut all pieces out.
9. Transfer notches, marking and placement points.
10. Get ready to sew.

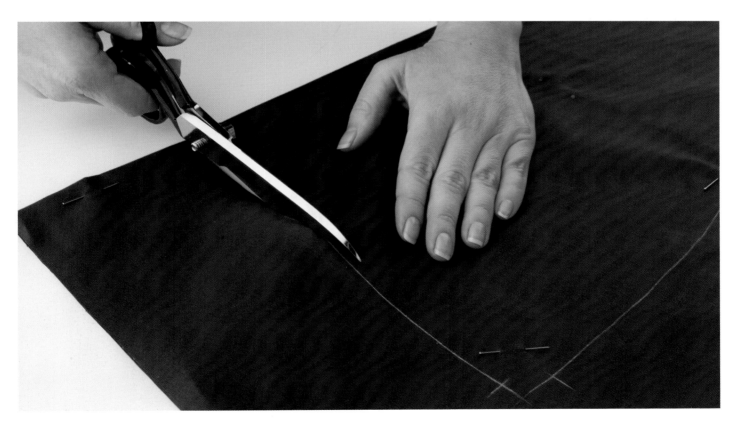

Place your hand on the fabric with the pattern shape to the left of the scissors.

Industry Production Methods

When designing for mass-production, or if you are working on your own label, you will be involved in the production process from start to finish. If you are working for a large company your involvement might be minimal. Mass-production of womenswear, menswear and childrenswear can be divided into lingerie and underwear, nightwear, sportswear and active wear, workwear, leather and fur. Tailoring and bridalwear can also be mass-produced although they are often bespoke. The techniques in this book cover professional best practice for sewing by hand and machine and will be useful for making any garment, whether it is a sample or a commission.

Producing samples

A pattern cutter produces pattern pieces from the designer's drawings and may also be involved in producing the size chart from which all samples are made. He or she will sew toiles that can be adjusted for style and fit. The pattern cutting is either done by hand or machine.

A sample machinist in a design studio or factory works closely with the designer and pattern cutter, developing construction methods and finishing ideas, and making garments on industrial sewing machines. They may work solely on selected ranges such as trousers or shirts, or within one or two areas of fabric. Many machinists working in factories are paid by the piece and specialization increases their speed. The sample machinist who works for a fashion house will produce the sample garments for collection development, the garments that will be shown on the catwalk and the garments that are presented to buyers in the showroom.

A sample machinist works within a fashion house producing garments for the catwalk and the showroom.

In the factory

Mass-production means producing one garment design in different sizes and/or colours, in large quantities. This is done using computerized patterns drafted to a size chart. The pattern pieces are cut through several layers by laser or industrial rotary cutters. The garments are assembled using specialized machinery for different areas: for example, buttonholes are made on an industrial buttonhole machine and hems are finished with an industrial blind-stitch machine. No hand sewing is used.

A machinist in a factory often works on only one part of a garment, which then moves on for the next stage in the production process.

Bespoke production

Bespoke and couture garments are made to measure, either as a one-off or a design reproduced for several clients. This area includes the bespoke tailor, the bridal business and some furriers and milliners. Fetish wear is mostly produced in a small range to a size chart or is bespoke. In bespoke tailoring, individual body measurements are taken and a pattern constructed to fit the client's shape. The fabric is cut by hand and some of the elements, such as buttonholes and hems, are hand finished.

Dummies are used during the initial construction of made-to-measure garments.

TIP

Different methods of production are reflected in the price of the end product. A bespoke jacket will take much more time to complete than a mass-produced one and be priced accordingly. However, it will also show a difference in individuality, fit, quality and garment life.

2

Materials and Sewing Supplies

Fabrics

Selecting the right fabric is essential for the success of a garment so a designer must understand the properties and qualities of different fabrics. The design process includes researching the fabric; the way it looks, hangs and feels can inspire a design.

It is crucial to choose the right fabric for the design – many beginners choose a fabric for its colour or pattern instead of its qualities, but the wrong fabric means the garment will not work. For example, wool crepe or silk jersey are perfect for a draped silhouette because they drape naturally around the body. For a more structured garment, choose a fabric with that quality, such as heavy or felted wool. When selecting fabric consider texture, drapability, structure, quality, colour, size and repeat of pattern, stretch direction, nap, transparency and price. Do not be put off if you have not worked with a material before; start by sampling the fabric and researching into finishing ideas before using it in your final garment. Sampling with unfamiliar materials will expand your knowledge of fabrics and may inspire new ideas.

S-twist (left) and Z-twist (right) yarns.

Fibres to yarn

Fibres are spun, twisted, cured, bulked or otherwise manipulated to create a continuous length of interlocked fibres known as yarn or thread. The direction the yarn is spun is called the twist and can be a 'Z' (right-hand) twist, or an 'S' (left-hand) twist. Two or more yarns can be twisted together with different degrees of tightness to the twist. Yarns are woven or knitted together to create fabric.

Natural fibres, man-made fibres and synthetics

Fibres are split into two main groups: natural and manufactured, or man-made, fibres. Natural fibres come from two main sources: cellulose from plants, such as cotton or flax, and protein from animals such as the silkworm or sheep. Manufactured fibres are produced using technology, with the raw material – which can be a natural or synthetic – in liquid form being spun or extruded to form a long-chain polymer.

Textile fibres can be staple, which are short fibres, or filament, which is a continuous strand of fibre. Most natural fibres are staple except cultivated silk, which is a natural filament. Manufactured fibres can be staple or filament – they always begin as filaments but can be broken into staples to simulate natural fibres. Contemporary fabrics are often blends of natural and synthetic fibres to overcome the limitation of a single component and to enhance the aesthetics and performance of a fabric or material.

Smart fabrics

Smart fabrics, also known as modern materials or e-textiles, are wearable technology. These materials contain digital components or electronics. Elements such as sensors, microcontrollers and power distributors are incorporated into wash-and-wear clothing. For example, warmX® fabric conducts heat and, when used with a power pack, will heat the body. NuMetrex® is a company that weaves heart-rate monitors into fitness clothing using smart-fabric technology. Smart fabrics can also sense and react to environmental conditions such as changes of temperature.

Smart technologies can be applied to woven, knitted and felted fabric as print or digital embroidery. The garments can be sewn traditionally or made with ultrasonic welding, where ultrasonic sound waves pass through the layers of fabric and fuse the fibres. Another method is web bonding (see page 93).

Fabric construction

Weaving

Weaving is a process where a minimum of two threads, a warp and a weft, are interwoven with each other on a loom or a weaving machine. The warp thread runs lengthwise to the grain and the weft thread crosswise. The three fundamental types of weave are plain weave, twill weave and satin/sateen weave.

Plain weave is the most basic weave; the weft thread is taken over and under alternating warp threads at right angles to each other. Plain weave fabrics are by no means plain – a vast variety of styles can be achieved. Plain weave fabric is firm, wears well and is a good base for printing or embroidery. It wrinkles more than other weaves but frays less and is easy to cut and sew.

Twill weave is one of the most durable weaves, creating hardwearing fabrics such as denim or gabardine, which are used for workwear, outerwear and suiting. The twill weave is easy to spot since it creates diagonal lines or ridges on the fabric surface. The fabric is compact, closely woven and quite heavy; it wears well and recovers well from wrinkling. However, the diagonal lines of twill weave give it a direction or nap, so care must be taken when cutting.

Satin weave is an unstable twill weave that can be costly in production, and snags and unravels easily. However, it has a high-lustre surface and produces some of the most luxurious fabrics, such as silk satin duchesse. Satin weave is favoured for linings and drapes because of its smoothness and drapability.

There are also variations or combinations of the three basic weaves, which are classified as complex or novelty weaves, such as Jacquard and pile weaving.

Jacquard weave can incorporate a combination of any or all of the three basic weaves and produces an unlimited variety of patterns. Jacquard not only refers to the weave technique but is also the name of a type of fabric.

Pile weave creates a three-dimensional effect. The fabric is constructed over rods to insert an extra set of weft or warp yarn into the basic structure to create loops. These loops can be cut after fabric construction to create a pile fabric, such as velvet, or left intact for a loop-back fabric such as terry. Fabric with a pile or loops has a nap or direction, which needs to be considered when cutting out and constructing a garment. For more information on pile fabric see page 276.

Knitting

Knitted fabric is constructed from a series of interlinking loops or stitches; a vertical row of stitches is called a wale and a horizontal row a course. Knitted fabric can be produced by hand knitting or machine knitting. Machine knitting creates two types of knit, warp or weft.

Warp knit fabrics: Milanese knit, raschel knit, kettenraschel knit, tricot knit, weft-insertion warp knit, Jacquard knit.

Weft/Filling knit fabrics: double knit, interlock-stitch knit, plain/single/jersey knit, purl knit, rib knit, weft-knit variations, Jacquard knit.

Plain weave.

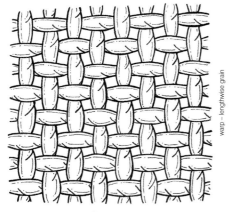

warp – lengthwise grain

weft – crosswise grain

Twill weave.

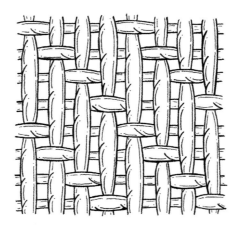

Satin weave.

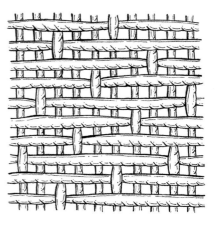

Stretch fabrics

Woven or knitted fabrics can incorporate elastane to increase the stretch and recovery of the fabric. Elastane and spandex are general names for a number of different stretch synthetic yarns, such as Lycra. Garments made out of stretch fabrics provide maximum elasticity, ease of movement and comfort. Knitted fabrics, such as nylon with Lycra, are a perfect choice for tight-fitting garments, while adding elastane to woven wool can provide a modern twist to a traditional fabric. The invention of elastane has enabled designers to experiment with new shapes without sacrificing comfort.

Felting and fulling

Felt is a non-woven fabric in which a minimum of 30% wool fibres are condensed and matted together, through wet felting or needle felting, until a sheet of fabric is formed. Felt has no direction or grain and comes in different thicknesses. It is very mouldable and can be shaped by heat and steam into any form. Felting should not be confused with fulling – felting creates fabric by pressing fibres together, whereas fulling is carried out after the fabric has been constructed.

Fulling is a finishing process for woollen fabrics using water, friction and pressure to create controlled felting of the fabric surface. The fabric is pre-shrunk and becomes denser with a fuller body. Melton is an example of a woollen fabric produced with a fulling finish.

Fabric finishing

Any combination of treatment or finishes can be applied to the fibre, yarn or finished fabric at any time during fabric production to enhance the performance, quality, look, feel or durability of a fabric. Finishing methods used to improve the visual effect of a fabric can include bleaching, dyeing, glazing, embossing, printing, fulling and mill-washing. To enhance the quality, a fabric can be pre-shrunk, mercerized, mothproofed, brushed, softened or stiff/crisp finished. A coating finish, such as waxing or water-repellent finishes, can be used to waterproof fabrics for protective wear. These are just a few examples of finishes and treatments available.

Fabric is best stored wrapped around a sturdy cardboard roll.

Cotton

Cotton is a natural yarn produced from the fibre of the boll (seedpod) of the cotton plant. The boll is picked, then the cotton fibre is separated from the seeds by a process known as ginning. The long-staple and finest cotton fibres are the most expensive and make the best quality fabrics, such as Egyptian, Sea Island, Pima and Supima cotton. Fibres too short for spinning are used in manufacturing rayon.

Cotton can be used on its own or blended with other natural or manufactured fibres to improve its durability, hand (also known as touch) or look. Mercerized cotton has been treated with a caustic alkali solution to improve strength, affinity to dye and lustre. Cotton fabrics are available in a variety of weights, surface structures, weaves, colours and patterns. They can be woven or knitted and can be as fine and transparent as organza, or a structured, hardwearing material such as cotton drill. This has made cotton a versatile and relevant fabric choice for many centuries; it is still popular in the fashion industry today.

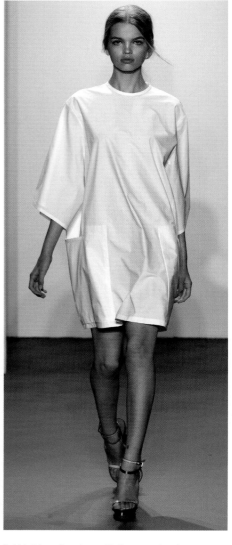

Detail of the boll (seedpod) of the cotton plant.

T-shirt style cotton dress with three-quarter sleeves. Calvin Klein, SS 2011.

The quality and characteristics of cotton fabrics

- Cotton fibres are absorbent; the fabric is breathable and comfortable to wear.
- The fabric is soft but durable and hardwearing.
- Most cotton fabrics are ideal for garment construction because they respond well to sewing and pressing.
- Cotton's versatility for garment styles is extensive; it can be used for almost everything including childrenswear and underwear/lingerie.
- Cotton fabric can be machine-washed or dry-cleaned depending on its finish or treatment.
- Cotton is stronger when wet than when dry.
- The fabric shrinks when washed so will need pre-shrinking by ironing with steam or treating before cutting out.
- Cotton wrinkles easily and has little elasticity and resiliency.
- It is very flammable and soils easily unless treated.

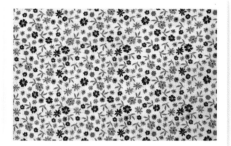

Floral Print Cotton in a light- to medium-weight quality. Cotton fabrics offer a good surface for printing. This type of fabric can be used for summer dresses, shirts or childrenswear.

100% Cotton Shirting in a panama or basket weave, which gives the surface its distinctive chequerboard appearance. This light- to medium-weight durable fabric comes mostly in pastel colours for shirting.

Fine Cotton Shirting in a Jacquard weave. This 100% cotton fabric has a silky feel and a satin sheen and is mainly used for men's special-occasion shirts. The Jacquard weave allows a wide range of complex patterns and designs to be produced.

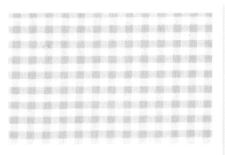

Gingham is a lightweight cotton fabric in an even, plain weave check pattern. Soft to the touch and strong, it is used for shirts, blouses, dresses, skirts and childrenswear.

Cotton Drill has a twill weave; it feels and looks like denim but with a more even colour quality. The twill lines run from the bottom right to the top left. Because of its durability it is often used for work clothes and uniforms.

Cotton Poplin is a fine, closely woven fabric with fine ribs running in the weft direction. It is a strong fabric that creases easily. When produced with a mercerized cotton yarn it has a soft sheen.

Wool

Wool is a natural animal fibre made of protein. Most wool comes from sheep; the living animal is shorn or clipped to remove its woolly fleece once a year. The fleece is then washed and treated to remove plant matter and dirt. Short fibres produce the finest wool whereas longer fibres create coarser fabrics. There are many different domestic breeds of sheep, but the Merino produces the finest wool.

There are also many types of speciality wool, including angora from rabbits, mohair and cashmere from goats, vicuña from a type of camel, and alpaca wool. Speciality wool is fine and very soft, creating a fabric with a luxury feel and look. It can be mixed with sheep's wool to keep the cost down and to improve the performance and drape.

Woollen fabric comes in different textures and can be woven, felted or knitted. It can be fine and cool for summer, or warm and cosy for winter.

Clockwise from top left: Merino sheep, alpaca, camel, angora goat.

Oversized cashmere coat with satin lining. MaxMara, AW 2013.

The quality and characteristics of wool fabrics

- Wool is the most absorbent fibre and takes up moisture without feeling wet, so it is comfortable to wear in any climate.
- Wool fabric insulates well and has great loft, giving warmth with little weight.
- The fabric is easy to use for garment construction because it responds well to sewing and pressing.
- It can be moulded or shaped with steam, which is used in tailoring on canvas interlinings to hold the structured shape of a jacket.
- It is resilient and has good elastic recovery, which makes it wrinkle-resistant.
- Wool can be machine-washed or dry-cleaned depending on its finish or treatment.
- Wool fibres can be blended with other fibres to improve performance and keep costs down.
- Wool felts easily when exposed to a combination of heat, moisture, pressure and abrasion.
- Incorrect pressing or the use of a hot iron can permanently damage wool fabric.
- Wool is damaged by sunlight, moths and bleach.

Melton is a firm fabric, traditionally made of wool, which does not fray and has a non-directional nap. The fabric is given a special finish to create a felted surface that looks matt and dense. It is used mainly for jackets and coats.

Tartan is a checked, woollen fabric in twill weave. It is particularly associated with Scotland, where it has a long history. It is a beautiful fabric to use for kilts, skirts, dresses, coats and suits.

Wool Gabardine is a closely woven twill with prominent diagonal ribs on the right side but not on the wrong side. Gabardine is water-repellent and hardwearing, which makes it a good choice for trousers, jackets and outerwear.

100% Pure Cashmere fabric has a luxurious feel, is warm and comfortable to wear and very soft to the touch. The fabric usually has a one-direction nap on the right side, which needs to be considered when cutting out.

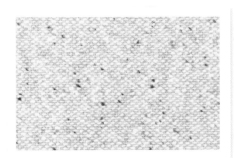

Tweed is a thick, heavyweight woollen fabric in plain or twill weave. Most tweeds have mixed colour effects, either speckled, checked, striped or a herringbone pattern. Tweeds have a rough surface so may need lining if made into garments.

Worsted Flannel is a lightweight twill weave fabric that is strong and soft to the touch with a slight nap. It is used in menswear tailoring.

Silk

Silk is valued for its shimmering beauty, luxurious feel and exclusivity. A protein fibre from an animal, it is the only natural continuous-filament fibre. Most silk is cultivated, a process known as sericulture, and comes from the cocoons made by the larvae of the *Bombyx mori* moth. Once the cocoon is spun the silkworm inside is killed with heat to prevent it maturing and exiting the cocoon, which would break the continuous-filament fibre. The cocoon is then degummed – placed into hot water to soften the protective sericin gum – since silk with less sericin makes better-quality fabric. After the softening process the filaments of many cocoons are unwound at the same time.

Wild silk is produced by other species of moth, either living in the wild or semi-domesticated, and is of lower quality because the silkworm larva is left to hatch, breaking the cocoon into short fibres. Fabrics woven from wild silk, such as Shantung silk, have a coarse, irregular surface. Some wild silks do not have sericin removed and show a knotted surface structure.

A silkworm cocoon.

Satin silk kimono-style jacket. Stella McCartney, SS 2010.

The quality and characteristics of silk fabrics

- Silk is regarded as the most luxurious and lavish material; it is soft to the touch and comfortable to wear.
- Silk fabrics are cool in summer and warm in winter, depending on the weave.
- It can be woven or knitted in different weights: sheer with good drape, or heavy, stiff and voluminous.
- It has little static build-up and absorbs moisture.

- Silk fabric is resilient, elastic and wrinkle-resistant, although it wrinkles more when wet.
- Most silks require dry-cleaning depending on the fabric structure, treatment or finish.
- Some silk fabrics are slippery and difficult to handle during garment construction. Skill is needed to avoid the fabric stretching or puckering when fed through a machine.

- For lightweight or medium-weight silk, choose a semi-fitted or loose draped, gathered or pleated style – avoid tightly fitted designs.
- Silk is resistant to mildew, but can be damaged by moths and insects. It yellows and weakens if exposed to the sun or excess heat.

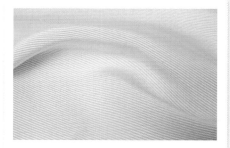

Silk Ottoman is a firm, stiff fabric with a smooth surface that shows pronounced ribs running crosswise. It can be used for suits and jackets, or for sculptural silhouettes that stand away from the body.

Satin Silk has a lustrous surface and excellent drape. It is constructed in satin weave so the right side is shiny and the wrong side is matt. Satin fabrics are mostly used for blouses, dresses, skirts and linings.

Silk Organza is a very fine, transparent, stiff plain weave fabric that creases easily. It is used for eveningwear, dresses, blouses and lingerie, and for small areas such as trims and panels. It is also used as an underlining to support lightweight fabrics.

Silk Taffeta is a fine, crisp and shimmering fabric in a plain weave with a papery feel. It makes a swishing noise as the garment moves. It is mainly used for womenswear such as formal-occasion garments, blouses, dresses and skirts.

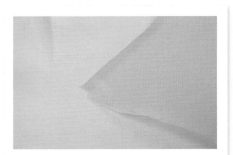

Silk Chiffon is a translucent, very lightweight fabric with a plain open weave. It drapes well and should be used for full silhouettes rather than for fitted or structured garments. It is beautiful used in multi-layers or for simple bias-cut garments.

Thai Silk is a fine, crisp fabric with a sheen, traditionally hand-woven in unique patterns and colours. It is used for dresses, skirts, blouses and linings. The sample shown is lining quality, very fine in a tight, plain weave.

Linen

Linen is made from the natural fibres of the flax plant; it has been around for many centuries and is valued for its visual appearance, strength and cooling properties. The flax fibres are harvested from the stem of the plant either by machine or manually, which maximizes the length of the fibre ensuring a better-quality yarn. Flax fibres are staple fibres that must be spun into yarns, which are then woven or knitted into fabric. The shorter fibres are made into household textiles and coarser fabrics, while longer fibres are used to produce finer materials for clothing and bed linen. Linen is labour-intensive to manufacture, which is what makes it expensive. Flax fibres are often blended with other staple fibres, but the term 'linen fabric' is only used for fabrics with a 100% flax fibre.

Flax plants have tall, slender stems; the fibres from the stems are harvested and spun to make linen yarn.

Summer suit in check suiting linen.
Michael Bastian, SS 2013.

The quality and characteristics of linen fabrics

- Linen is cool to the touch with good moisture absorbency, which makes it ideal to wear in hot weather.
- The fabric has poor elasticity and wrinkles easily, which is considered part of its natural charm. However, it can be treated with liquid ammonia, which makes it wrinkle less.
- Linen fabric will soften with each wash.
- It shrinks so needs to be pre-washed before cutting.
- The fabric frays and seam slippage can be a problem.
- Choose loose silhouettes, unstructured jackets and semi-fitted, casual garment shapes when using linen.
- When creased or folded in the same place, such as for collar folds or hemlines, the fibres will tend to break. Pressed-in creases are difficult to remove.
- Linen changes colour with age.

100% Linen This fine, lightweight fabric feels soft and cool to the touch and can be used for spring and summer garments such as blouses, skirts, shorts and dresses or casual menswear shirts.

Suiting Linen in a closely set plain weave has a crisp finish. It is very absorbent, strong and soft and comfortable to wear. It is used for skirts, shorts or suits.

Cotton and Linen Blend in a plain weave. Flax fibres can be blended with other natural fibres to improve the quality, price and texture of the fabric. This fabric blend can be used for a wide range of garment types.

Coated Linen fabric in a plain weave. Linen fabrics can be treated to improve the look or expand the range of use. This fabric has been treated with a water-resistant finish and can be used for outerwear such as jackets and coats.

Linen Hopsacking is a heavyweight linen fabric in a basket weave. This type of fabric is rough in texture, bulky and heavy. It is loosely woven showing the lumpy or uneven flax fibres. These fabrics are easy to shape but fray badly.

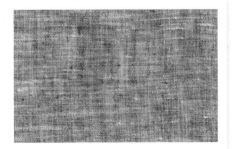

Handkerchief Linen is a fine plain weave fabric that is soft and lightweight with a satin sheen. It creases like all linen fabrics and shows the typical irregular surface. This fabric is used for dresses, skirts and blouses or casual menswear shirts.

Man-made and synthetic fibres

The first artificial fibre, rayon (viscose), was developed in the late nineteenth century to replace expensive silk. The manufacturing process was inspired by the way the silkworm produces silk fibres: the liquid raw material is extruded through spinneret holes to form a long-chain polymer. The filament fibres can be broken into staples to copy natural fibres. Manufactured fibres are divided into two categories:

- Artificial or man-made fibres, made by regenerating a natural material, such as cellulose, to create fibres such as viscose/rayon and acetate.

- Synthetics made entirely from chemical compounds – mostly petroleum – to create fibres such as nylon/polyamide, acrylic/polyamide, polyester and elastane.

Many manufactured fibres are finished to duplicate the feel, look, texture and/or structure of natural fibres. What started as a low-cost alternative has become a sophisticated and innovative textile industry, developing desirable contemporary fabrics for the fashion industry.

The quality and characteristics of rayon, acetate, nylon and polyester

Rayon
- Rayon is a soft, comfortable fabric made to imitate cotton, silk, wool or linen.
- It does not collect static.
- Some rayon fabrics shrink and must be washed before cutting out.
- Some rayon fabrics have little elasticity and recovery and therefore wrinkle.
- Rayon can be damaged with a hot iron. Always press from the wrong side or use a pressing cloth on the right side.

Nylon
- Nylon is a strong, durable material originally used for stockings and lingerie.
- It is elastic, easy-care, wrinkle-resistant and water-repellent.
- It can be woven, knitted or non-woven.
- Nylon does not ease well, sticks to the sewing machine needle and is prone to skipped stitches and puckered seams.
- A hot iron easily damages nylon fabrics.

Acetate
- Acetate drapes well with a luxurious texture and look.
- It resists pilling.
- Acetate can melt under a hot iron.
- Acetate fabrics are easily damaged by pinholes or ripping.

Polyester
- Polyester fabrics are resilient, have good elasticity and do not wrinkle. They are easy to care for and need little ironing.
- 100% polyester has poor absorbency and can be uncomfortable to wear, so it is often blended with other natural or man-made fibres.
- Polyester does not ease well and is prone to skipped stitches and puckered seams.
- Pre-pressed polyester fabrics become softer and easier to sew, but are easily damaged by a hot iron and difficult to press.
- Polyester fabrics wear at garment edges and folds.

Layered, transparent synthetic organza dress. Marc Jacobs, SS 2012.

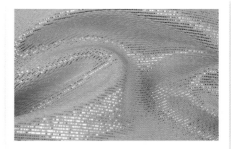

Lurex has metallic yarns blended with other fibres, such as polyester or silk, and is lightweight, smooth and shiny. It is selected for beauty, not durability. Lurex should be used for loosely fitted garment designs and drapes.

Neoprene is a soft, foam-like fabric in a range of thicknesses, constructed of two fabrics laminated together – the backing is either polyester or nylon warp-knitted tricot. It is waterproof with very good abrasion strength and elasticity, and is used for protective clothing, wetsuits and waders.

Crushed Polyester Taffeta with a subtle gold foil detail and irregular crushed pattern. It is made from silk or synthetic fibres and is crisp and smooth woven. It drapes well and has the swishing sound typical of taffeta. It is mostly used for special-occasion womenswear, blouses, dresses and skirts.

Satin Polyester is constructed of synthetic fibre polyester and is the cheaper version of satin silk (see page 67). Its texture is not as smooth as satin silk but it also has a shiny right side and is good for draped or bias-cut garments.

Net is a sheer, open-mesh fabric, usually made in nylon or polyester. Net fabrics are constructed in different ways and range from soft to very stiff. It is used for special-occasion wear, as an interlayer or underlining, as a petticoat or under-structuring or as trimming.

PVC, also called **Vinyl**, is an elastomer manufactured from petrochemicals. A synthetic PVC coating can be applied to woven, knitted or non-woven fabric to give protection from water, abrasion or chemicals. PVC is ideal for rainwear and protective wear, or to create complex silhouettes.

Textured fabrics

Textured fabrics are experimental or unusual textiles, or those that have been treated with a finish at some point during fabric construction, which can make it difficult for the fabric to be cut, sewn or pressed. These include, for example, plastic materials, napped fabric, latex or sequined fabrics – but also skins such as leather, suede and fur. For more information on special construction techniques for these fabrics, see Chapter 5, Fabric- and Cut-Specific Techniques.

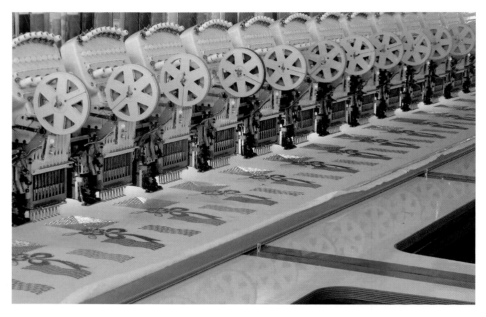

An industrial embroidery machine can reproduce many copies of the same design in different colourways.

Sequin-effect metallic printed jumper and trousers. Akris, AW 2012.

The quality and characteristics of textured fabrics

These depend on the material, but generally speaking:

- Pinning the fabric may leave a permanent mark, so test first.
- Test pressing – usually these materials cannot take a hot iron or pressure because the surface could be flattened. Some need to be pressed on the wrong side or with a pressing cloth, while others, such as latex or leather, cannot be pressed at all, so seams must be topstitched or glued in place.
- Most textured materials can only be dry-cleaned.
- Always make up a sewing sample first; most textured materials have a tendency to skipped stitches or puckering on seams.
- You may need specific cutting equipment, or sewing equipment such as a Teflon foot or walking foot for sticky materials.
- Consider the garment style and cut; some designs are not suitable for textured fabrics. A sequined fabric, for instance, should not be used for a garment with too many seams because these could interrupt the sequin pattern.

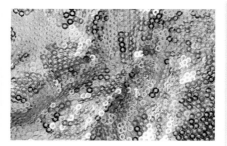

Sequined Fabric is one of the most glamorous fabrics. The sequins are sewn or glued onto a knit or woven background fabric in either an individual motif or an all-over pattern. Special sewing and cutting methods are required for sequined fabric.

Leather is the natural skin or hide of an animal, for example a cow, sheep or pig. Leather needs specialized equipment for garment construction. It can be treated with different finishing techniques to reflect fashion trends – the sample shown has a metallic finish. A broad range of imitation leathers is now available by the metre, meaning it is no longer necessary to work around the size of a skin.

Fur Fabric imitates real fur, which is the skin of an animal with the hair still attached. Fur fabric has a pile made from long-staple synthetic fibres attached to a backing fabric. The imitations of real fur are often so well done that it is very difficult to tell the difference between real and fake – often the only giveaway is the reverse side.

Brocade is a detailed Jacquard weave fabric with a richly figured pattern created by the weaving method. It has a three-dimensional look on the right side, with a less pronounced design on the wrong side. Most brocades are heavyweight, often with metallic or colourful threads giving the fabric a luxurious appearance.

Plastic Fabric is a non-woven material that comes in different thicknesses and colours and can be transparent to opaque. It is waterproof and can be used for whole garments, such as raincoats, or as inserts/part of a garment. A thin transparent layer of plastic fabric used over another fabric can create an interesting effect.

Honeycomb is a woven fabric constructed using a honeycomb weave method, which gives the fabric a repeating three-dimensional cellular effect on both sides. It is very absorbent and is often used for childrenswear, sportswear and casual wear.

Knitted and jersey fabrics

Knitted fabrics are available in many weights, textures and designs, in natural or synthetic fibre or a blend. Knits have more stretch than woven fabrics so they can mould to the body; some also contain spandex, which increases stretch capacity for a tighter fit while retaining good shape recovery. Like woven fabric, knits have a grain, but the lengthwise grain is called the wale and the crosswise grain is called the course.

Knitted fabrics are produced using needles to interweave yarn into a series of interlinking loops. Machine knitting can be weft knitted – with one yarn that travels horizontally back and forth – or warp knitted – with a separate yarn for each wale running vertically. A hand-knitted fabric is always weft knitted.

The right side of knitted fabric is referred to as plain stitch/knit and the wrong side as purl stitch/knit, while the texture depends on the size of needle and yarn thickness. The term jersey is applied to all types of weft-knitted fabric: single jersey has plain knit on one side and purl knit on the other, while double jersey looks the same on both sides and can be double the weight. Knitted fabrics can also be produced with elaborate patterns by fitting the knitting machine with a Jacquard mechanism.

Knitted fabrics are in general manufactured using a different approach to woven fabrics; for more information see Knitted and Stretch-Woven Fabrics, page 254.

A circular knitting machine can produce single or double jersey.

A flatbed knitting machine, which can be fitted with a Jacquard mechanism.

Panelled top and skirt made of different patterned, knitted fabric. Louise Goldin, AW 2013.

The quality and characteristics of knitted fabrics

- Knitted fabrics stretch more than woven fabrics, in one or both directions.
- Knits are soft to touch, comfortable to wear and drape well.
- Knitted fabrics are resistant to wrinkling, but do not crease well.
- Depending on the fibre content, knitted fabrics can be machine-washed or dry-cleaned.

- Do not apply the iron directly onto the surface of a knitted fabric because it may create a permanent shine.
- Knitted fabrics need specific sewing equipment, such as overlockers/sergers and cover stitch machines, to accommodate the natural stretch of the fabric.
- Use a ballpoint needle to avoid skipped stitches and holes.

- Knitted fabric works best on designs without fussy details.
- Jersey curls to one side once cut and will not retain a crisp, structured shape.
- Double jersey is easier to cut and sew, will retain a structured shape and does not run and unravel as jersey does.

Single Jersey is a fine knit with plain knit one side showing vertical ribs and a flat purl knit on the other side. It is mainly used for casual wear and sportswear. The sample shows a wool single jersey.

Double Jersey has vertical ribs on both sides and is firmer and heavier than single jersey. It is used for sophisticated knitwear pieces such as tops, dresses and jackets. The sample shows cotton double jersey.

Sweatshirting is a single knit fabric showing vertical ribs on one side and a napped fleece surface on the other that makes it comfortable to wear. It is used for active wear and casual wear. The sample shows cashmere-mix sweatshirting.

Mesh fabric has an open structure and can be knitted, lace or sometimes woven. A soft fabric with stretch, it can be used in sportswear as a lining or for garment sections and is popular for lingerie and casual wear. The sample shows a fine knitted mesh.

Ribbed Knits have a weft double-knit construction, using knit and purl stitches in regular repetition. This knit is more elastic than other weft knits so is ideal for tight garments. It is often used in casual wear to finish garment edges as well as for constructing tops and dresses. This sample shows a wool ribbed knit.

Viscose Jersey with Lycra has an increased stretch capacity for a tighter fit, but retains its shape with good recovery. It has a soft feel and is comfortable to wear. This fabric is used for foundation garments and swimwear, as well as any body-conscious garments.

Lining fabrics

Linings cover the inside of a garment to protect seams from fraying, to help a garment retain its shape and improve its durability, feel, comfort and quality. Garments can be fully or partially lined depending on function and design. It is important to choose the right lining, taking into consideration fibre content, fabric type, structure and weight, colour and pattern. Lining comes in different fibres such as silk, cotton, polyester, nylon, viscose and microfibres; for a light, breathable lining choose silk or viscose over nylon or polyester, or to add extra insulation use a quilted or fleece lining. When considering fabric type keep in mind the garment function – pocket bags for a coat are better in pocketing fabric for improved durability, whereas for a luxurious finish to a skirt a satin lining is better.

Lining fabrics may be woven or knitted to match the outer fabric structure: woven fabric needs a woven lining and knitted fabric a knit lining. For stretch fabric, use either a woven-stretch lining or a knit lining. A woven-stretch lining can also sometimes be used for knits, but test beforehand. Linings also come in different weights; ideally the lining should be lighter in weight than the outer fabric otherwise it will alter the look of the garment and feel bulky. Finally consider colour or pattern: although linings are on the inside of a garment, they should be an important design feature. Some designers use the lining as their trademark. An example is Ozwald Boateng, who adds brightly coloured linings into his suit jackets. For more information on how to apply a lining into a garment see Lining, page 212.

A jacket with its contrast lining used as a design feature at front facing, hood and cuffs. Fendi, SS 2014.

The quality and characteristics of linings

- A lining covers and neatens the inside of a garment, but also helps to retain shape and prolong its life.
- Linings are usually smooth fabrics to help a garment slip on and off easily.
- They can add warmth and insulation to a garment.
- Linings can be added to prevent a garment from stretching.

- Lining a garment creates a quality finish because it adds body and reduces wrinkling of the outer fabric, and stops the garment from clinging to the body so it hangs well.
- Linings can protect the skin from potentially irritating materials such as wool or sequined fabrics.
- Adding a lining to a garment gives it

a luxurious feeling and makes it more comfortable to wear.
- A lining fabric should be lighter in weight than the outer fabric, colourfast and static-free.

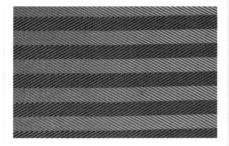

Herringbone Lining with a twill weave is a very durable fabric, which has a striped weaving pattern, making it popular as a lining in tailored outfits.

Pocketing is a tight, plain weave of cotton or cotton-blend fibres. It is a hardwearing fabric mainly used for constructing pocket bags.

Satin Lining in a satin weave with a polka dot design. The satin weave gives the lining a luxurious and shiny surface on the right side, with a matt surface on the reverse. This fabric is used for lining dresses, jackets, coats and skirts.

Heavy Viscose Lining in twill weave. This lining is very durable; it is used in jackets and coats to line the sleeves, and for pocket bags.

Cotton Lining in a plain weave. This is used in casual and sportswear because it is breathable and comfortable on the skin, although a garment lined in cotton is not as easy to slip on and off as one lined in slippery silk or viscose.

Quilted Lining is made of two layers – fabric and wadding – stitched together, so it is heavy and bulky. This needs to be considered when cutting the pattern for the garment to be lined. Quilted linings add insulation and can be decorative, creating complex silhouettes.

Lace

Lace is an open-structured, decorative fabric available in qualities from very fine, soft and sheer to heavy, stiff and coarse. Handmade lace, which can be either bobbin lace or needlepoint lace, is one of the most expensive and complex textile constructions and requires skill and time. Machine-made lace is produced on a variety of machines using twisting, knitting or embroidery techniques. Most fibres can be used for lace making, including Lycra blends for stretch-lace, which is ideal for tight-fitted garments and lingerie. Traditionally lace was used as a fabric for special occasions or as a trimming or appliqué, but has become more affordable and popular so is now widely used.

Most lace fabrics fall into the following categories:

- *Chantilly lace* has flowers and branches in the design and the pattern is outlined with a thick, silky thread.
- *Alençon lace* has a delicate flower and swag design on a netting base with motifs outlined in fine cord. Alençon motifs are more delicate than Chantilly.
- *Allover lace* has a repeating pattern across a wide width and can be cut and sewn like other fabrics. It is an inexpensive lace fabric and can be used for whole garments.
- *Guipure*, also called *Venise*, is a firm, stiff cotton lace with an embroidered design. It is made on a foundation material, which is later dissolved.
- *Cluny lace* is a coarse cotton lace used for trimmings or combined with less formal fabrics.
- *Schiffli* is a delicate, transparent chain-stitch embroidery lace on fine netting. It comes in a narrow width or as a trim.

For more information on special construction techniques for lace see Lace, Sequined and Beaded Fabrics, page 270.

Alençon lace blouse with a tiered lace-bordered dress. Erdem, SS 2011.

The quality and characteristics of lace fabrics

- Lace is mostly transparent and delicate.
- Some have scalloping instead of a selvedge, which can be used as a finished edge.
- Lace fabric is usually narrow.
- Lace is fragile and can snag easily.
- Minimize seaming when using intricate lace to avoid interrupting the lace pattern.
- Lace fabric does not have a grain but the pattern often shows a direction, which must be considered when cutting out.
- Some lace fabrics must be lined or stabilized with a backing such as organza or netting.
- Lace fabric stretches more in the width than in the length.

The bobbinet machine passes flat round bobbins through and around vertical threads to make lace.

Chantilly Lace is a fine bobbin lace with a scalloped edge that can be used for neckline and hemline finishing. Chantilly-style trims are also used on lingerie, nightwear and other garments.

Alençon Lace was originally a needlepoint lace with classical flowers and swags on a net ground. Instead of a selvedge, each side is finished with a scalloped edge.

Crochet Lace can be heavy and chunky with a rustic look.

Val Lace, also called **Valenciennes**, is a narrow flat lace with a floral design on a diamond- or circular-net base.

Guipure Lace starts as an embroidered material. The lace is made on a foundation, which is then dissolved. It is available as fabric or trimming.

Bordered Lace is finished on both lengthwise edges, usually with scallops, which can be used as a decorative edge finish. Bordered lace can be used for a whole garment or for only part.

Haberdashery

Closures

Closures enable garments to open and close for ease of access, and should be selected to suit the garment design. The range of different fastenings is vast; it includes many types of button, zips, Velcro, snaps, hooks-and-eyes, sewn-in magnets, buckles and eyelets. Garments can be closed edge-to-edge – in which edges are butted together – or with one edge extended to overlap the other to accommodate, for example, a button and buttonhole. Closures can be applied to the surface of a garment or as a structural element. They should be considered at the beginning of the design and construction process – they cannot be treated as an afterthought.

What to consider when selecting a closure

- Garment design.
- Closure design, location and purpose.
- Use and care of the garment.
- Fabric quality, pattern, weight and transparency.
- Durability and security of the closure.
- Type of sewing machine and skill involved in application.
- Cost.
- Current fashion trends.

Buttons

Buttons are used with buttonholes or button loops and can be functional or decorative. They come in a range of materials, including wood, mother-of-pearl, bone, leather, glass, ivory, silver, gold, brass, pewter, ceramic, rubber and plastic – and can also be covered with fabric. Button shapes and sizes also vary widely. There are two basic types: the sew-through button, which usually has either two or four holes to stitch through, and the shanked button, which has an eyelet on the underside. Buttons can be sewn on by hand or using a machine with a button-sew facility. When placing buttons, do not forget key positions at stress areas, such as across the chest or bust point and at the waistline. Find more information on how to apply buttons and on buttonhole placement in Fastenings, page 224.

Flat sew-through button with two holes.

Flat sew-through button with four holes.

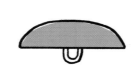

Domed shank button.

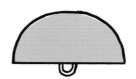

Half-ball shank button.

Full-ball shank button.

Button diameter is measured in *lignes* (abbreviated L), an internationally recognized standard measurement. See the diagram below.

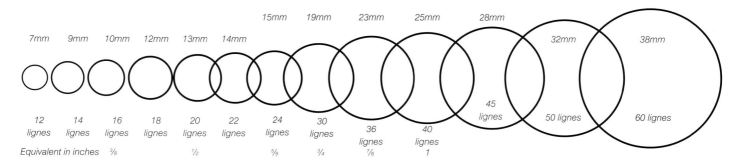

Shirt Buttons are small and usually plain and flat, with two sewing holes.

Mother-of-Pearl Buttons are also popular for shirts and blouses.

Jacket and Coat Buttons are medium to large and can be sew-through or a shank type, depending on the garment design – a military-style coat is likely to need a shank button, for instance.

Decorative Buttons come in all sizes and shapes and can be used on almost everything – enjoy the vast variety.

Fabric-Covered Buttons are available already covered or in a kit to be covered with the garment fabric. They include the Chinese ball type.

Trouser and Skirt Buttons are usually flat to allow a belt to sit on top and for the wearer's comfort.

Dress Buttons vary widely depending on the garment design and whether the opening is at the front or the back.

Backing Buttons are positioned inside a coat or jacket behind the closure button on the outside. They stop the outer button from pulling through and ripping the fabric due to the stress on a small area when fastened.

CHOOSE THE RIGHT BUTTON

- Consider the garment design – some traditional styles need a traditional button to look right, such as the duffle coat with its wooden toggles.
- Make sure the button size fits the closure area and is in proportion to the garment.
- Do not use a full-ball button on the centre back of a garment, since this could be uncomfortable for the wearer when leaning back.
- Make sure the buttonhole type fits the button style.

Zips

The zip is a slide fastener consisting of a pair of woven tapes holding metal or synthetic teeth that interlock. Since it is low cost, comes in a wide range of styles, colours, lengths and weights, and is quick and easy to use, the zip is a popular fastening device for skirts, dresses, trousers, jackets and coats. The two basic types of zip are coil or chain. Coil zips are usually lighter in weight; the coils that form the teeth are polyester or nylon. The chain zip has individual moulded teeth of metal or plastic. Metal chain zips are mainly used in jeans, workwear or any garment under stress.

Zips can be inserted into a garment in different ways to suit the design, material, usage and zip type. Concealed zips are inserted within a seam and are invisible on the outside of the garment. Other types of zip can be exposed – so the tape and teeth are visible on the outside of the garment – or concealed, either by covering the teeth with both edges of the seam fold or with a fly.

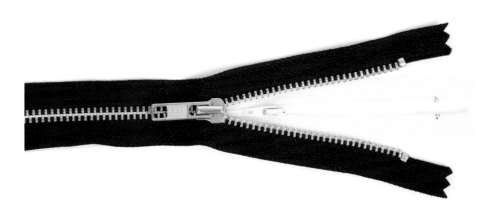

Metallic chain zip with individual moulded teeth (in black) and coil zip with plastic teeth (in white).

APPLYING A ZIP

- Choose the right zip type and construction method for the garment design, fabric and quality.
- Cut the pattern to suit the construction method used – a pattern for a zip with a fly will be cut differently to the pattern for a concealed zip.
- The zip length can define the length of a garment.
- Make sure the topstitching method and thread are appropriate to the garment design and fabric choice.
- Always ease the fabric slightly onto the zip and not the other way around.

Conventional Zips open at the top and are closed at the base, and may be coil or chain. They are used on garments requiring a one-way opening, such as trousers or skirts, and may be exposed or concealed.

Open-End/Separating Zips open at both ends; some types have two zip heads so can be operated from either end. They can be chain or coil and are available in light- to heavyweight. This type of zip is generally used in jackets and coats and may be exposed or concealed.

Concealed/Invisible Zips are a type of coil zip with teeth concealed on the underside. They are applied using a special sewing foot. Once inserted, the opening looks from the outside like a continuous seam with no stitching or zip showing. This type of zip may be conventional or open-ended and is used where a visible zip would detract from the design or where a smooth finished line is required.

Velcro

Velcro consists of two woven nylon strips, one side with hooks and the other with loops, which lock into place when pressed together but pull apart when required. The hook strip is placed on the under-wrap and the loop strip on the over-wrap of a garment, aligned with each other. Velcro fastenings can be used instead of buttons or a zip, but are not always suitable because the hooks can catch and damage the garment material. On loose-woven fabric the hooks may also clog up with loose fibres.

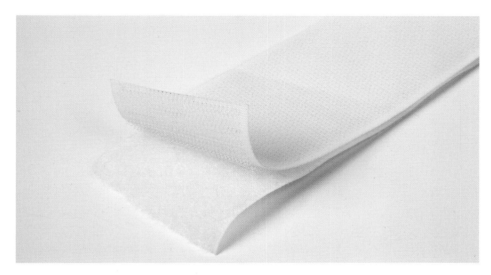

Sew-on Velcro is available in tape form or as individual circular spots.

Snap fastenings

A snap fastening, also called a popper or press stud, can be used instead of a button or where a flat and smooth closure is required. It consists of a pair of plastic or metal discs with a ball-stud (male, top part) and a socket-stud (female, bottom part), which interlock. Snaps are available in many sizes but are one of the weakest fastenings since they can be pulled apart easily. Sew-on snaps are hand stitched on the inside of a garment. A non-sew snap fastening has a decorative cap on top, which shows on the face of the garment, and a rivet on the bottom and is attached using special snap pliers. The fabric on the over-wrap is held between the cap and socket stud and on the under-wrap between rivet and ball stud. This type of snap is common on casual outerwear.

1 A plastic snap fastening, which is applied by hand sewing.

2 A metal snap fastening, which is applied by hand sewing.

3 A non-sew snap fastening.

4 A snap fastening on tape. This fastening tape has the ball-stud on one side and the socket-stud on the other side. The two sides snap together.

Hooks-and-eyes

Hook-and-eye fastenings consist of a hook and an eye or bar. They can be used alone, in pairs or in multiples and come in several sizes and types. They are mainly used at necklines or in skirt and trouser waistbands, often in combination with another fastening such as at the top of a zip.

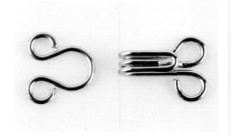

General-Purpose Hooks-and-Eyes have either a straight or round eye. The straight eye is used on overlapping edges, such as waistbands, and the round eye on adjoining fabric edges. Both are attached by hand sewing.

Covered Hooks-and-Eyes are larger and are used mainly on deep-pile fabrics or fur. They are hand stitched in place.

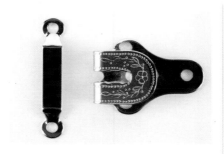

Heavy-Duty Hooks-and-Bars are used on the inside of trouser and skirt waistbands so are invisible on the face of the garment. They are hand stitched or hammered in using a special device and are very secure.

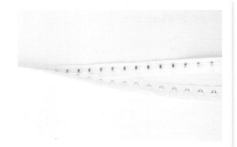

Hook-and-Eye Tape is available with cotton, organza, satin and nylon tape containing a single or double row of hooks. It is bought by the metre and used mainly in corsetry and underwear.

Magnetic fastenings

A sew-in magnet fastener consists of two magnetic discs that are concealed between a facing and the outer fabric, so are invisible on the face of the garment. They can be hand or machine stitched in place. A magnetic popper fastener, with concealed magnetic discs combined with ball-stud and socket-stud on the fabric surface, is also available.

A clip-in metallic (left) and sew-in magnetic (right) fastening. The clip-in fastening can be used where machine or hand stitching is not wanted.

Buckles and clasps

These are usually found on belts to fasten the two loose ends. They come in different designs, some with a prong and others designed to slide on. They can be purchased ready for use or for covering with fabric to match the garment. Vintage fairs and antique shops often have unusual buckles or clasps.

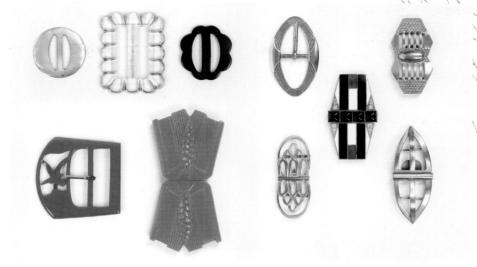

Buckles and clasps from the 1920s.

Other fasteners

Other devices are available to fasten and/or control the shape and volume of a garment.

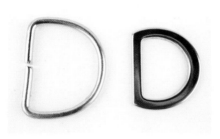

D-Rings in different sizes and materials can be used as an attachment point for straps or as a belt buckle.

Frog Fastenings are available ready-made, or you can design your own in your choice of material.

Swivel Hooks, Trigger Locks and Clasps are used as attachment points or as belt fastenings.

Brace Clips are attached to each end of an elasticated strap and then clipped to the front and back of a garment, such as trousers, to hold it up.

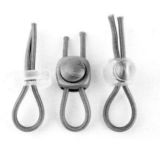

Toggles come in different sizes and materials and are used to control volume on garments at waistlines, hemlines or around hoods.

Threads

Thread is formed of short fibres or continuous filaments twisted together. The fibres may be natural or synthetic – natural fibres mildew or rot over time whereas 100% polyester threads will not. Thread stitches hold material pieces together temporarily or permanently; the correct thread is essential for a good seam and a professional finish. Always use quality thread because poor thread leads to weak seams and stitching problems. Thread is supplied on spools, cones, cards or in bundles and is available for hand and machine sewing in different colours, thicknesses and qualities. Specialized threads include invisible, fusible and water-soluble basting thread.

What to consider when selecting thread

- Garment design.
- Garment life expectancy and use.
- Fabric weight, colour and quality.
- Seam type.
- Type of sewing machine, machine speed and needle size.
- Cost.

Cotton Thread is available in a vast range of colours and is suitable for most light- to medium-weight fabrics, but does not stretch. A mercerized finish provides strength and smoothness. Cotton tacking thread is used in tailoring and couture work for temporary hand stitching and thread marking.

Polyester Thread is suitable for most fabric weights and qualities, including man-made fibres, leather, suede, knitted and waterproof fabrics. It is elastic, resilient and durable. Most polyester threads have a wax or silicone finish so they slip through material and machine with minimum resistance.

Cotton-Wrapped Polyester Thread is a popular all-purpose thread used on stretch and non-stretch materials, both natural and man-made. Its polyester core gives elasticity and strength and the cotton wrapping a heat-resistant surface.

Silk Thread is made of 100% silk fibres for strength and elasticity. It is mainly used for silk, wool and knit fabrics. Its fine quality makes it ideal for hand sewing – it is the tailor's first choice of thread.

Nylon Thread is fine, stretchy and strong and is used for sewing light- to medium-weight materials. It is transparent so is used for invisible hems, embroidery, appliqué and beading. It may melt if pressed on a high temperature.

Metallic Threads are for decorative sewing such as quilting, embroidery and appliqué. They can be used for machine and hand sewing but are fragile and heat sensitive so are not recommended for garments subject to heavy use.

Wool and Linen Yarns are available in a wide range of colours and sizes. They are used for darning and strengthening as well as decorative stitching such as tapestry, embroidery and edge finishing.

Elastic Thread is used for stitching that needs to stretch, including decorative shirring and smocking. Always wind elastic thread onto the bobbin by hand to avoid tension.

Decorative Yarn is used for embroidery, weaving, knitting and crochet.

Thread finishing

Thread may be finished to enhance its suitability for various sewing tasks. Cotton threads are treated with either a soft finish such as bleaching or dyeing, a glacé finish using special chemicals, a hard finish using wax/starches to strengthen and protect the thread, a glazed finish by passing through a flame at high speed, or a mercerized finish to add strength and create a smooth, lustrous thread. Polyester and nylon threads are treated with a special resin to encase the filaments and add a tough, smooth coating to resist abrasion.

Thread size

Threads are available in many sizes. If no size is specified, look at the thickness of the thread; the general rule is the higher the number the finer the thread. Tailor the weight of the thread to the weight of the material: lightweight for lightweight fabrics and heavier, topstitching or embroidery thread for heavy materials and decorative sewing. Most fabrics can be sewn with a medium-weight all-purpose thread, which is also used for topstitching on medium-weight fabrics.

MATCHING THE THREAD COLOUR TO THE FABRIC

- For printed or woven patterned fabric select the thread to match the dominant colour in the design.
- On plain colour fabric use the same colour thread or a shade darker because the thread will be a tone lighter when stitched.
- Always take a large swatch of fabric when buying thread to match.

- Choose the colour in daylight, not under artificial lighting.
- When choosing a contrast topstitching thread consider traditional usage, such as orange on denim materials.

Tapes and bindings

Tapes and bindings are used for decoration or to strengthen and support garment parts. There is a vast selection, available by the metre. Some are fusible, others are hand or machine sewn in place.

Tapes

Tapes are often used inside a garment to stabilize or hold parts together. They may be cut on the straight grain to prevent stretching or on the bias for more give.

Sew-in tapes

Cotton Tape is a woven tape to strengthen hemlines and seams.

Twill and Herringbone Tape is for stabilizing seams in cotton fabric.

Petersham Tape is a corded tape used for finishing and facing waist edges and as waistbanding inside corsets, dresses (waistline stay/belting) or for crinolines.

Pre-Fabricated Waistband Tape is sturdy, hardwearing and comes in different designs and widths. It is used mainly in tailored trousers.

Non-Fusible Tape comes in different sizes and is used to strengthen seams or openings anywhere on the garment.

Fusible tapes

Fusing Web Tape is used to fix hemlines without stitching.

Bonding Web is a thin sheet of adhesive webbing used to bond fabrics together.

Slotted Waistband Tape is used for interfacing waistbands to strengthen the material. It is pre-cut and the pre-marked folding lines provide a crisp waistband edge.

Belt-Backing Tape is a stiff hardwearing tape used to stiffen fabric belts.

Waistband-Stiffening Tape is for stabilizing waistbands and is available in a range of different widths.

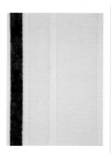

Fusible Tape comes in various sizes and is used to strengthen seams or openings. **Fusible Cotton Tape** is a stable cotton tape with a fusible backing. It is used for support.

Elastic

Elastic comes in a range of widths and styles and can be functional or decorative. It can be pulled through a casing or stitched to the fabric and left exposed. Elasticated sections add a casual look to a garment and make it more comfortable to wear.

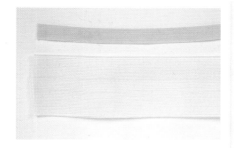

Flat Elastic comes in different widths and is threaded through a casing. It is sometimes stitched through once inserted to hold the gathers evenly.

Elastic Cord can be threaded through a casing or zigzag stitched into place.

Framilon® Elastic Tape has more elasticity than most tapes. It does not need casing and can be stitched or overlocked directly to the fabric.

Knitted Shirring Elastic or **Shirring Band Elastic** is an open-weave elasticated tape used for lingerie and light fabrics.

Lingerie Elastic is used as an edge finish for underwear. It is soft on the side to be worn next to the skin.

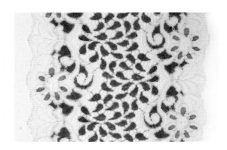

Lace Elastic is used for lingerie and outerwear. It is flexible and soft and moulds around the body. As it has good stretch it can be used for detail work in combination with other stretch fabrics or knits.

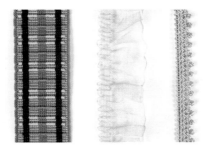

Decorative Elastic sits on the outside of a garment to enhance the style while adding stretch.

Bias bindings

Bias bindings are used to finish raw edges such as necklines or to strengthen seams. The binding replaces the facing, adds a decorative border and can be used as a casing for elastic or a drawstring. It can also be used to create button loops, belts and spaghetti straps. Fabric bindings are strips cut on the true bias from any fabric, or can be purchased pre-cut and folded. See pages 122–23 for how to sew a bias binding and attach tapes and trimmings.

Right: Cotton bias binding.
Far right: Satin bias binding.

Trims and decorations

Trims and decorations are used to emphasize the design of a garment and can change its style. Trimming designers cater for different styles in clothing and they use materials including netting, feathers, sequins, metal and wood. Some trims are elasticated, others are non-stretch. Trims and decorations can be hand or machine stitched or glued in place – it depends on the trim and the garment material. Choosing the right trim or decorative piece depends upon what is in fashion and finding the right balance is not easy. Research original garment styles for decoration and trim ideas.

Sew-on trims and pom-pom tape.

Decorations

Embroidery can be used as a stitch design to decorate a garment or to add beads, pearls or sequins. Many designers have used non-traditional materials in embroidery, such as screws or other small DIY parts. Ready-made decorations include bows, appliqué, fringes, tassels, rivets and snaps.

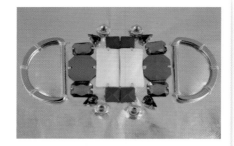

Embroidery sample with stones, studs, D-rings and screws by Christina Ruby Walton, above, and used to embellish a biker-style leather dress, right.

Supporting Materials

Fusible (iron-on) and non-fusible (sew-in) supporting materials are used to stabilize and add substance to parts such as fastenings, pocket openings and necklines to prevent stretching. Materials such as boning and canvas may be used to emphasize the natural body contour, as in corsetry, while a netting underskirt will hold the garment away from the body. Underlining can provide support and structure. Supporting materials are applied before or during the construction process – they can be added in different ways so should be considered at toiling stage before final cutting out. The variety available is vast, covering light support to reshaping, so experiment to achieve the best result.

When to use supporting materials

- Analyse the design. A garment gets shaping and support from the human body; parts that cannot be supported must be stabilized with supporting materials.
- Feel the texture and analyse the hang of the fabric; if it needs support to realize the garment shape use a suitable stabilizer.
- Consider garment edges such as necklines, armholes, pocket openings and hemlines – if cut on the bias they may stretch. Stabilize with interfacing, tape or interlining. For more information on how to stabilize openings see The Neckline, page 156.

Inside-out constructed jacket with exposed tailoring, showing canvas interlining and taped edges. Maison Martin Margiela Haute Couture, AW 2011.

WHY USE SUPPORTING MATERIALS?

- To reinforce shape and structure.
- Improve the fit and hang of a garment and extend its life.
- To help prevent stretching, so garments retain their shape.
- Prevent seam slippage.
- Prevent clipped areas from fraying.

Fusible and non-fusible interfacings

Interfacings are some of the most popular supporting materials. They come in different weights and colours, may be woven, non-woven, knitted or a combination, and can be fusible or non-fusible. Interfacings are traditionally applied to the wrong side of the fabric or sewn between outer fabric and facing or lining, but to achieve the best effect sample alternative techniques. For example, traditionally silk satin duchesse is supported with organza silk, which gives a big, soft drape. Using a light- to medium-weight knitted fusible interfacing would allow for stretch and drape and give a lighter, crisper, more modern look.

Woven Interfacing has a stable warp/weft construction with slight give crosswise. It is available as fusible or non-fusible and gives firm support. It is generally cut in the same grain direction as the garment fabric to avoid fitting problems.

Non-Woven Interfacings are lightweight, bonded, felt-like materials with no direction or grain. They do not fray, come in basic colours and qualities – from almost transparent to firm – and are reasonably priced.

Non-Woven Interfacing with Stitching has a non-woven base with reinforcement stitching running lengthwise, but with give crosswise.

Knitted Interfacing can be manufactured as a tricot, stabilized tricot, weft-insertion or warp-insertion knit. Tricot has crosswise stretch, stabilized tricot gives support lengthwise and crosswise with stretch on the bias. Knitted interfacings are mostly fusible and are lightweight and soft, with good flexibility and drape.

Fusible interfacing

Fusible interfacings can be woven, non-woven or tricot knitted, with an adhesive on one side. Heat, pressure and time are required to bond fusible interfacing to the fabric. It can be done with a domestic or industrial iron, but for best results use a fusing press, which can be closely monitored and is more accurate. Fusible interfacing should not be chosen by feel, as the property will change once ironed onto the material.

Fusible Interfacing may have adhesive in an even layer over the surface. The shiny side contains the adhesive.

Closely Spaced Adhesive Dots (left) offer better cover and less movement than widely spaced dots. **Widely Spaced Adhesive Dots** (right) create a softer appearance and more flexibility and drape.

Non-fusible interfacing

Non-fusible interfacings can be woven or non-woven and must be stitched in place by hand or by machine.

Organza and *Organdie* are transparent woven silk or cotton, used underneath fine fabrics for support and a luxury appearance.

Muslin is a light, open-weave cotton suitable as a supporting layer for all light- to medium-weight fabrics.

Batiste is a fine, woven cotton fabric suitable for any light- to medium-weight fabric.

Canvas is made from hair and wool threads with horsehair twist or viscose filaments. It is a light- to heavyweight woven interfacing used for building structure and to support sections of tailored jackets and coats.

Vilene is a non-woven interfacing available in light- to heavyweight. It is economic to use because it has no grain so can be cut out in any direction.

Fleece is a soft interlining used to add warmth or to pad quilting.

Wadding is a bulky material available in different weights, used for quilting and padding. It can be applied for warmth or effect.

Above: Vilene non-woven, sew-in interfacing.

Stabilizing tape

This can be used to prevent garment edges from stretching and deforming. See pages 139–41 for more information on how to tape a garment edge.

Web bonding

Fusible web is used to join two layers of material together. A very thin, net-like layer of adhesive only, it is available in strips or in larger pieces by the metre. It is used to fix hemlines and apply appliqué and trims, but can also be used to position pieces before stitching instead of tacking them in place. For an unconventional look try bonding different material types together to create a unique fabric. Read the manufacturer's instructions before using because it is very hard to correct mistakes once applied.

Right: Samples of satin and leather bonded with wool using fusible web.
Far right: All-in-one made with bonded satin and wool fabric by designer Iryna Mikhailovich.

How to apply interfacing

Interfacings can be applied to the whole garment or only parts. The fabric can be block fused before cutting or the interfacing can be cut out separately and applied to individual garment parts before construction.

Sewn-in interfacing (left) and ironed-on interfacing (right).

WHAT TO CONSIDER WHEN SELECTING INTERFACING

- Garment design and end use.
- Material structure, weight, stretch, colour and transparency.
- Quality of material and end product.
- Production and material cost.
- Matching interfacing care requirements to fabric care.
- Equipment available.

Selecting the right interfacing

Let the fabric guide you – interfacings should support and enhance, not change its appearance. For example, choose fusible interfacing with a low melting point for leather so the leather does not shrink or change colour, while fabrics with a pile, such as velvet, are damaged by pressing so reinforce with non-fusible interfacing.

Pre-shrinking interfacings

Interfacings such as cotton or wool need pre-shrinking to avoid shrinkage after application. There are three different methods: steaming, pressing, or washing by hand in hot water, after soaking for about 30 minutes, then drying.

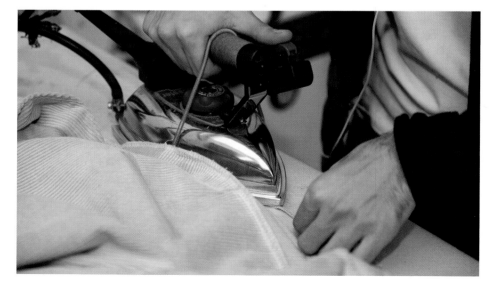

TIP

The fashion industry provides extra pattern pieces for interfacings since they are generally cut slightly smaller than the outer fabric piece and in bulk in a separate process. A separate pattern piece should always be provided if the interfacing is a different shape, clearly marked as 'cut interfacing only'. It is possible to use the same pattern for fabric and underlining but make sure the pattern is clearly labelled, for example 'cut 2 x fabric and cut 2 x underlining'.

Industrial iron used to apply interfacing.

Sampling

Always take time to sample with different types of interfacing to avoid disappointment with the finished result.

Step by step sampling

- Cut a minimum 10 x 10cm (3⅞ x 3⅞in) square of fabric.
- Cut the interfacing half the size of the fabric sample.
- Apply the interfacing to half the fabric by pressing or sewing, depending on the interfacing type.
- For fusible interfacing, leave to rest at least 30 minutes after application so the adhesive can settle and bond with the fabric.
- Drape the fabric over your hand to see if it has changed or if adhesive is showing. Some transparent fabrics cannot be fused and need sew-in interfacing.
- Roll the sample to see if it creates a smooth roll without creasing.
- If the fabric is too limp try a crisper or heavier interfacing; if it is too heavy choose a lighter interfacing.
- Experiment with different qualities of interfacing; save the most successful samples, labelled, for future reference.

Applying iron-on interfacing

Follow the manufacturer's instructions. If these are not available regulate the temperature according to the fabric. Sampling (see above) will identify the temperature, time and pressure required to make the adhesive stick.

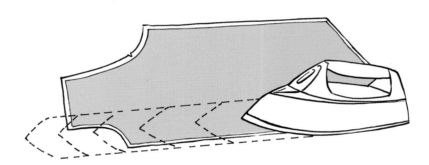

Step by step application of fusible interfacing

- Cut the interfacing up to 5mm (³⁄₁₆in) smaller than the fabric piece to avoid any excess hanging over the edge. Working in layers also creates a staggered edge for a smoother finish.

- Set the temperature of the iron or fusing press to the manufacturer's instruction, or to match the fabric.
- Place the interfacing with adhesive side to the wrong side of the fabric and smooth into place, aligning the grain if required.
- Place a large piece of paper or a pressing cloth between iron/fusing press and interfacing to avoid getting adhesive onto the equipment.
- Press the interfacing to the fabric. If using a domestic iron do not glide it back and forward – place it down at one edge and lean into it to add pressure for about 10–20 seconds, depending on the fabric. Lift the iron and place down on the next area, slightly overlapping the first to avoid gaps (see above).
- Once all the interfacing has been applied, turn the fabric over and press from the right side.
- Leave the fabric to rest for about 30 minutes to bond.
- Test the bonding by trying to peel the interfacing from the fabric at one corner. If it comes away press again, increasing either temperature or time.
- Place the pattern pieces back onto the fabric and transfer markings. Fabric and interfacing can now be stitched as one piece of fabric.

Block fusing

Block fusing involves fusing the interfacing to the fabric before cutting out the pattern pieces. It is recommended for many small pieces because it is easier, saves time and reduces cost. A fusing press will cover a large area at once.

Step by step block fusing

- Choose the pattern pieces to be interfaced and estimate the amount of fabric needed.
- Cut a suitable piece of fabric and a piece of interfacing slightly smaller.
- Place the interfacing with adhesive side onto the wrong side of the fabric and smooth in place, aligning the grain if required.
- Place a piece of paper or pressing cloth between press and interfacing to avoid getting adhesive on the equipment.
- Press the interfacing to the fabric.
- Leave the fabric to rest for about 30 minutes to bond.
- Place the pattern pieces onto the block-fused fabric, mark and cut out fabric and interfacing at the same time.

Problem solving

The surface of the outer fabric is bubbling so the interfacing has not fully attached:
- Check the temperature of the iron or fusing press and repeat the fusing process.
- Increase the pressure when pressing the interfacing onto the fabric.
- Try sampling another type of interfacing with a different bonding agent.
- Check if the fabric has been pre-shrunk because this can affect the sizing and stop the adhesive bonding evenly.
- Do not pull the interfacing when applying it.

The interfacing melts when pressed:
- Lower the temperature on the iron or fusing press.
- Try another type of interfacing with a different bonding agent.
- Try sampling with a sew-in interfacing.

The fusible interfacing has been wrongly placed:
- Hold a steam iron just above the fusible interfacing to liquefy the adhesive, then carefully peel it off.
- Cut a new piece of fusible interfacing and reapply.

The fusible interfacing is peeling away from the fabric:
- Repeat the fusing process on a new sample, changing the temperature of the iron or fusing press.
- Make sure the pressure is evenly applied to the surface.
- Try sampling another type of interfacing with a different bonding agent, or a sew-in interfacing.

Applying sew-in interfacing

Sew-in interfacing has no adhesive and is hand or machine stitched directly onto the garment fabric, usually before garment construction begins. Tacking stitches are removed after the garment has been assembled. Sew-in interfacing requires more time for cutting and preparation than fusible interfacing.

Step by step application of sew-in interfacing

- Pre-shrink the interfacing, unless it is polyester or nylon, to avoid shrinkage after the garment has been constructed.
- Cut the interfacing slightly smaller than the fabric piece.
- Smooth the interfacing to the wrong side of the garment fabric, aligning the grain if required, and pin in place.
- Attach the interfacing to the garment fabric by machine or hand-tacking inside the seam allowance.
- Always work on a flat surface when hand-tacking, use a thin thread to match the garment colour and sew with fairly large stitches unless the fabric is very fine and slippery. See page 114 for more on hand-tacking.
- If machine stitching, choose the largest stitch and sew around the fabric edges.
- Place the pattern pieces back onto the fabric piece to transfer any lost markings, then proceed with garment construction.

Underlinings

An underlining covers an entire fabric piece; it can also be called a backing or mounting. It can be a layer of fabric or interfacing to add stability and structure, or an insulator to add warmth without bulk. Underlining materials include organza, batiste, muslin, canvas, netting, lining and fleece. Experiment to see what works – there are no rules except it must suit the design and material.

When and why to use underlining or backing techniques

- As a base for fusible interfacing, acting as a protective layer between garment fabric and interfacing adhesive on fabrics that cannot be fused.
- Underlining reduces wrinkling and clinging, adds body and durability and supports the garment shape.
- As a buffer for seams and hems.
- Behind a transparent fabric it can change the colour or pattern of the outer fabric to create a new fabric design. Experiment to create interesting effects.
- As a base and support for open-weave fabrics.
- A lining backing can be applied to a trouser front to control pleats, or added between waist and knee for comfort.
- The underlining should have the same care requirement as the outer material.

Step by step application of underlining

- Pre-shrink the underlining, unless it is polyester or nylon, to avoid shrinkage after the garment has been constructed.
- Cut the underlining the same size as the garment material.
- If using fusible interfacing, add this to the underlining before it is attached to the outer fabric.
- Smooth the wrong side of the underlining against the wrong side of the outer fabric, aligning the grain if required, and pin together.
- Tack the underlining and outer fabric together inside the seam allowance.
- Place the pattern pieces back onto the fabric and transfer all markings.
- Tack around dart and pocket areas to secure the fabrics together so they do not shift when stitching.
- Work with open seams pressed flat instead of to one side. Avoid working with closed seams, which can add bulk that shows on the outside and creates puckered seams.
- If seams are bulky, trim away the underlining leaving a couple of millimetres. Darts can be cut and pressed open after stitching. Find more information about darts on pages 151–54.

TIP

The illustration (right) shows the order in which underlining and interfacing can be used. Each component may be used together or separately.

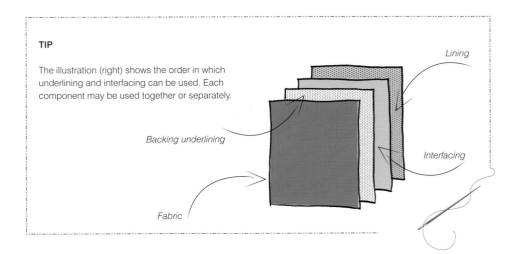

Lining

Backing underlining

Interfacing

Fabric

Examples of where to apply interfacing on garments

These are only guidelines – there is always an exception to every rule.

Skirt

- *Waistband:* Completely interfaced.
- *Vent:* Only vent area interfaced, both under- and over-wrap.
- *Zip:* On some loosely woven fabrics, support the end of the zip with a small circle of interfacing.
- *Hem:* May be interfaced 1cm (⅜in) over the hem fold line.
- *Pockets:* Interface pocket pieces and opening to support hardwearing areas.

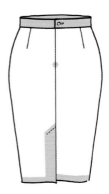

Dress

- *Neck and armhole facings:* Interface completely. Sometimes the neckline and armhole need taping before the facing is applied.
- *Vent, zip, hem* and *pockets:* As skirt.

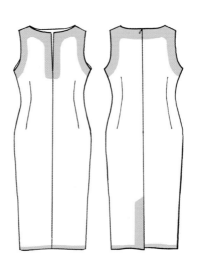

Trouser

- *Waistband:* Completely interfaced.
- *Belt loops:* Interface only if the fabric is unstable.
- *Zip fly:* Interface the under- and over-wrap.
- *Pockets:* Interface pocket pieces and opening to support hardwearing areas.

Shirt

- *Collar:* Interface top collar, under collar and collar stand. If only one collar requires fusing, fuse the top collar.
- *Button stand:* Completely interfaced.
- *Cuffs:* Completely interfaced, including cuff fly.

Jacket

- *Front:* Interface the complete front using light/medium-weight interfacing.
- *Front:* Interface the collar, hem and pocket opening with an extra layer of thread/stitch-reinforced interfacing.
- *Front facing:* Interface completely with thread/stitch-reinforced interfacing.
- *Side panel:* Interface under the arm area with light/medium-weight and the hem and pocket area with thread/stitch-reinforced interfacing.

- *Back:* Interface the top back area with light/medium-weight and the hem with thread/stitch-reinforced interfacing.
- *Sleeve:* Interface the sleeve head with light/medium-weight and the hem with thread/stitch-reinforced interfacing.
- *Collar:* Interface completely with thread/stitch-reinforced interfacing.
- *Pocket pieces:* Interface completely.
- *Neckline, armhole and break line of lapel:* Add cotton tape. These areas are easier to control with a sew-in tape.

General fusing plan for a fused jacket

This can be altered to suit the fabric of your choice. The jacket shown below was made using this fusing plan.

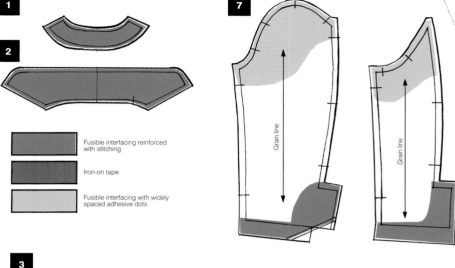

	Fusible interfacing reinforced with stitching
	Iron-on tape
	Fusible interfacing with widely spaced adhesive dots

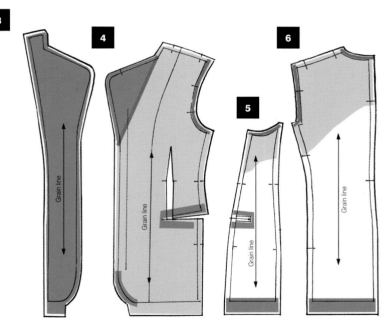

1 *Back neckline facing*

2 *Collar*

3 *Front facing*

4 *Front panel:* Use additional fusible interfacing reinforced with stitching on the lapel area up to the break line, 2cm (¾in) around the pocket opening, and at the curve of the hemline. Ease iron-on tape onto the break line of the lapel.

5 *Side panel:* Interfacing with widely spaced dots is applied to the underarm; finish with a curve to avoid a break line showing on the right side. Use interfacing reinforced with stitching 2cm (¾in) around the pocket opening and at the hem finishing 1cm (⅜in) above the hemline.

6 *Back panel:* Interfacing with widely spaced dots is applied across the shoulders ending with a curved line. Use interfacing reinforced with stitching at the hem, finishing 1cm (⅜in) above the hemline. Apply iron-on tape at the neck.

Apply iron-on tape around the armhole once the front, side and back panels are stitched together and before the shoulder seams are joined. Take the measurement from the pattern, not the fabric piece.

7 *Top and undersleeve:* Interfacing with widely spaced dots across the top third of the sleeve ending with a curved line. Use fusible interfacing with reinforced stitching at the hem and vent finishing 1cm (⅜in) above the hemline.

Netting, organza and organdie

Netting

Netting is a sheer open-mesh fabric available in silk, cotton, polyester or nylon in qualities from fine and soft to rigid and heavy. It has no grain line and more give crosswise, and can be used to create volume and shape or stabilize without adding weight. It does not unravel when cut but a raw edge can irritate the skin and should be finished with a binding, trim or facing. Stiff netting will stand away from the body and can be multilayered into underskirts to support a skirt shape, or used in a single layer as underlining to add lightweight support. Take care when working with netting; it rips easily and may be damaged with a hot iron.

Polyester or nylon net is inexpensive and mostly used for petticoats and underlining. Silk netting can be used as an outer fabric to add volume to a garment, evoke a certain mood or exaggerate parts of the body with a soft look.

Point d'esprit is a fine net with rectangular dots in a regular pattern. It is used for millinery and garment decoration.

Organza and organdie

Organza is a plain weave, transparent fabric manufactured in silk, rayon and polyester. It is expensive to use as a stabilizer, but will add a luxury finish when used as an underlining.

Organdie is a sheer, crisp, plain weave cotton fabric. It is used for interfacing and underlining garment pieces.

Both organza and organdie can be tacked or machine stitched to the wrong side of the outer fabric as an underlining or sew-in interfacing, or used as garment fabrics to lend a luxurious look and feel to special-occasion wear. They are also used to create shapes and design details or add body without adding weight.

Tulle

Tulle is a fine, soft hexagonal net fabric with a small hole size. It can be used as an outer fabric or as an underlining for light support.

Illusion is very fine tulle, mostly used as decoration for millinery and veils.

For more information on how to work with netting, organza and organdie see Transparent and Semi-Transparent Fabrics on page 262.

Above left: Layered netting skirt. Alexis Mabille, SS 2013.

Above centre: Blouse with layered organza detail in front panel. Lanvin, Fall 2013.

Above right: From left to right, samples of netting, tulle, organza and organdie.

Quilting and padding

Quilting

Quilting is a technique where fabric and wadding are stitched together for insulation and decorative effect. Quilted fabrics are readily available in two-layer or three-layer versions, or can be custom made. The two-layer version has a face fabric with a wadding backing held together with lines of machine stitching, traditionally in a diamond pattern. The three-layer version can be single- or double-face: single-face quilted fabric has a face fabric and backing material with a layer of wadding between; double-face has a face fabric on either side of the wadding so it is reversible. Again the layers are stitched together in a decorative pattern. When making custom quilting, the stitching technique depends on the design of the garment. Each layer of fabric must be considered carefully as well as the degree of bulk required. Quilted fabrics are used to insulate garments but also lend themselves to creative ideas with silhouette and dimension.

Padding

Padding is a method of enhancing shape by stuffing certain areas for support or to contour the surface for decorative effect. In quality garments padding may be used in hemlines, for example, to avoid over-pressing, to create softness and add weight and body. Tailors use wadding, canvas or fleece to pad garments in areas such as the shoulder and chest. In bespoke tailoring the body can be corrected or enhanced using padding – for example a sloping shoulder can be built up to correct it visually when the garment is worn.

Above left and centre: Kimono-style jacket with striped stitching pattern on quilted panel, designed by Nadine El-Oun.

Above right: Jacket with padded front and sleeves. Comme des Garçons, AW 2010, Ready-to-Wear.

Quilting and padding materials

The traditional material for quilting and padding is wadding, which comes in a variety of thicknesses and weights and can easily be tailored to requirement. Wadding is manufactured from polyester, cotton, wool or a mixed blend; note that wadding made from natural fibres can shrink. A more expensive filler is down and feathers, which is often used in winter outerwear garments for lightweight thermal insulation. However, it is costly in production and garment care, so has partly been replaced with polyester fibrefill wadding.

How to quilt

As always, sampling is key. Try different colours and thicknesses of thread and experiment with stitching patterns. Test different fabrics – woven fabrics behave differently to knitted fabrics.

Step by step quilting

1 Cut the fabric and wadding to shape, leaving a generous extra allowance around the edges.

2 Iron the face fabric if required.

3 Draw the stitching design onto the face fabric using chalk or a disappearing pencil with a ruler. For more complex designs, draw the pattern onto a template of thin paper and attach this on top of the face fabric.

4 Place the face fabric right side up on top of the wadding and tack together around the edges. On larger pieces, secure the layers with pins or tacking across the piece, at intervals, to avoid the face fabric shifting while stitching.

5 Stitch the layers together, following the marked stitching lines.

6 Remove the tacking and the paper template, if used.

WHAT TO CONSIDER WHEN QUILTING

- Make up sample garments that include the quilting material and fit the garment before cutting out in final fabric. The pattern needs to be generous to allow for the extra bulk added by the quilting.
- Experiment with different types of fabric and quilting methods, including other quilting stitch patterns that may complement your garment design better than the traditional diamond trellis.
- Test out different thread qualities and colours.

- Loosen the pressure of the machine foot or use a walking foot to keep the layers from shifting or puckering as you stitch.
- Use a large stitch length, such as 3.5–4mm.
- Consider the seam allowance and how the quilted piece is attached to a non-quilted piece. Make sure the quilting pattern is not interrupted so there is a flow from one piece to the other.

Corsetry and Underpinnings

A corset is a close-fitted garment worn to contour the natural body shape, using boning and supporting materials such as canvas and interfacing. It shapes or supports three main areas – bust, waist and hips – and can be worn as outer clothing or as an undergarment. Corsets often work against the natural body shape and have been used throughout history to achieve the desired fashion silhouette.

Supporting undergarments

The corset has been reworked following changes in fashion, or with the invention of different materials, such as elastic and rubber, so a variety of styles has developed.

Satin corset dress with pointed cups and netting skirt. Jean Paul Gaultier Haute Couture, SS 2013.

Corset: A closely fitted bodice, stiffened with boning to reshape the torso.

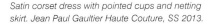

Basque: This shapes the upper body down to the hip and has added suspenders.

Bustier: This shapes the bust area to the waistline. It can be worn with or without shoulder straps.

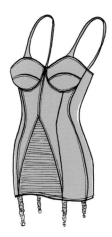

Corsolette/Corselet: A tubular garment with shoulder straps and suspenders, which gives support to the bust, waist and hip.

Girdle: Supports from the waist down to the lower hip and often has added suspenders.

Bra or *brassiere:* For the bust only. It can be made with or without wire channelling, depending on the support needed.

Supporting materials for corsetry

The choice of material depends on the style of corset and the support needed. Boning made of metal or plastic is the most frequently used support in corsetry. Metal boning needs a casing so the bone is covered; plastic boning can be encased or stitched directly onto the foundation and is used for straight seams. Different types of boning include rigilene boning, covered boning, lacing bones, spiral steel bones, flex stays (for curved seams), extra wide boning and fusion coated boning for under the bust. Spiral steel bones are the most flexible, and are used for curved seams because they follow contours.

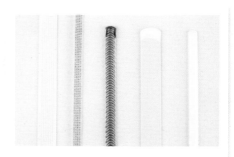

From left to right: **Rigilene Boning**, **Decorative Rigilene Boning**, **Spiral Steel Boning**, **Extra Wide Plastic Boning**, **Thin Plastic Boning**.

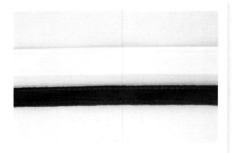

Bone Casing in black and white. If a casing tape is not available, use a bias cotton tape.

Under-Bust Wire for cup support.

Under-Bust Wire Casing is stitched along the under-bust cup seam to cover the wire.

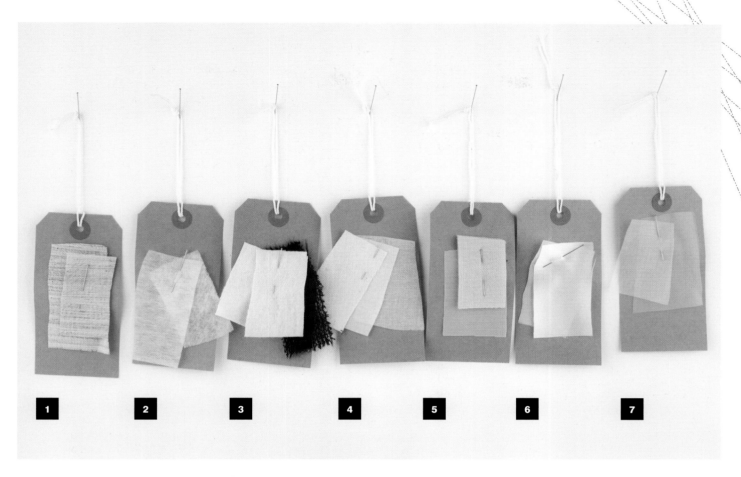

1 *Canvas* is used as an underlining to support the shape of contour-fitted garments and to prevent the outer fabric stretching.

2 *Interfacing* is used as a stabilizer and can be sewn in or ironed on. It may be attached to the outer fabric directly or to a supporting material if the outer fabric cannot be interfaced.

3 *Brushed Cotton* and *Domette* are soft, light materials brushed on one side that can be used as an underlining between the boned foundation and outer fabric to prevent the boning from showing on the outside. If they are too thick, cotton batiste or muslin can be used instead.

Brushed cotton and domette can also be used as padding under hair canvas to prevent skin irritation. *Icewool* is a more flexible half knit and loosely woven underlining, used in the same way as brushed cotton and domette.

4 *Cotton Drill* or *Herringbone Coutil* is a twill weave fabric used as a supporting material and as a base for boning. When used as a foundation for boning, it sits between the outer fabric and lining.

5 *Mesh* is a stretch power-net in synthetic fibre that can be used in the side panels of a corset for more flexibility. *Neoprene* is used to make bra cups.

6 *Lining* is a fine material of silk, viscose or synthetic fibre used to protect the skin from the boning structure and stabilizing material. A lining provides a good-quality finish to the inside of a corset.

7 *Muslin, Batiste, Organza* and *Organdie* are used to support the outer fabric when it is not strong enough or to prevent stretching and wrinkling. They are mounted to the outer fabric.

Fastening options

Hook-and-eye fastenings for corsetry come on a tape or as single hooks-and-eyes to sew in, and as steel busk fasteners.

Lacing requires eyelets or loops in fabric or metal to take a tape or lacing cord. This fastening is flexible since it can be altered to suit size and shape when lacing the corset. Lacing and hook-and-eye fastenings are traditionally combined in one corset.

Zips are a modern way to fasten the corset to a fixed size. Alternatively, a zip at the front can be combined with lacing at the back.

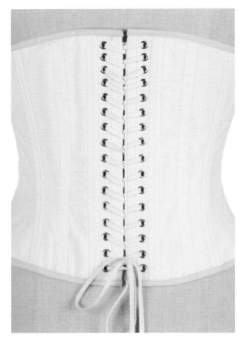

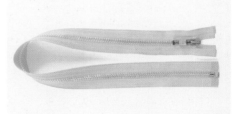

Top left to top right: Corset fastening methods shown before use and in situ. All can be used in front or back panels.

Above left: Hook-and-eye fastening on ready-to-sew tape.

Above centre: Metal eyelet in two parts. Follow the manufacturer's instructions to apply.

Above right: A metallic chain zip offers more stability than a plastic coil zip. Zip fastening can also be combined with lacing.

Construction of a corset with bones

These instructions are for a basic boned corset with lacing and a zip.

Materials:
- Outer fabric of choice
- Underlining/interfacing that suits the outer fabric and construction purpose
- Lining
- Boning
- Bone casing tape
- Bias binding
- Open-ended zip
- Eyelet tool set and eyelets
- Lacing cord

Step by step construction of a basic corset

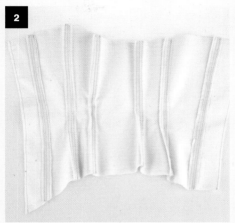

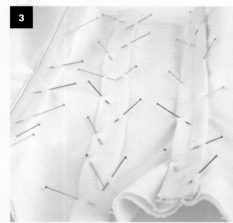

- Choose a pattern that suits your design and cut out the fabric, underlining and interfacing as required.
- Prepare the lining pattern and cut out the lining pieces (refer to Lining on page 212).
- Mark lines for the bone casing onto the underlining using tailor's chalk or thread marks.
- If interfacing is required, attach it to the underlining or outer fabric.
- With wrong side of outer fabric facing wrong side of underlining, machine stitch the underlining to the outer fabric at the seam allowance using a large stitch of about 4mm. **1**
- Machine stitch the pieces together, clip the seams if necessary and press open the seam allowance. **2**

- Use a ready-made casing or a bias-cut tape for the bone casing, or use the seam allowance.
- Pin the casing onto the wrong side of the corset along the seam allowance and the marked lines. Machine stitch through the layers with an edge stitch of 2.5–3mm. Press the corset after stitching. **3**
- Any type of boning can be used with a casing but make sure it is slightly shorter than the casing to allow for finishing of the top and bottom edges. Pre-cut bones define the length of the corset, or cut and cap the boning to size, then insert into the casings. **4**
- Attach one side of the zip at a time by machine stitching with a stitch size of 2.5–3mm. For more information on

how to attach an open-ended zip see page 244. Alternatively use a steel busk fastener instead of a zip. **5** *Shows the right side of the corset and* **6** *the wrong side.*
- Use the pattern to cut a wide facing from the outer fabric to cover the inside of the zip area up to the first seam allowance. Add fusible interfacing to the facing pieces. With wrong side upward, sew the facing down along the zip using a machine stitch of 2.5–3mm. Fold the facing back and stay-stitch in place. Trim any bulk from the seam allowance if necessary, then press. Attach the opposite side of the facing to the seam allowance.

continues on page 108...

Step by step construction of a basic corset (continued)

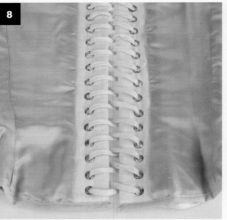

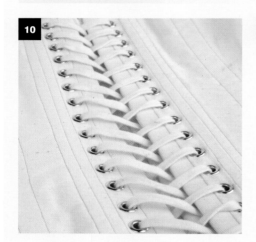

- To prepare a facing for the lacing, interface the pieces and attach with a machine stitch of 2.5–3mm. Fold the facing back and stay-stitch. **7**
- Add the lining by bagging it onto the zip facing and lacing facing with machine stitching.
- Cut bias binding for the top and bottom edges from the outer fabric, or use pre-cut bias binding. Lay the corset flat and pin top and bottom layers of fabric and lining together. Bind the top and bottom edge using a machine stitch of 2.5–3mm, folding the ends of the binding in before finishing the last few stitches. For more information on how to attach a bias binding see

pages 122–23. **8** *Shows a close-up of the lining attached to the lace fastening and the bias binding finish.* **9** *Shows a corset from the inside front.*
- Alternatively, finish the edges with facings top and bottom. Use the pattern to cut out the facing in fabric. Add fusible interfacing to the facing pieces. Pin the corset to the facing right sides together and machine with a stitch size of 2.5–3mm. Fold the fabric up and stay-stitch the facing. Turn the facing to the inside of the corset and press.
- As an option, add a modesty panel in the back. This is a strip of fabric behind the lacing to cover any exposed skin.

- Reduce the size of the lining by the size of the facing, then add the lining to the corset.
- Mark the position of the eyelets and punch or cut the holes. Insert the eyelets and use an eyelet tool and hammer to fix them into place. **10**
- Give your corset a final press, trim off loose threads and add the lacing cord to the eyelets. **11** *Shows the finished corset from the front, and* **12** *shows the back.*

Corset variations

Right and far right: A foundation corset structure from a Vivienne Westwood dress. Power-net mesh is used on side panels and shoulder straps for more flexibility, and cotton drill for the centre front and back with rigilene boning attached to one layer and covered with a second layer of cotton drill. This type of corset would be worked into a top or dress, covered with an outer fabric.

Right: A black velvet Vivienne Westwood corset from the inside, with exposed boning in the centre panel.

Far right: A foundation corset structure from a dress by Julien Macdonald. The corset has power-net mesh body panels and neoprene for the cups, with a cup wire to support the bust. The bodice has boning casings with plastic bones. The corset is attached to the dress neckline facing and hangs loose at the waist, fastened with hooks-and-eyes (see page 84) at the centre back.

TAKE YOUR TIME

Constructing a corset takes time and attention to detail; you will not be able to finish a corset you can be proud of in a day. Planning the materials, testing the layers of underlining, interfacing and supporting materials and practising the attaching of the bones will take time. You should also allow for one or two fittings, especially when trying a pattern for the first time. To construct a basic corset shape takes up to 30 hours.

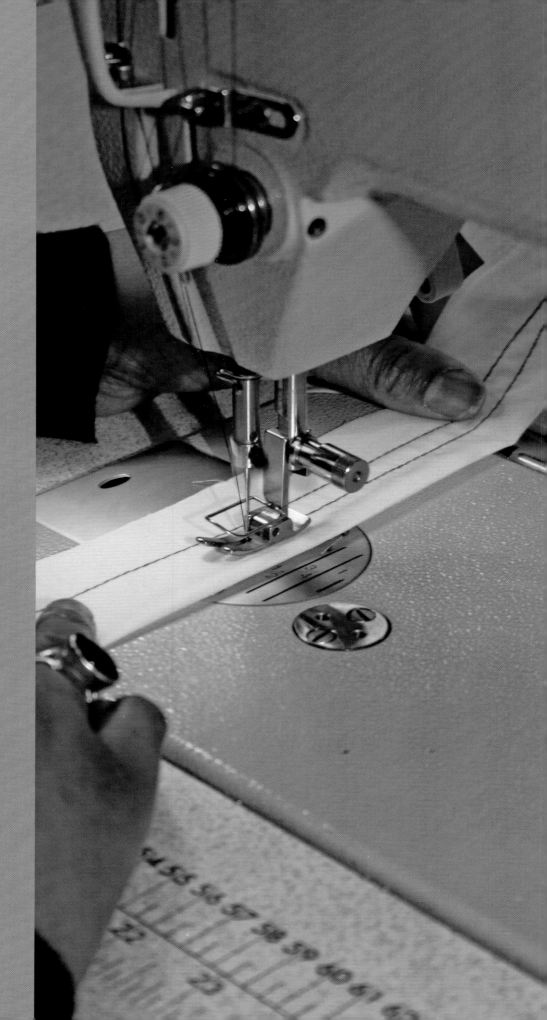

3 The Basic Stitches

Hand-Sewing Techniques

Most garments on the high street are finished to a high standard using machine stitching, with very little hand sewing. Hand stitching adds cost to a garment because of the time involved so it is usually confined to sample making, high-end ready-to-wear, haute couture and bespoke tailoring. However, it is important to have a basic knowledge of hand-sewing skills because some parts of a garment should be hand stitched for a quality finish.

Hand-sewing techniques are split into two categories: temporary stitches and permanent stitches. A temporary stitch is used to hold two or more pieces of material together during construction and is removed after the garment is finished, or to transfer pattern markings to the fabric – for example tailor's tacks (see Thread marking, page 54). A permanent hand-sewing stitch is part of the garment construction – for example blind hemstitch for a trouser hem, which gives an invisible finish. Hand-sewing techniques are also used for decorative stitching such as beading and embroidery work.

Getting started

- Choose a needle for hand sewing that suits the material, texture and weight of the fabric. See pages 12–13 for more information about hand-sewing needles.
- Choose the right thread thickness and colour to suit your fabric. The best thread for hand sewing is a pure silk thread, which glides effortlessly through the fabric. See page 86 for more information about threads.
- Cut your thread shorter rather than longer because a short thread is easier to control. Long threads become tangled and knotted during the sewing process and it takes more time to pull them through the fabric.
- Cut the thread at an angle before inserting it into the eye of the needle; this makes it easier to thread than if the end is broken or bitten off. If it is still difficult to thread the needle use a needle threader (see page 13).
- Always use a thimble to protect your finger.
- Choose a comfortable sitting position on a chair and use a foot rest to avoid bending over your work and hurting your back. Stretch between bouts of sewing.
- Work from right to left, unless you are left-handed.
- Do not pull the thread too tight because this can create puckering that shows on the outside.

WAXING THE THREAD

Some types of hand sewing benefit from the thread being coated with beeswax, which strengthens it and makes it easier to thread into the needle. This method is used in tailoring to keep the thread smooth and stop it from knotting. It is also advisable to wax the thread before sewing on metal fasteners or attaching beads with sharp edges. Run the length of thread through a block of beeswax to apply a layer of wax.

SEWING WITH A DOUBLE THREAD

Most hand sewing is done with a single thread, but when sewing on fasteners the thread is doubled up to provide more stability. It can be tricky to sew with a double thread because the strands can knot and twist more easily. To avoid this, lock the two threads together.

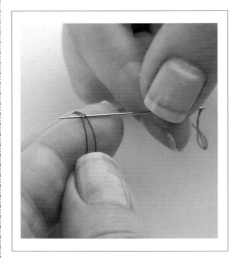

Step 1
Insert the needle into both strands of thread.

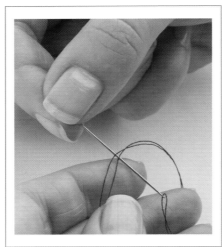

Step 2
Pull the needle through the strands.

Step 3
The two strands are now interlocked.

Starting and finishing

The thread must be secured at the beginning and end of a line of stitching, especially when using a permanent hand stitch. Usually this is done with a knot.

Waste knot

A waste knot is a temporary knot that is used at the start but clipped away after the stitching is complete, hence its name.
- Thread the needle and tie a knot at the end of the thread.
- Insert the threaded needle into the fabric a distance away from where you want to begin sewing and pull through – do not pull too hard or the knot will slip though the material.

- Secure the thread at the beginning of the line of stitching with one or more backstitches.
- Snip the knot off when the sewing is done.

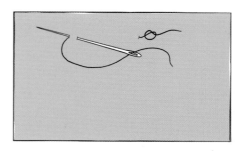

A waste knot.

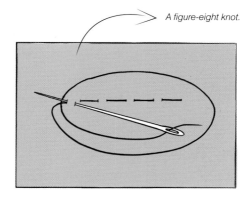
A figure-eight knot.

Figure-eight knot

A figure-eight knot is used at the end of the stitching for a firm and secure finish to the thread end.

- Take a small backstitch and wrap the thread under and around the needle before pulling the needle through.
- Repeat this process a couple of times on one spot then cut the thread off.

A tailor's knot.

Tailor's knot

The tailor's knot secures the end of the stitching and can be used with hand sewing or machine sewing. It gives a flat finish – unlike a backstitch tack, which can sometimes create slight bulk.

- Form a loop with the thread end.
- Insert needle into the back of the loop.

- Hold the loop flat against the material and pull the thread so the loop begins to tighten. Try to get the knot as close as possible to the end of the stitching.
- Cut off the excess thread leaving a short thread end of 5mm (³⁄₁₆in).

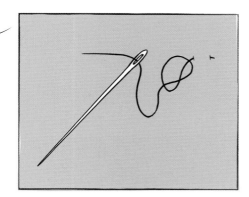

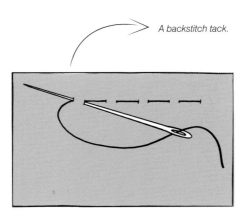
A backstitch tack.

Backstitch tack

A backstitch tack is the most secure and strongest way to start and finish a line of hand sewing. It can begin with or without a waste knot.

- Take a small stitch into the fabric with the needle and thread.
- If you are not using a knot, hold on to the short end of the thread to avoid pulling it right through the material.

- Take a couple more small stitches over the same points on the fabric to secure the thread end firmly.
- Repeat this process at the end of the thread or line of stitching.
- Cut the thread end so that it is even with the other stitches.

Temporary and permanent hand stitches

The following hand stitches are those most commonly used during the making of a garment, either to temporarily hold layers together or as a permanent part of the construction.

Tacking stitch

Tacking stitches, also known as basting stitches, are used to hold two or more layers of fabric together temporarily in preparation for permanent stitching. They are removed after the final seam has been stitched. For tacking seams temporarily use a contrast colour thread or a tacking thread. When sewing in stabilizer use a thread that matches the colour of the fabric. For more information on how to tack sew-in interfacing see page 96.

- Always work on a flat surface and use a long, fine, hand-sewing needle.
- Pin the seams or layers of material together.
- Start by securing the thread with one backstitch, without a knot.
- Take the needle in and out to create large stitches.
- Finish with one backstitch, or leave the end unsecured so the tacking is easy to remove later.

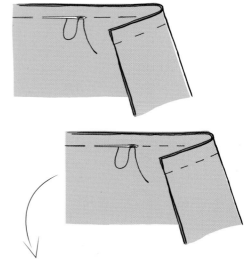

Tacking stitches can be long and short, alternately, or be regular in size.

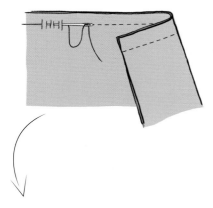

Working running stitch by taking several stitches at the same time before pulling the thread through.

Running stitch

The running stitch is a permanent stitch that can be used for seaming, gathering or attaching pieces such as shoulder pads. It is also used as a simple embroidery stitch. A short and even stitch, it is quick to work but not as strong as backstitch.
- Use a short needle and a thread colour to suit the material.
- Sew from right to left.
- Secure the thread to the fabric by using a knot and/or backstitching.

- Pass the needle in and out through all layers and pull the thread through. Make small stitches of equal length.
- Several short stitches can be picked up before pulling the thread through, as illustrated, or complete single stitches can be made. Both methods are correct; the only difference is that single stitches take longer.
- At the end, secure the thread with a couple of backstitches.

Backstitch

Backstitch is a strong and elastic stitch mainly used for seaming, but also as an embroidery stitch for outlining motifs.

- Use a short needle and match the thread colour to suit the material.
- Sew from right to left.
- Secure the thread to the fabric using a knot and/or backstitching.
- Pull the needle through the fabric and take a small stitch through all layers.
- Insert the needle at the start of the previous stitch, taking a small backward stitch, then bring the needle through again, a little in front of the first stitch.
- Repeat the sequence, always inserting the needle into the end of the previous stitch.
- At the end, secure the thread with a couple of backstitches.

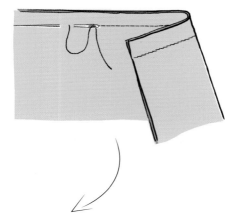

A backstitch.

Prick stitch

Prick stitch is sewn from the right side and is a variation of backstitch that creates thread dots on one side of the garment and long stitches on the other. It is used as a decorative stitch instead of topstitching, as a retaining stitch to keep facings and linings from rolling to the outside – such as at collar and lapel edges – and to attach a zip by hand.

- Match the thread colour and needle type to the material.
- Sew from right to left on the right side of the garment.
- Secure the thread to the fabric using a knot and/or backstitching.
- Pull the thread through to the right side of the garment. Insert the needle just behind (1–2 threads away) where the thread comes out as if working backwards.
- When installing a zip insert the needle through all layers and bring it out of the fabric about 0.6–1cm (¼–⅜in) away and to the left.
- When using prick stitch as a retaining stitch, do not sew through the outside layer.
- Sew in a straight line keeping the same distance from the edge.
- At the end, secure the thread with a couple of backstitches.

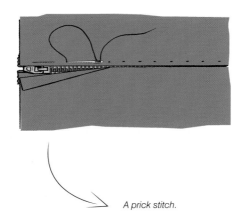

A prick stitch.

Slipstitch

Slipstitch is used to sew a folded edge to another layer of fabric invisibly and as a fine edge finish. It is mostly used to attach a lining hem to a garment and is also often seen as a finish on silk scarves.

- Match the thread colour and needle type to the material.
- Secure the thread to the fabric edge with a knot and/or backstitching.
- Sew on the wrong side of the fabric.
- Pick up a single thread or two from the garment side with the needle and pull the thread through. Make sure the thread cannot be seen on the outside/right side of the garment.

- Insert the needle into the folded edge directly below, take a 6mm (¼in) stitch and then pull the thread through.
- Pick up a thread or two from the fabric directly above and pull the thread through.
- Repeat these stitches, alternating between the fabric fold and the garment.
- Make sure the thread is invisible from the right and wrong side of the garment.
- Secure the thread at the end of the sewing.

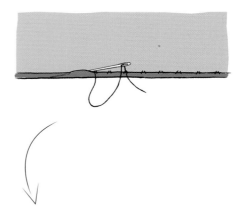

Slipstitch worked as an edge finish.

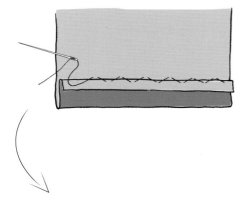

Hemming stitch.

Hemming stitch

Hemming stitch, also called blind stitch, is mainly used to hold up hemlines but can also be used to hold facings in place. It is invisible on the right side of the fabric and only a small stitch is visible on the inside of the hemline. Hemming stitch is used on woven fabrics and non-stretch materials.

- Fold the hem edge back by about 5–7mm (³⁄₁₆–⁹⁄₃₂in).
- Match the thread colour and needle type to suit the material.
- Sew from right to left.
- Secure the thread to the hem edge using a knot and/or backstitching.

- Pick up a single thread or two from the garment side with the needle and pull the thread through. Make sure the thread cannot be seen on the outside/right side of the garment.
- Take a small stitch through the hem edge, leaving a space of 0.7–1cm (⁹⁄₃₂–³⁄₈in) between stitches.
- Alternate between the hem and the garment, leaving the stitches relatively loose.
- At the end, secure the thread with a couple of backstitches.

Herringbone stitch

Herringbone stitch, also called catch stitch, is mostly used for stretch fabrics such as jersey because it offers more stretch than hemming stitch. It can be sewn as a blind stitch hidden between the garment and hem, or on top of the hemline so it is visible.

- For blind herringbone stitch turn the hem edge back by approximately 5–7mm (³⁄₁₆–⁹⁄₃₂in).
- Match the thread colour and needle type to suit the material.
- Sew from left to right.
- Secure the thread to the hem edge using a knot and/or backstitching.
- Pick up a single thread or two from the garment side with the needle and pull the thread through. Make sure the thread cannot be seen on the outside/right side of the garment.
- Take a small stitch through the hem edge, leaving 0.7–1cm (⁹⁄₃₂–³⁄₈in) between stitches.
- Because you are working left to right the stitches cross to form an X pattern hidden between the garment and hem layer, which allows for extra thread length and stretch.
- Alternate between the hem and the garment, leaving the stitches relatively loose.
- At the end, secure the thread with a couple of backstitches.

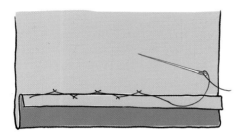

Herringbone stitch worked as a blind stitch.

Overcast stitch

Overcast stitch is a diagonal stitch applied over the edge of a single or double layer as a raw edge finish. It is rarely used these days, having been replaced by an overlocker machine edge finish, which is quicker and more efficient. However, there may be areas that cannot be finished by machine and so must be overcast to prevent the edge from fraying.

- Use a short needle and match the thread colour to suit the material.
- Sew from right to left with the raw edge positioned horizontally.
- Secure the thread to the fabric edge using a knot and/or backstitching.
- Insert the needle from back to front about 3–4mm (¹⁄₈–⁵⁄₃₂in) below the raw edge and pull the thread through.
- Move the needle to the left and take another stitch from back to front, leaving a 5mm (³⁄₁₆in) gap between stitches, and pull the thread through.
- The stitches should be evenly spaced in a slanted pattern.
- At the end, secure the thread with a couple of backstitches.

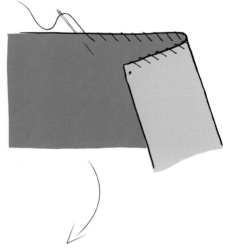

Overcast stitch.

Blanket stitch

Blanket stitch is used as a decorative edge finish to neaten a raw edge, to attach hooks-and-eyes, and to make thread chains and bars. It is often used as decoration along a woollen edge using wool yarn in a contrasting colour.

- Use a needle that suits the material and yarn or thread.
- Sew from right to left with the right side facing you and the raw edge horizontal.
- Secure the thread to the fabric edge using a knot and/or backstitching.
- Bring the needle through from front to back about 5mm (³⁄₁₆in) below the edge and loop the thread under the needle point. Pull the thread through.
- Move the needle to the left and take another stitch 5mm (³⁄₁₆in) below the edge, from front to back, leaving a 5mm (³⁄₁₆in) gap between stitches. Pass the needle over the thread loop and pull the thread through.
- Keep an even space between stitches and work to an even depth, with the thread loop sitting along the edge.
- At the end, secure the thread with a couple of backstitches.

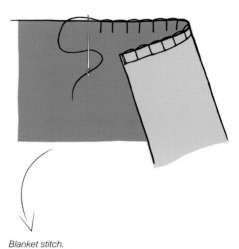

Blanket stitch.

Buttonhole stitch

Buttonhole stitch is used for hand-sewn buttonholes, for sewing on poppers and hooks-and-eyes and for button loops. For how to hand stitch a buttonhole, see page 230.

- Match the thread colour and use a needle that suits the material.
- Secure the thread with a knot.
- Take a small stitch to bring the needle through to the front of the fabric about 2–3mm (³⁄₃₂–¹⁄₈in) in from the edge. Pull the needle through to create a loop.
- Pass the needle through the loop from the back and pull the thread tight. When tightening the thread, position the purl part on top of the fabric edge to close the gap between stitches.
- Insert the next stitch close to the first and continue working stitches and purls closely together.
- At the end, secure the thread with a couple of backstitches.

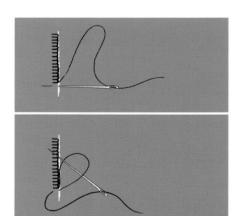

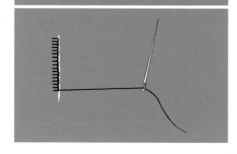

Working buttonhole stitch.

Machine Seams
and Seam Finishes

Seams are used to join the parts of a garment together. They are needed to create shape and strengthen the garment, and may also be decorative and support the design. It is vital to place seam lines correctly when designing and constructing a garment, taking into consideration body shape, style and choice of material. Seams can be joined in different ways, such as by sewing, stapling, gluing or fusing. In this part we look at the different machine stitched seams: which one you use will depend on the garment design, material and end use.

Seam allowances vary in depth depending on the type of seam used. For more information on seam allowance see page 39. Some seams, such as the plain seam, need a finish to the seam allowance to make sure the fabric does not fray, while other seams are self-enclosed and do not need further finishing, such as the French seam. A good way to find the right seam and seam finish is by researching traditional garment finishing and sampling with the final material. This must be done right at the beginning, because the type of seam will influence the pattern construction. There are plenty of seams and seam finishes to suit all kinds of materials and you can also create your own. Choosing the right seam is discussed on page 125.

Preparing to stitch a seam

Some preparation work will need to be done on both the sewing machine and the garment before you can stitch a seam.

Setting up the machine
- Make sure the correct size and type of needle is installed.
- Thread the machine and check the tension.
- Check the stitch length and adjust if necessary.

- Sew a sample seam using two layers of scrap fabric and check for faults.
- If needed, place a sewing gauge or a strip of masking tape on the machine as a guide to help you sew a straight line with the correct seam allowance.
- Always keep a tape measure, a small pair of scissors and spare pins to hand.
- Make sure your chair is the right height so you sit up straight. Avoid bending over with your head too close to the machine.

- Remove any jewellery or scarves that could get caught in the machine and tie back long hair.

If you encounter any problems with stitching, see pages 26–27.

A flatbed machine with sewing guidelines engraved onto the throat plate.

Alternatively, or if the sewing machine is not equipped with a sewing guide, place a strip of masking tape onto the throat plate as a guide for the sewing line.

Step by step stitching the seam

Place the fabric under the machine with the bulk to the left. Align the seam under the presser foot and lower the needle to anchor the fabric.

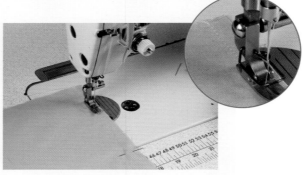

Step 1

Hold the threads towards the back to avoid them being pulled under when starting to stitch.

Step 2

Secure the stitching at the beginning and end by backstitching. To backstitch go backward for a couple of stitches and then continue stitching the seam forwards. At the end go backwards for a couple of stitches to secure the end of the seam. The backward stitches should sit directly on top of the seam line.

Step 3

Make sure your hands are placed in front of the presser foot when stitching. Avoid pulling the fabric from the back – only guide the seam through the sewing process, because the machine will move the fabric at the right speed.

Step 4

Check the stitching for faults, cut off loose threads and press each seam as you work.

Stitch length and usage

Both industrial and domestic sewing machines can be adjusted to sew different stitch lengths. Most machines offer a variation of between 1 and 5, which indicates the length in millimetres.

1–2mm stitches are the smallest and strongest as well as the hardest to unpick if something has gone wrong. This size is used for fine fabrics, pin hem finishing, retain stitching, for stitching curved seams and corners and for pre-stitching hand-sewn buttonholes and bound buttonholes.

2.5–3.5mm stitches are for permanent stitching on most fabric qualities, from medium-weight to heavyweight. This length can also be used for topstitching light- to medium-weight fabrics.

It is important to consider the length of stitch required at the start of a new sewing project – it will depend on the fabric quality and the purpose of the stitching.

4–5mm or more is a large stitch size. This length will not hold a garment together securely so is mostly used for temporary stitching. However, this stitch length is used for gathering and to stitch toiles together, because the seams can be opened fairly easily to correct fitting errors. Outerwear is usually topstitched with a large stitch length, as are heavyweight materials such as denim or leather.

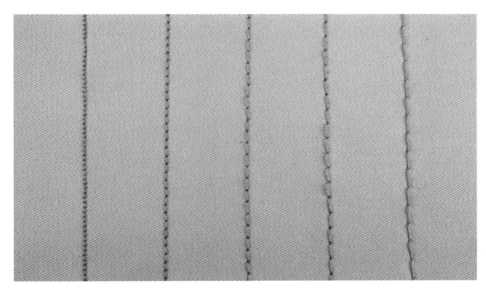

From left to right: Stitching lines with a stitch length of 1mm, 2mm, 3mm, 4mm and 5mm.

PREPARING GARMENT PIECES

- Marking seam lines on the wrong side of the fabric with chalk can help to achieve accurate seams.
- Secure fabric pieces with pins to make sure layers do not move out of place when stitching. Pins can be placed horizontally or vertically but should be removed as you stitch up to them. The professionals stitch over horizontal pins, but this is not good practice as it could result in a broken machine needle. Vertical pins can provide a stitching guide if correctly placed. Always remember not to over-pin.
- Some fabrics are best hand-tacked together to avoid seam movement.

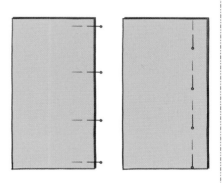

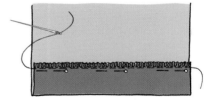

Seams pinned together horizontally (top left) and vertically (top right).

A hem allowance first pinned and then tacked in place before stitching (above).

Neatening the seam allowance

A structural plain seam has raw seam allowance edges that may fray if not finished. A professional seam finish can also add quality to the garment. There are different finishes to choose from depending on the fabric structure and type, design of the garment, end use and garment care.

Overlocked finish

Overlocking, also known as serging, is a finish most often used on woven and knitted fabrics. It is an easy and inexpensive way of finishing the seam allowance without adding bulk, and can be used on open and closed seams. Most overlocker machines have a cutting blade that trims off overhanging threads and the edge of the fabric as they stitch, so take extra care not to overlock any seam allowance away.

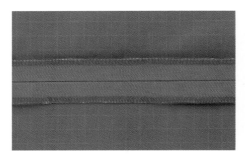

For an open seam finish, overlock the edge of the seam allowance first before stitching the seam. Then press the seam open.

For a closed overlocked seam finish, stitch the seam first then overlock the seam allowances together and press to one side.

Bound finish

A bound seam is a high-end seam finish in which the raw edges are encased with a bias-cut strip; it is used mainly on partially lined or unlined jackets and coats, or on tailored trousers. Although costly and time-consuming it adds quality to a garment and can be used to add colour or pattern as a design feature. The binding can be purchased ready-made or cut from fabric and can be attached to the seam by hand sewing or by machine stitching.

Step by step cutting and preparing bias binding

When cutting your own bias binding, use a fine lightweight fabric to avoid adding bulk to the seam finish.

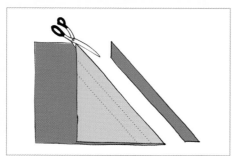

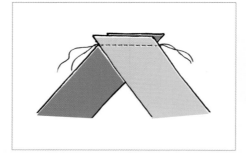

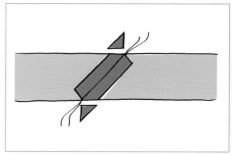

Step 1

Bring the lengthwise and crosswise grain together. The folded edge is the 45-degree bias grain, also called the true bias. Draw a line parallel to the bias and the desired width of your bias strip; repeat as many times as necessary. Cut the bias strips.

Step 2

Usually strips must be joined to achieve the required length of binding. Place the strips right sides together, matching the lengthwise grain. Stitch the seam as illustrated using a 5mm (³⁄₁₆in) seam allowance. Repeat to join as many strips together as necessary.

Step 3

Press all joining seams open and trim off the extended points on either side, as illustrated.

Step by step applying the binding by machine

This is how to apply the binding if there is no binding attachment on the sewing machine. The binding is 3.5cm (1⁵⁄₁₆in).

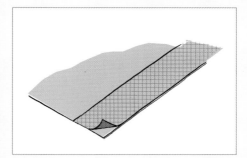

Step 1
Place the bias strip along the edge of the seam allowance, with the right side facing the wrong side of the fabric.

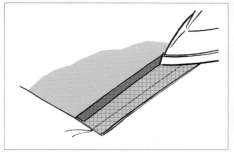

Step 2
Stitch the bias strip onto the fabric using a 7mm (⁹⁄₃₂in) seam allowance. Press the unsewn edge of the binding over by 1cm (³⁄₈in).

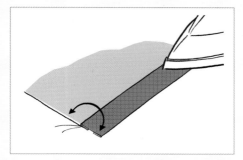

Step 3
Fold the bias strip right over along the stitching line, as shown in the illustration, and press down.

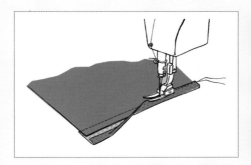

Step 4
Turn the garment over and fold the bias strip to cover the stitching line. Stitch along the edge of the binding – sometimes, pinning or tacking the edge before edge stitching can be helpful.

Step 5
Press the bound seam allowance before continuing the sewing process.

Pinked finish

A pinked finish to a seam allowance produces a zigzag cut edge that adds no bulk, is quick and easy to do and costs little. It is not suitable for all fabric types; it is mainly used on linings or as a decorative edge finish on non-fraying materials.

- You will need at least 1.5cm (⁹⁄₁₆in) seam allowance.
- Use pinking shears to cut along the edge.
- The raw edges can be pinked before or after the plain seam is stitched.
- Press the seam open after the edge has been pinked.

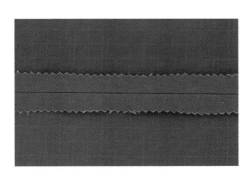

Clean-finished

A clean-finish has a folded and stitched edge on each side of the seam allowance; it is not suitable for heavyweight fabric because it adds bulk. It is time-consuming to apply but may be used when only a straight-stitch machine is available. It adds durability to the garment and is seen in designer garments as a high-end finish on lightweight fabrics.

- You will need at least 1.5cm (⁹⁄₁₆in) seam allowance.
- Construct a plain seam and press open.
- Fold each outer edge under by 5mm (³⁄₁₆in).
- Edge stitch the folded edges with a 2mm stitch.
- Press lightly to avoid ridges on the right side of the fabric; under-press the seam allowance if needed (see page 245).

Overcast finish

Overcasting is hand sewn and is mostly used on heavyweight materials to stop the edge from fraying. It is used when machine finishing is not available or on areas that cannot be reached by machine.

- Overcasting can be applied before or after stitching the plain seam.
- Construct the plain seam and press open or closed on one side.
- See page 117 for detailed instructions on how to overcast stitch.
- Press lightly over the stitching to avoid leaving a ridge on the right side of the fabric.

Zigzag finish

The zigzag finish is the machine version of an overcast finish; it is easy and quick to work and adds little bulk. It is a poorer quality finish than overlocking so is only used if an overlocker is not available. It can be applied to an open or closed plain seam.

- The zigzag finish can be applied before or after stitching the plain seam.
- Construct the plain seam and press either open or closed to one side.
- Sew the zigzag stitch close to the raw edge of the seam allowance.
- Press lightly over the stitching to avoid creating a ridge on the right side.

Raw edge finish

A raw edge finish can be used on any fabric that does not fray, such as felted wool, leather or non-woven materials. The raw edge can be topstitched or glued, for support or to neaten it. If the seam allowance is on the outside, a raw edge finish with a frayed edge can be used as a design feature to add a distressed look to the garment. Some fine jerseys can be cut and left with a raw edge finish because the edge will roll to create a finishing effect.

- When using a raw edge, cut the edge straight with the seam allowance at a consistent width.
- Consider a variety of seam options, such as an abutted seam. Seams for non-woven materials are discussed on page 292.

Choosing the right seam

It is vital to have a good understanding of seam construction in order to design and manufacture a professional-looking garment. Study the history of haute couture and tailoring crafts and compare those with techniques used by the manufacturing industry today. Here are some points to consider when choosing the seam finish:

- Garment design, style, quality and end use.
- Fabric type, texture, stretch, transparency, wear and tendency to fray.
- Durability and care needs.
- Current fashion trends.
- Skill level and equipment available.
- Manufacturing costs.

For more detailed information on fabric-specific seams, see Chapter 5, Fabric- and Cut-Specific Techniques.

Step by step plain seam

The plain seam can be used on most materials except knitted fabrics, which makes it the most used seam when stitching garment pieces together.

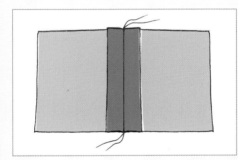 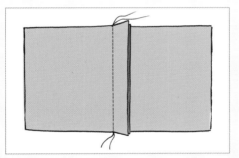 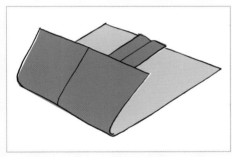

Step 1
Choose a stitch length from 2–5mm depending on the end use. Place the garment pieces right sides together and secure along the sewing edge with pins or hand-tacking. Place under the machine and stitch together, starting and finishing with a backstitch. Press the seam open.

Step 2
Alternatively, the plain seam can be pressed closed with both seam allowances to one side.

Step 3
The seam allowances are raw and can be finished with overlocking, bias binding or overcasting, or clean-finished to stop the edge from fraying. Depending on the material, the plain seam can also be glued or topstitched down.

Step by step French seam

A French seam is used on fine fabrics such as chiffon and georgette and is an enclosed seam that needs no further finishing to stop the edge from fraying. The seam shows a clean finish on the outside and inside of a garment.

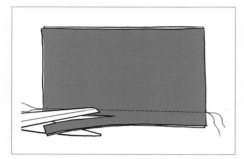

Step 1

Choose a stitch length between 2–2.5mm depending on the fabric. Place the garment pieces wrong sides together and secure along the sewing edge with pins if necessary. Stitch the pieces together with a 5mm (³⁄₁₆in) seam allowance, starting and finishing with a backstitch, then trim the seam allowances to 3mm (⅛in).

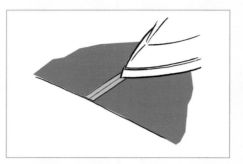

Step 2

Press the seam allowance open.

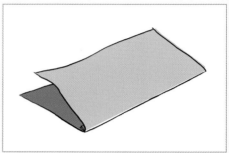

Step 3

Fold the garment pieces with right sides together along this seam.

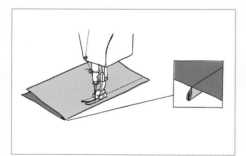

Step 4

Stitch another seam taking a 5–7mm (³⁄₁₆–⁹⁄₃₂in) seam allowance and encasing the first seam allowance. Start and end with a backstitch to secure the stitching. The aim is to produce a very thin seam allowance, because this seam is often used for transparent and fine fabrics.

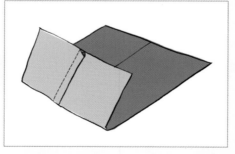

Step 5

Press the seam flat to one side.

Step by step French seam turned around a corner

This is a seam construction for experienced sewers.

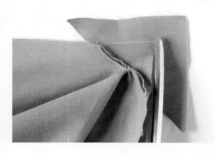

Step 1
Add 1–1.5cm (⅜–⁹⁄₁₆in) seam allowance to both inward and outward corner. Cut into the inward corner and cut a small triangular piece of matching fabric.

Step 2
Open out the inward corner and sew the triangular piece onto the cut line, wrong sides together, with a 2mm (³⁄₃₂in) seam allowance and using a 2mm stitch length.

Step 3
Cut the inserted triangular piece down to match the seam allowance of the inward corner and press the seam allowance outwards.

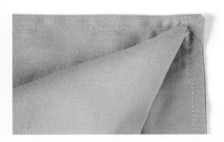

Step 4
Sew the inward and outward corners wrong sides together. Trim the seam allowance to 5mm (³⁄₁₆in).

Step 5
Turn right sides together and stitch a 7mm (⁹⁄₃₂in) seam, encasing the seam allowance.

Step 6
Press the French seam towards the inward corner piece.

Step by step flat fell seam

The flat fell seam is a hardwearing and durable seam that provides a neat finish on the outside and inside of a garment. It shows two rows of stitching on one side and one row of stitching on the other and is used in shirting on side seams, for workwear and on denim garments such as jeans.

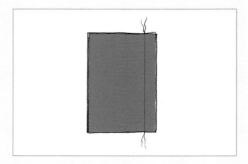

Step 1

Choose a stitch length between 2.5–3.5mm depending on the fabric. Place the garment pieces with wrong sides together and secure along the sewing edge with pins if necessary. Stitch the pieces together with a 1.5–2cm (⁹⁄₁₆–¾in) seam allowance, depending on the garment and fabric weight, starting and finishing with a backstitch.

Step 2

Trim one seam allowance to 5–7mm (³⁄₁₆–⁹⁄₃₂in). Another option is to prepare the pattern pieces with a flat fell seam allowance from the start, so one allowance is cut narrower than the other instead of being trimmed off after the seam has been stitched.

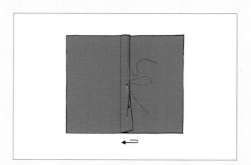

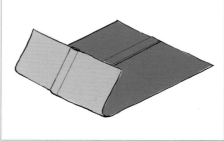

Step 3

Press the seam allowance to one side with the uncut seam covering the trimmed seam. Fold the uncut seam edge under to enclose the trimmed edge and press. Secure the seam with pins or tacking stitches, as shown in red in the illustration, to stop the seam moving. Topstitch close to the folded edge.

Step 4

Press the flat fell seam from both sides.

Step by step welt seam

The welt seam is similar to the flat fell seam, but with one side showing a raw edge. It is a strong seam used for sportswear, outerwear and on bulky fabrics where a flat fell seam would be too heavy. The welt seam can be made with the raw edge on the right side of the garment as a design feature.

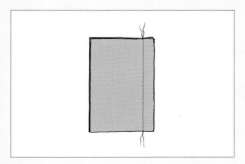

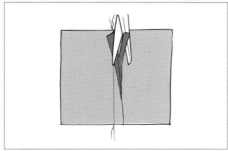

Step 1

Choose a stitch length between 2.5–3.5mm depending on the fabric. Place the garment pieces with right sides together and secure along the sewing edge with pins if necessary. Stitch the pieces together with a 1.5–2cm (⁹⁄₁₆–¾in) seam allowance depending on the garment and fabric weight. Start and finish with a backstitch.

Step 2

Trim one seam allowance to 5–7mm (³⁄₁₆–⁹⁄₃₂in). Alternatively the pieces can be cut from the start with one allowance shorter than the other, instead of it being trimmed off after the seams have been stitched.

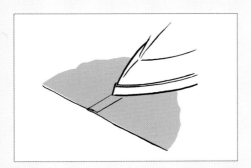

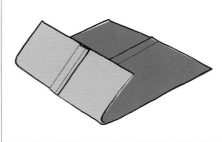

Step 3

Press the seam allowance to one side with the uncut seam covering the trimmed seam.

Step 4

Consider overlocking the raw edge if the fabric frays a lot, then secure it with pins or tacking to cover the trimmed seam allowance. Topstitch the raw edge onto the garment, covering the trimmed seam allowance. Press the welt seam from both sides.

Matching up seams

Matching or marking points to indicate width of seam, placement points and balance points are marked on the pattern by notches or punched holes and transferred to garment pieces using cut notches, thread or chalk marks. For more information on how to apply marking points see How to Mark the Pattern onto the Fabric, page 52 and Understanding Symbols on Patterns, page 36.

How to pin notches and placement points together

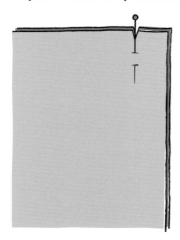

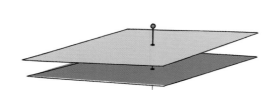

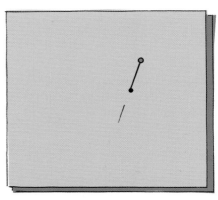

1 Place the two garment pieces on top of each other, lining up the notch marks that indicate both seam width and which pieces go together. Pin through both pieces of fabric in line with the seam width.

2 To match up placement points put the tip of the pin through the two layers of fabric to make sure that the marks sit on top of each other.

3 Once the points are lined up, pin in place.

Secure adjoining garment pieces by pinning in place before sewing.

Intersecting seams

In some places two seams may intersect and create bulk, such as at the crotch of trousers or under the arm where side and sleeve seams meet.

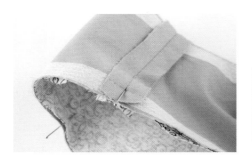

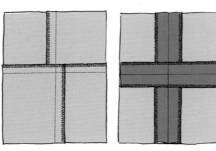

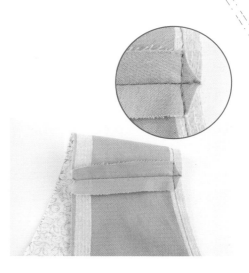

Match the seam junction by pinning the seam allowance together directly in the seam line. When stitching the intersecting seam, only remove the pin when close to the section.

Intersecting seams can be pre-pressed open or to one side. With a closed seam pressed to one side the seam allowance creates bulk at the seam junction, so press the seam allowances in opposite directions (left) to reduce the bulk. Use open seams (right) for heavyweight materials to keep bulk to a minimum.

Some intersecting seams at hemlines and facings are clipped at the seam allowance to avoid bulk. Clip off all corners of the seam allowance.

Ease stitching

When the edge of one garment piece is longer than the other, ease stitching can be used to fit the longer piece onto the shorter without pleating or puckering.

This method is used often on sleeve heads, shoulders, waistline, bust area and necklines. An eased seam can also be used to create subtle fullness and shape.

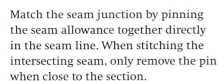

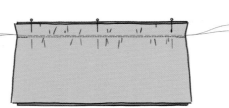

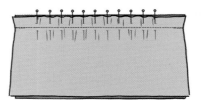

1 Prepare the longer piece by machine stitching with a large stitch length slightly inside the seam allowance – do not secure with backstitching.

2 Pull the bobbin thread only to ease the fullness. Place the pieces right sides together and pin with the ease stitching facing up and evenly distributed. Stitch the seam, taking care that no pleating or puckering shows on the right side of the garment.

3 Some adjoining pieces can be stitched together without ease stitching if the ease is moderate. Pin the edges together, matching notches, and distribute the fullness evenly. Secure with plenty of pins. Stitch slowly to control the fullness from the eased side.

Enhancing and securing the seam

The following types of stitching are used to enhance and secure the seam and to prevent facings coming round to the right side.

Topstitch

Topstitching is a single or multiple line of stitching on the right side of a garment to support and strengthen a seam and also enhance the design. It can be done in the same colour thread as the garment, or a contrast colour to highlight the seam, or as a design feature. Research iconic garments to study traditional topstitching techniques, and sample with different threads and stitching styles, since topstitching can make or break a garment.

1 Take your time when topstitching because the stitching is visible on the outside of the garment. The stitch length must be chosen with the fabric texture and garment style in mind.

2 Double topstitching can be done with a twin needle (see page 21) or with a single needle. When using one needle, make a line of edge stitching and then line up the presser foot to the edge, or to the edge stitching, and stitch a parallel line of stitching.

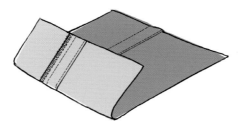

TOPSTITCHING OR EDGE STITCHING SHAPED SEAMS

- Take your time on shaped seams, working in short sections.
- Stop with the machine needle down in the material. Lift the machine presser foot and turn the material slightly, then stitch another short distance. Repeat the process to the end of the seam.

- If the curved seam is very tight, hand-walk the sewing machine by turning the hand-wheel for better control. Make sure your feet are off the pedal when using the hand-wheel.

Edge stitch

This stitch is one row of topstitch, stitched very close to the seam line to highlight and flatten a seam. It keeps the seam allowance facing the same way and adds strength to the seam.

Press the seam allowance to one side of the garment. Place the garment right side up under the machine and stitch not more than a couple of millimetres away from the seam line.

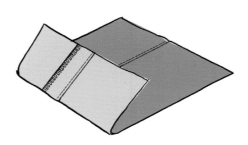

TIP

If the topstitching or edge-stitching thread breaks or runs out halfway there is no need to unpick and start again.

1 Pull the broken thread through to the wrong side. Tie the two threads together and thread through a hand-sewing needle. Insert the needle as shown in the illustration to hide the thread ends in the seam allowance.

2 Put the machine needle into the last stitching hole and continue topstitching to the end. Pull the thread to the wrong side at the re-joining point, thread the two ends into a hand-sewing needle and hide in the seam allowance as before.

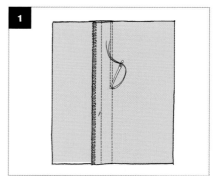

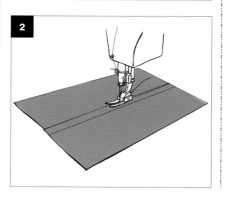

Retain stitch

Retain stitching, also called under stitching, is a row of stitching close to the seam line onto a facing, lining or under layer to prevent these pieces from rolling to the right side of the garment. Retain stitching provides a crisp edge to the facing without any stitching showing on the right side.

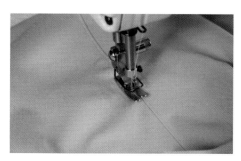

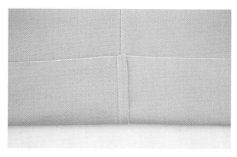

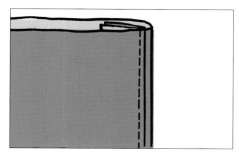

Press the seam allowance towards the facing, lining or under layer side. Place the material under the sewing machine with the garment side to one side and the facing, lining or under layer to the other side.

Sew the seam allowance to the facing, lining or under layer a couple of millimetres from the seam line.

Retain/under stitching shown from the inside of a garment edge. The stitching shows only on the inside of the garment.

Sink stitch

Sink stitching or 'stitching in the ditch' is a line of stitching made into a seam line so it is concealed; it is used when you do not want the stitching to be visible on the right side of the garment. Sink stitching is mainly used on facings, waistbands, cuffs, collars and bindings. Always use a matching colour of thread and match the stitch length to the weight of the material.

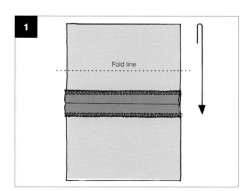

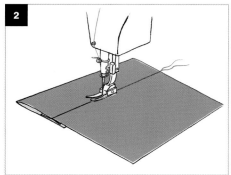

1 Use a standard machine foot or a zip foot. Prepare the garment pieces by pressing, pinning or tacking to hold in place. Here a waistband is being folded over in preparation for sink stitching.

2 Place the garment right side up under the machine. Carefully stitch along the seam line so the stitching sinks in and becomes almost invisible on the right side of the garment.

Raw edge deconstructed finish

Using raw edges for a deconstructed or distressed look has been fashionable for some time. This type of finish can be found on an external seam allowance, as an edge finish at the hem, neck or armhole, or as a decorative trim on parts such as pockets or collars. Some fabrics lend themselves more to this technique than others, such as loosely woven fabrics, woollen and linen fabrics, or denim and canvas. For more information on a raw edge seam allowance finish see page 124.

For a deconstructed look, the edges of a woven fabric can be distressed with a toothbrush, wire chenille brush, pumice stone or any other abrasive tool. You can also use your fingernails if working on a small area. Deconstructed edges can also be achieved by pulling either the warp or weft thread out to create a fringe. Some fabrics, such as denim, are best distressed by machine-washing; cut the garment pieces and assemble before the washing process.

Bleached denim coat with raw, distressed finish by Vania Gouveia.

STAY-STITCHING

This is a row of stitching on a single layer of fabric using a long stitch, made to reinforce notched or clipped seams and to prevent seams from stretching out of shape during the sewing process – see Stay-stitching on page 141. Apply stay-stitching within the seam allowance so it does not need to be taken out. As an alternative to stay-stitching, a seam can be taped (see page 139).

Trimming seams and reducing bulk

Seam allowances on enclosed garment parts, such as collars and facings, will need trimming or layering to reduce bulk and improve the quality of the finish. Curved and shaped seams need clipping and trimming to lie flat in a smooth line. Reduce the bulk straight after stitching the seam – it is not always possible to do it once parts of the garment have been completed.

Trimming
Cut both sides of the seam allowance down to half the original width or down to a couple of millimetres depending on the shape of seam and weight of fabric. Fused seam allowances can be trimmed much further because the interfacing adds stability to the fabric and stops it from fraying.

Layering
Also known as grading, this entails trimming one seam allowance more than the other to give a staggered edge for a thin, crisp seam or edge finish. The wider seam allowance is the one next to the garment and cushions the trimmed layer so the layering will not show on the right side of the garment.

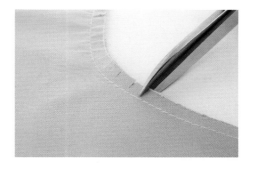

Clipping
Inward curves are clipped to allow the seam allowance to open up so the seam will lie flat around the curved area. Clip into the seam allowance almost to the stitching line every 0.5–1cm (³⁄₁₆–³⁄₈in).

Notching
Notching means to cut V-shaped wedges from the seam allowance on an outward curve to reduce bulk for a flat and smooth shaped curve.

Bagging out
Bagging out is a method of cleaning up garment edges at neckline, hemline or around sleeveless armholes using a tape or a facing. To bag out a garment edge, place two pieces of fabric right sides together and stitch along the

seam allowance. After trimming and pressing the seam allowance, turn the garment piece inside out and press again. The process of bagging out is further explained in the Step by step all-in-one neckline facing on page 163.

Shaped seams

Shaped seams can be hard to stitch and will need some preparation to achieve
a good result.

Curves

Curved seams are found in many
different places – almost every garment
has a curved area somewhere.

- Clip or notch curved seam allowances
  on enclosed seams. Concave curves are
  clipped and convex curves are notched.
  The number of clips/notches increases
  with the tightness of the curve.

- Some curved seams will need stay-
  stitching and clipping before stitching.
- Take your time when stitching a curved
  seam. Sew in short bursts.
- If the curved seam is very tight hand-
  walk the sewing machine.
- Use a small stitch length for a curved
  seam – the tighter the curve the

smaller the stitch length.
- Some curved seams should be taped or
  interfaced to stop the seam stretching.
- Press a curved seam over a tailor's ham
  with a similar shape, or a sleeve board.

Step by step inserting a semi-circular seam

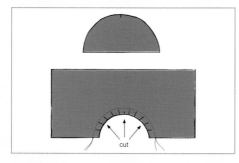

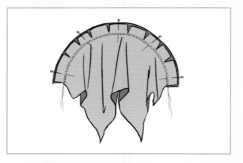

Step 1
Stay-stitch inside the seam allowance on
one side of the semi-circle using a long
stitch. Clip the inward seam allowance
up to the stay-stitch, with clips equally
spaced – this will allow the seam
allowance to open up for the two seams to
be stitched together.

Step 2
With the clipped side working around
the other pattern piece, pin the two
pieces right side together. Stitch together
just behind the stay-stitching, starting
and ending with backstitching to secure
the seam. Press the seam allowance
to one side so that the clipped side is
underneath.

Sewing corner seams

Angled seams are found in many areas of garment construction. The art is to make sharp and defined corners that are not rounded and soft. Outward corners are found on collars and cuffs and need trimming to reduce bulk. Inward corners may be found on necklines or styled as part of the seam design. The corners on inward angled seams are clipped so are weak and need reinforcement.

Step by step stitching an inward corner

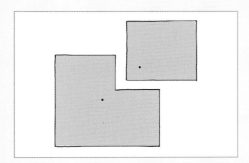

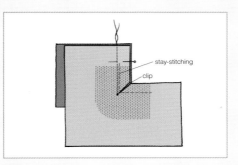

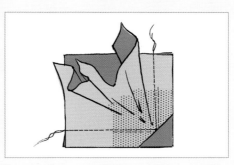

Step 1

Mark the turning point on the corner of both garment pieces on the wrong side of the fabric, using either a hole punch, thread mark or chalk mark.

Step 2

Stay-stitch or reinforce the corner with interfacing to avoid it deforming and fraying. Some materials will need both reinforcement techniques. Sample beforehand to establish the best result. Place the pieces right sides together, matching the turning points, with the layer to be clipped on top. Pin up to the matching point then stitch the seam up to the matching point. Leaving the needle down in the fabric, clip the corner up to the stitching.

Step 3

Pivot the top layer of fabric to align with the bottom layer at the edges and seam allowance. Continue stitching the rest of the seam. Press the seam to one side so that the clipped-in corner is underneath. Proceed with a seam finish that suits the material and style.

Step by step bagged out corner

Step 1
Place the two garment pieces right sides together. Stitch to the corner, stopping the width of the seam allowance from the raw edge.

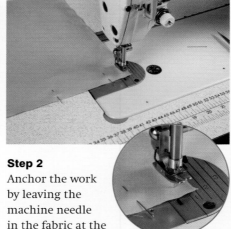

Step 2
Anchor the work by leaving the machine needle in the fabric at the corner.

Step 3
Pivot the fabric on the needle at the corner to line up with the seam allowance in the other direction and continue stitching until the end of the seam.

Step 4
Trim or layer the seam allowance and trim the corner off to reduce bulk.

Step 5
Press the seam allowance open. Turn the garment to the right side and press carefully from the right side. Some fabrics need to be protected by a pressing cloth when ironed from the right side.

Step 6
To achieve a sharp and defined corner, use a pin to pull the tip of the corner out but be careful not to pull too much and fray the corner. You may prefer to leave the pin in place to straighten the corner when pressing from the right side.

Step 7
Alternatively, use a hand-sewing needle and strong thread to straighten the corner: from the right side, insert the needle and thread into the tip of the corner, pull the needle through and gently pull the thread ends to straighten the corner out.

Taped seams

Necklines, shoulders, armholes, edges of lapels and pocket openings are some garment areas that might be taped for support. Tape is used to stabilize seam lines and prevent them from stretching during and after construction, and also to prevent seam slippage when working with loosely woven fabrics or those woven with smooth, silky yarn. Not every seam will be affected – just those under stress such as at armholes. The tape comes in different materials, weights and colours and should be matched to the material of the garment. Stabilizing tapes are narrow and can be applied by sewing or ironed on within the seam allowance. Tapes and bindings on page 88 looks at the different tapes available and their use.

Selecting the tape

Select the right tape before beginning and sample with the final material first – there is nothing more disheartening than constructing a garment only to realize that the tape adds too much bulk or shows on the right side when it is too late to do something about it. Alternatives include straight-grain or bias-cotton and polyester tape, fabric selvedge, clear elastic tape for sewing in, and iron-on tapes – most of which come in a variety of widths, colours, textures and weights. The type of seam used and the fabric texture and weight will influence your choice. For knitted fabric use a clear elastic tape such as Framilon®, which allows the seam to stretch but will return to its original length.

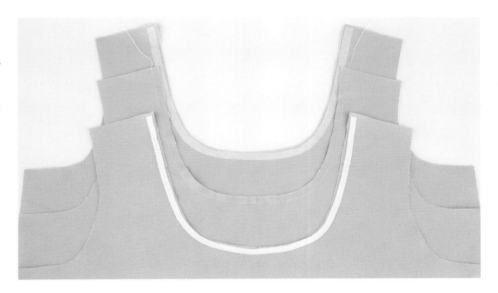

From top to bottom: Iron-on, stay-stitched and taped necklines.

SELF-MADE TAPE

Cut off the selvedge of a viscose or silk lining fabric and use this as an alternative lightweight tape. The selvedge of a fabric is tightly woven with no stretch, so it is ideal for taping the seams of a lightweight or medium-weight fabric. The selvedge of organza or organdie is good for sheer fabrics. Try using the selvedge of the fabric you are working with as a stabilizing tape, since this will perfectly match the fabric weight and colour without adding bulk to the seams.

Sew-in tape

This section shows how to apply a woven cotton tape to a neckline. Parts of the neckline are on the bias so the tape is applied to prevent the neckline from stretching during construction and afterwards when the garment is worn and washed. Sometimes the tape is cut shorter than the neckline measurement and must be eased on; this will make the neckline fit closely to the body. Using a sew-in tape is the strongest and most durable option and will contribute to the quality and long life of a garment.

 Step by step applying sew-in tape to a neckline

Step 1

Measure the pattern piece along the neckline and cut the tape to that measurement – in some cases the neckline (or any seam line that needs taping) may have stretched during cutting out and preparation. Lay the garment piece flat on a table and pin or hand-tack the wrong side of the tape to the wrong side of the neckline. Keep hand-tacking within the seam allowance. Do not stretch the tape.

Step 2

Stitch the tape to the seam allowance along the centre of the tape using a medium stitch length. Some tapes are applied solely within the seam allowance; others slightly overlap the seam line, to be reinforced when the seam is stitched.

Step 3

After the tape has been sewn on, the front and back panel can be stitched together and the facing can be applied. Seams with sew-in tapes can be clipped, retain stitched and pressed open or to one side just like any other seam.

Applying iron-on tape to a neckline

1 Measure the pattern piece along the neckline and cut the tape to that measurement – in some cases the neckline (or any seam line that needs taping) may have stretched during cutting out and preparation. Lay the garment piece flat on a table or on the ironing board and pin or hand-tack the adhesive side of the tape to the wrong side of the neckline. Keep hand-tacking within the seam allowance. Do not stretch the tape. Some tapes are applied within the seam allowance and others are ironed slightly over the seam line to be reinforced when the seam is stitched.

2 Iron the tape onto the seam allowance using the correct temperature to suit both iron-on tape and the garment material.

3 Continue with the garment construction after the tape has been applied. Seams with iron-on tapes can be clipped, retain stitched and pressed open or to one side just like any other seam.

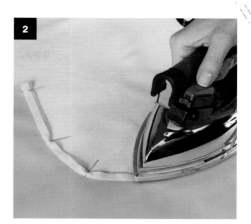

Stay-stitching

If tape adds too much bulk to the seam, consider using stay-stitching to reinforce the neckline instead.

Step by step stay-stitching a neckline

Step 1
With the garment right side up, apply a line of stay-stitching within the seam allowance along the neckline, using a long stitch.

Step 2
Take the measurement of the neckline from the pattern piece and pull the bobbin thread to ease the neckline to fit the measurement of the pattern. Distribute the ease equally around the neckline.

Step 3
Always double-check that the measurement of the garment neckline after stay-stitching is the same as the measurement of the pattern piece. Take a tape measure and place it along the stitching line to make sure that both sides measure the same from centre front to shoulder seam.

Facings

A facing is applied to a garment edge at openings and may be functional, decorative or both. Facings are either separated or extended. A separate facing is cut as an individual part and can be the shape of the garment piece, or a bias strip stitched to the garment edge.

An extended facing is cut as part of the garment. A separate facing is more versatile because it can be applied to any shaped edge; an extended facing can only be used on straight edges. Facings can be used on the inside or show partly on the outside as a trim.

What to watch for when applying facings

- The facing for inside a garment is cut slightly smaller to prevent it from rolling over to the right side of the garment and showing.
- If the facing is used as a decorative trim, cut it slightly larger so it sits comfortably without pulling on the outside of the garment.
- Cut a separate facing on the same grain line as the garment piece to which it will be attached.
- Consider the weight and texture of the fabric for the facing and allow more for a heavyweight or pile fabric to accommodate bulk.
- Facings provide strength and support to a garment edge and should be interfaced with an appropriate stabilizer. See page 92.

- Always reduce the bulk on the seam allowance once the facing has been applied by clipping and notching shaped seams, and layering or trimming excess seam allowance.
- Retain stitch the seam allowance to prevent it from rolling over to the right side of the garment.
- Consider the edge finish of a facing if it is not attached to a lining. Options include a bound edge or a clean-finished edge.
- Some garment edges need taping before the facing is applied to prevent the edge from stretching.
- Make sure the facing lies flat, is not twisted and is not visible at the edge on the outside.

Sailor-style top with a neckline bagged out for a clean finish. Derek Lam, AW 2013.

All-in-one facing

The all-in-one facing is a separate facing used to finish both neckline and armhole edges on garments without sleeves, such as vests or summer dresses. It can be applied by different methods and can be used on lined or unlined garments. An all-in-one facing is cut to the same shape as the garment part to which it is attached. See page 163 for how to apply an all-in-one facing.

Shaped facing

The shaped facing is cut in the same way as the garment part to which it is attached. This type of facing is used on waistlines, hemlines, necklines and armholes or any garment openings requiring an edge finish with a facing. The width of the shaped facing on the inside of a garment is defined by the type of garment, but should be at least 2cm (¾in) wide plus seam allowance. If the garment type and fabric allow, always consider a wider facing because these tend to stay invisible on the inside of a garment. This shaped facing is usually cut in the same fabric as the garment, but could be in a contrast colour or in a different fabric type to enhance the garment design.

Outside or decorative facing

An outside facing is not only functional but also adds a decorative finish to any garment edge. This type of separate facing sits on the outside and is cut to the same shape as the garment part to which it is attached. It can be cut to any width, depending on the design, and is usually made in a contrast colour, pattern or fabric texture as a design feature.

Bias facing

Bias facings are narrow strips of self-cut bias, or purchased pre-finished bias strips, used on necklines, armholes and hemlines as a quick and inexpensive way of finishing these edges. The strip must be cut on the true bias so it will lie smoothly around curved edges without pulling. The bias facing is either turned inside the garment and secured by hand or machine stitching, or used as a trim on the right side of the garment. To stop the bias facing from rolling around to the right side, consider topstitching on casual garments, or hand stitch or sink stitch it in place for a more invisible finish.

Extended facing

An extended facing is cut as one with a garment piece and then folded to the inside to create the facing. This method avoids having to stitch on a separate facing, creating a bulky seam, which makes it a good choice for heavy material. However, the extended facing can only be used on straight edges such as front and back openings.

4 Sewing Techniques

Garment Construction

The construction methods introduced in this chapter are basic and based on traditional techniques, but they can be changed to suit individual designs and reformatted into innovative ideas. Additional techniques specific to different fabrics can be found in Chapter 5. The chapter is arranged in the order in which a garment is sewn, beginning with finishes, such as tucks, that are sewn onto individual pattern pieces before making up.

Gathers, Pleats, Tucks and Darts .... page 146
The Neckline.. page 156
The Waistline.. page 165
Pockets .... page 177
The Sleeve .... page 192
Hemlines .... page 204
Lining .... page 212
Fastenings.. page 224
The Finishing Touch .... page 245

Gathers, Pleats, Tucks and Darts

These elements control and add fullness to shape the garment and create interesting features in the design.

Asymmetric neckline with a wide crochet trim gathered and stitched on top. Missoni, SS 2012.

Gathers

Gathers are small irregular pleats that regulate fullness, for fit or decorative effect. They look best in light- or medium-weight fabric – heavyweight fabrics can be bulky, so fullness is best controlled with pleats, darts or seaming.

Preparing the fabric

- For the best result use the straight grain.
- Assemble all seams and press the garment part well before applying gathering stitches – pressing heavily afterwards may squash the gathers.
- Special gathering threads are stronger, but ordinary sewing thread is fine in most cases.

Gathering

Use twice the length of fabric for soft gathering and three times, or more depending on the fabric, for maximum gathers. Gathering can also be done on a sewing machine using a gathering foot.

1 Use the largest straight stitch length, leaving long thread tails at start and end. Stitch two parallel rows either side of the seam line so the gathers will form evenly.

2 Pull the bobbin thread only to create evenly distributed gathers.

3 Secure the thread tails at each end with a knot and pin the gathered seam to the adjoining seam.

4 Sew from the gathered side, controlling the gathers using your fingers or with thread clippers in front of the foot. Press the seam allowance only, facing away from the gathers.

Skirt by Julien Macdonald in washed silk with gathered layers.

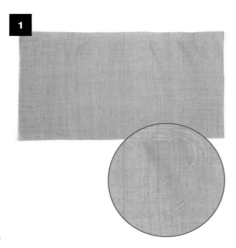

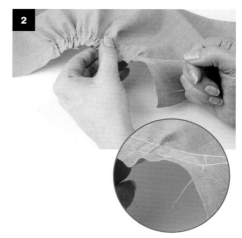

Pleats

Pleating takes in fullness creating even folds in the fabric, which can be left to fall softly or pressed sharply. They are used in various ways, from small pleats either side of a trouser waistline to a full pleated skirt. Specialist companies provide pleating. Designers, such as Issey Miyake, who is famous for his pleated designs, use pre-pleated fabric or have finished garments pleated to a specific design.

Preparing the fabric

- For best results use pre-shrunk fabric that can hold a crease.
- Transfer the pleat position and fold line marks from the pattern to the fabric, using thread or chalk marking (see pages 52–54).
- For pleats that will be pressed to the hem, finish the hemline first.

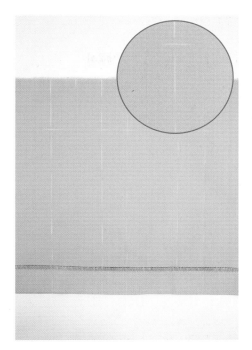

Chalk marking: Use a ruler to mark the pleat lines with chalk or a disappearing pen on the wrong side of the fabric.

Thread mark: Mark with a tacking stitch along the pleating lines. Take a couple of small stitches every 5cm (2in) and clip the thread between stitches.

Dress with a combination of box pleats on the underskirt, knife pleats on the overskirt and pin tucks on the bodice. Dior, AW 2012.

Unpressed soft pleats are caught in the seam without being fixed. This will create volume and a soft look. J.W. Anderson, SS 2014.

Professionally applied structured pleats imitating a herringbone pattern. The process uses heat, pressure and sometimes a type of liquid chemical to fix the pleats permanently. J.W. Anderson, SS 2014.

Box pleat

Box pleats can be used alone or grouped.
Each box pleat consists of two pleats of
the same width turned towards each
other, either folded outwards or inverted.

Step by step box pleat

Step 1
Apply marking lines. With right side up,
press both pleats to each other, meeting
in the centre.

Step 2
Alternatively, fold the pleat through the
centre, matching marking points, and
pin along the pleat line.

Step 3
Stitch the pleat line to the desired length.

Step 4
Press open, aligning the centreline with
the stitch line. Stitch across the top to
hold the pleat in place.

*Dress with a giant box pleat in the centre front.
Simone Rocha, AW 2013.*

Knife pleat

Knife pleats are a series of pleats folded in the same direction, either overlapping regularly or at spaced intervals, and running right round the garment or in grouped sections. They can be left unpressed or fully pressed – in either case, stitch the beginning of the pleat in place.

Edge-stitched pleats

Alternatively, the fold can be edge stitched to reinforce the break line. Construct the pleat and press the fold line. Right side up, place only the fold line under the machine and edge stitch the edge of the pleat. Either backstitch at the end of the pleat or pull the threads through to the wrong side and secure with hand stitching or a knot.

Overlapping pleats

Bulk can be a problem when pleats overlap. Cut out the pleat depth from the top to the end of the closed section, leaving a 1cm (⅜in) seam allowance. This can be done on the pattern before the fabric is cut or after the pleat has been constructed.

 Step by step knife pleat

Step 1

Mark the pleat start and end and fold it over, making sure any seam is hidden within the fold. Do not press the seam open – press it to one side.

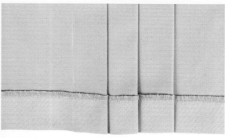

Step 2

If the pleats are fully pressed, finish the hemline first. From the wrong side, pin and stitch the top part of each pleat for at least 4cm (1⅝in), so the pleat is constructed without any stitching showing on the right side.

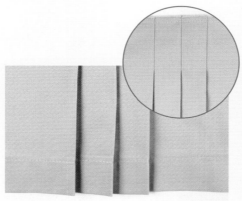

Step 3

Press the stitched section only if the rest is remaining soft, but press the entire fold line for a crisp look. Fold the pleats in one direction and stitch across the top to hold them in place.

Structured pleat combination: sunray pleats in the bodice with trapezoid pleating in the centre section and knife pleats in the skirt. Jaimee McKenna, Central St Martins, AW 2013.

Step by step topstitched pleats

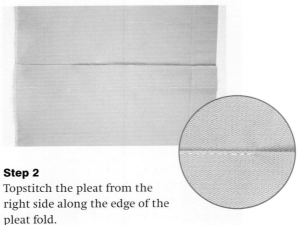

Step 1
Mark the pleat position and form each pleat by pressing along the fold line. Pin or hand-tack each pleat in place and mark the end of the topstitching.

Step 2
Topstitch the pleat from the right side along the edge of the pleat fold.

Tucks

Tucks are rows of small pleats partly or entirely stitched down. They can be used decoratively or to add fullness: tucks around the waist, for example, can release fullness to the bust and hip. Blind tucks overlap and pin tucks are very narrow – for a different look consider tucks that cross over, scalloped tucks or corded tucks.

- Use a light- to medium-weight fabric.
- Stitch on a straight grain because tucks stretch on the bias.
- Tucks, particularly pin tucks, can be sewn into the fabric before the garment piece is cut out.
- If they are to be stitched after the garment is cut out, the tuck allowance must be included in the pattern.

Pin tucks

Pin tucks are spaced slightly apart and are stitched along their length. They can be used on sheer fabrics for modesty – over the bust for instance – or to add detail and texture.

1 To stitch before cutting out, estimate the amount of fabric needed to fit the pattern piece plus allowance for tucks. Cut the fabric and mark the tucks.

2 Press the tuck fold line and stitch to the desired width. Repeat the process until all tucks have been stitched in place.

3 Place the pattern onto the tucked fabric, matching where tucks will fall across garment parts. Cut out the pattern pieces and continue constructing the garment.

Blouse by Ulyana Danyleyko with tucks around the neck and the top part of the sleeves.

Darts

Darts are inserted to control the silhouette and shape a garment to the body, as well as being used as a design feature. They are usually placed at the bust and waist, but also at the neck, shoulder and elbow. Darts can be straight or shaped to fit closely to the body and are mostly used on woven fabrics or non-woven materials.

Bust darts are placed at the underarm, side seam or coming from the shoulder, running towards the bust point. A bust dart is never stitched right up to the bust point but stops a couple of centimetres short. For fitted garments two bust darts can be used, perhaps one up from the waist and the other across from the underarm.

Waist darts shape the fabric in at the waist but allow fullness at the hip and are used on skirt and trouser waistlines. Usually two darts are placed at the front and two to four at the back. Shape the waist dart slightly inwards for a better fit.

Neck darts provide a close fit to the neckline. The neck and bust dart can be combined to shape both areas by placing the neck dart so that it runs towards the bust point.

Shoulder darts are small darts from the shoulder seam or top armhole area to shape the shoulder plate.

Elbow darts on a two-piece sleeve run from the underarm seam towards the elbow, or on a one-piece sleeve from the wrist/hemline of the sleeve towards the elbow. They allow for comfort on tight sleeves and a tailored fit on jackets and coats.

Shaped darts are curved to fit the body closely.

A dart is wedge shaped with two equal length dart legs ending in a dart point. Couture or double-pointed darts run in opposite directions from the widest part, with a dart point at each end. See also page 37.

Couture or *double-pointed darts* sit at the waistline running upwards to the bust point and downwards to the hipline and are used on jackets, coats and dresses without a waistline seam.

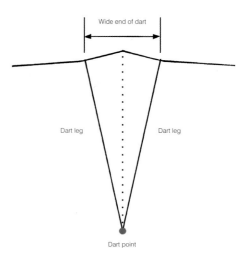

Marking the dart position

- See How to Mark the Pattern onto the Fabric, page 52.
- Chalk mark from the wrong side of the garment. Draw the dart legs from the wide end to the dart point with a ruler.
- Clip the wide ends of the dart on the fabric edge and mark the dart end with a chalk pen from the wrong side or thread mark with a tailor's tack.
- On fabrics that cannot be chalk marked or clipped, use thread marking on the dart legs to the dart point.

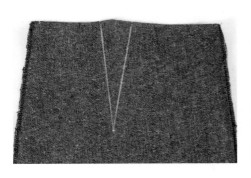

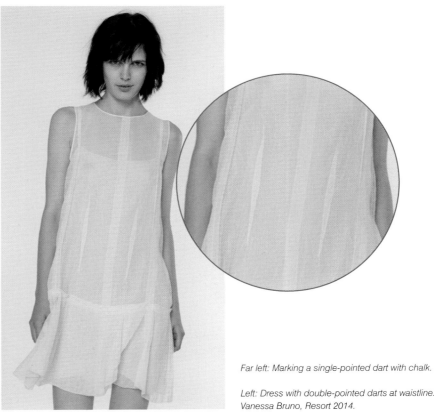

Far left: Marking a single-pointed dart with chalk.

Left: Dress with double-pointed darts at waistline. Vanessa Bruno, Resort 2014.

Step by step single-pointed darts

These can be stitched and pressed in several ways to suit the fabric weight.

Step 1
Mark the dart onto the fabric. Wrong side up, fold the fabric through the point of the dart, matching up marks at the wide end. Pin the dart legs together and pin-mark the dart point.

Step 2
Stitch the dart legs from the wide end to the dart point. Finish with backstitching.

Step 3
Press the dart to one side and check from the right side that the dart point is pressed out nicely and not puckering.

Step by step securing the dart point

In most cases the dart point can be secured with backstitching.

Step 1
On fine and sheer fabrics finish the end with a knot by running the stitching out and leaving a long thread tail. Form a loop and pull the thread through.

Step 2
Make the knot as close as possible to the dart point. The finished knot is small and unobtrusive.

Pressing a single-pointed dart

Darts can easily leave an impression or shine mark on the right side of the garment when pressed, so place a strip of paper between the dart and garment beforehand (see page 245). Press darts over a tailor's ham or sleeve board to avoid flattening the shaping.

Press to one side
Press vertical darts towards the centre and horizontal darts downwards.

Pressing flat
1 Single-pointed darts may also be pressed flat over the stitching, as above.

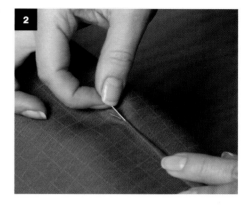

2 To do this, put a pin in the dart point and manipulate the fabric apart by moving the pin to each side.

Dealing with heavy fabrics
Darts in heavyweight fabrics can be cut open to reduce bulk. Cut along the fold line, stopping 1–2cm (⅜–¾in) before the dart point, and cut into the corners if necessary. Press the dart open and the remaining dart point flat.

Dealing with shaped darts
1 On shaped darts cut the dart down to a 1cm (⅜in) seam allowance.

2 Stitch the dart and press open or to one side.

Step by step double-pointed darts

These can be stitched and pressed in different ways to suit the fabric quality.

Step 1

Mark the dart onto the fabric. Wrong side up, fold the fabric through the dart points, matching markings. Pin the dart legs together and pin-mark each dart point.

Step 2

On fine and sheer fabrics, stitch the dart from the centre to each dart point and secure the end with a knot. Alternatively, stitch from one dart point to the other, backstitching at both ends.

Step 3

Press the dart to one side or cut along the fold and press open to reduce bulk. It may be necessary to snip into the dart centre to allow it to lie flat.

Taped dart

1 Consider taping darts on a bias grain to stop them stretching. Cut a strip of straight grain lightweight fabric or a strip of iron-on interfacing the length of the dart. Wrong side up, pin the tape to one side of the dart leg, or iron the interfacing, centred on the stitching line.

2 Pin and stitch the dart with the tape at the same time. Press the dart to one side to cover the tape.

MAKING DARTS THE SAME LENGTH

Making two darts the same length can be a challenge – even more so when they must match either side of a garment. After pinning the darts, place them on top of each other, lining up the wide end and the centre fold. Pin the end of each dart point, making sure they line up. Darts are stitched from the wide end to the dart point for a good tapered shape, but this can be tricky – stitching from the dart point towards the wide end makes it easier to achieve darts the same length. Test using both methods to see which one is best for you.

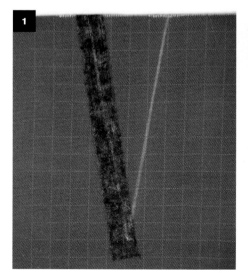

Shaping techniques

Other techniques that can be explored to shape a garment onto the body include smocking, shirring or elastic shirring.

They can be done by machine or hand, and are used to create a decorative gathering effect and to release fullness

above and below decorative stitching. Here is a variety of fabric types with different shaping techniques.

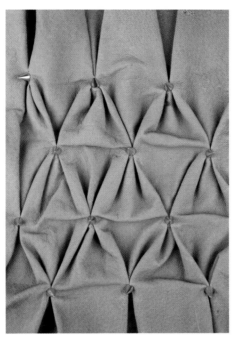

Sample of smocking on suede by Vania Gouveia.

Shirring used around the waist to create body contour and texture. Louis Vuitton, Ready-to-Wear AW 2009.

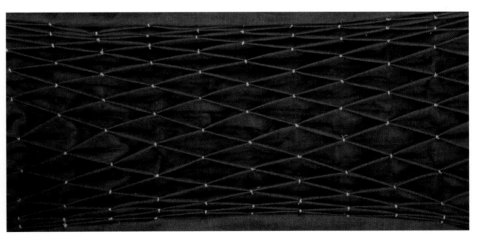

Sample of smocking on cotton fabric by Vania Gouveia.

Smocking creates a yoke around the neckline of this silk dress. The fabric falls free from the last row of the smocking, creating volume. Preen, SS 2011.

The Neckline

The collar can be a significant focal point. Collars come in different shapes, sizes and designs but are divided into three categories: the stand-up collar, roll collar and flat collar. A collar can be a separate piece attached to the neckline, such as a shirt collar, or be a part of the bodice, like a shawl collar. They can be combined, for example a notched collar with a lapel and separate collar. The methods of constructing and attaching a collar are the same for a separate collar, a grown-on collar or a notched collar.

Stand-up collars stand up all around the neckline. The front can be edge-to-edge or extended with a button fastening, rounded or squared off. An example is the mandarin collar.

Stand-up collar cut away from the centre front. Chanel, SS 2012.

Roll collars stand up for a certain height at the back but then roll over onto the garment with the outer edge wider then the neckline – examples include shawl and lapel collars.

Jacket with lapel. Akris, Resort 2014.

Flat collars lie flat against the garment with very little lift. A classic example is the Peter Pan collar.

Large flat collar extending over the shoulder. Erdem, AW 2013.

Collar features

Stand: The stand of a collar rises from the neckline and helps the collar to stand up. All collar types need a stand, even the flat collar, which has a small stand included in the pattern that enables it to roll over to the garment side.

Break line: This is the line where the collar stand breaks into the collar fall.

Fall: The visible part of the collar that turns down from the break line.

Style line: The outside edge of a collar, which defines its extent.

Lapel: Lapel or revers are turned-back facings on the front of a garment.

Gorge line: The seam that joins the collar and lapel/revers.

Break point: The point at which the lapel/revers begin to fold back from the edge.

Top collar: The top collar is the outer or upper layer of the collar. It is slightly larger than the under collar to make sure the seam line does not roll round to the top surface. Add 2mm (³⁄₃₂in) to the top collar for a lightweight fabric, 3mm (⅛in) for a medium-weight and 4–6mm (⁵⁄₃₂–¼in) for a heavyweight – this is only a guideline and should be tested using the final fabric.

Under collar: This is the facing on the underside of the collar.

— Break line

····· Gorge line

— Style line

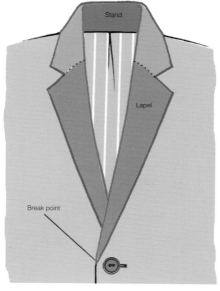

Stabilizing the collar

Collars are interfaced to retain their shape and add body and stability. The type and amount of interfacing depends on the final look and comfort factor needed. If only one layer is interfaced, it should be the top collar. A stand collar is usually interfaced on both top and under collar.

Tailored shirt collars are usually firm to the touch and crisp so are interfaced with collar canvas on the top collar with one layer in the stand. The canvas is cut to the size of the finished collar and stand, not taken into the seam allowance.

There is no rule to fit all eventualities – sample different qualities and types of interfacing to find the most suitable.

Attaching a collar

1. Make sure the inner collar edge measures the same as the neckline. Once the collar is bagged out and pressed, the inner collar edge is stitched onto the garment neckline. A good pattern has notch marking for centre front and back, shoulder and – in the case of shawl or lapel collars – a notch for the break point.

2. The seam allowance is usually 0.5–1cm (³⁄₁₆–³⁄₈in) for collar and neckline. Pin the collar to the neckline and match up all marking points. A collar or stand can have either the top or the under collar attached first.

3. Once stitched onto the neckline, carefully press the seam allowance into the collar or stand. Fold in the seam allowance of the under or top collar into the collar or stand, and pin – if necessary hand-tack in place.

4. Finish the collar and choose between sink stitching or edge/topstitching, when the top collar is stitched on first, or edge stitching when the under collar is attached first. In both cases, stitch from the top collar side.

An unusual construction with the collar ends draped under and inserted into the button stand. Issey Miyake, AW 2012.

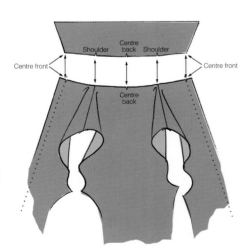

The shirt collar

This collar can be constructed as a two-piece with separate stand or with stand and collar in one piece. The two-piece gives a better fit and adds a professional look. The one-piece is used for leisurewear and informal fashion. The collar itself can be cut in different ways, such as button-down, spread, pinned, cut-away, wing-tip, Italian or classic collar. Most separate collar styles, such as the Mandarin collar, Peter Pan collar and tie collar, can be constructed using this method.

Shirt collar with separate stand

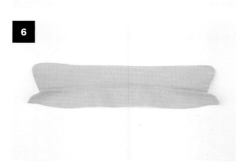

1 Cut out top and under collar and two collar stands and interface them. The collar and stand shown are fused with reinforced interfacing to the top collar and both collar stand pieces.

2 Prepare the collar first. Place the top and under collar right sides together and stitch the style line seam only, not the neckline. Layer the seam allowance and clip the corners on a pointed-style collar – see Trimming seams, page 135.

3 Turn the collar to the right side and press. Make sure the shape is symmetrical on both sides and topstitch if required. If it is a button-down style, add the buttonholes before it is attached to the stand.

4 With right sides together, sandwich the collar between the collar stand pieces, matching up all marking points, and pin.

5 Stitch together and then layer the seam allowance to reduce bulk.

6 Turn the stand to the right side. Press.

7 Stitch the outside of the collar stand to the garment neckline, matching all marking points.

8 Press the seam allowance into the stand from the inside of the garment and pin the inside collar stand to the neckline seam.

9 Edge stitch through all layers and around all edges of the collar stand. Press to finish.

Lapel collar

The lapel collar, also called a revers, notched or tailored collar, is found on jackets and coats. This collar style is formed of two parts, the collar and lapel. The shape of the collar and lapel and the angle of the gorge line define the collar style, such as a peak lapel or notched lapel.

A tailored lapel collar can be constructed using traditional tailoring techniques by attaching the stabilizer, such as canvas, with pad-stitching by hand, or by following industrial techniques by using iron-on interfacing. It is essential to get the stabilizer right to achieve a professional-looking lapel collar – for more details see page 92. The same method can be applied to construct other collar styles, such as the shawl collar, revers collar and peak lapel.

Step by step notched collar with fusible interfacing

The under collar is cut in two pieces on the bias to make the collar roll and sit better underneath the top collar.

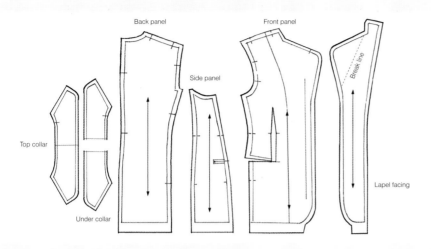

Step 1

Apply stabilizer to the top and under collar. Fuse the complete front panels, top part of the back and side panels and the lapel facings. Tape the break line of the lapel with fusible tape.

Step 2

Stitch the under collar parts together and press the seam open. Place the top collar and under collar right sides together and stitch around the style line, but not the neckline. Layer the seam allowance and clip the corners to reduce bulk. Turn the collar to the right side and press, then check the points and general shape.

Step 3

With right sides facing, pin the lapel facing to the front panel up to the break-point notch. Stitch in place from hem to break-point notch, layer the seam allowance and clip the corner and into the curved hem edge. Stitch the side seams of both front and back and the shoulder seams.

Step 4

Tape the neckline of the garment to stabilize the seam and stop it stretching – see pages 140–41. Pin the under collar to the back neckline of the garment, past the shoulder to the step of the lapel facing. Stitch in place.

Step 5

Pin the top collar to the facing and up to the step in the lapel facing. Stitch from the step in the lapel facing, stopping about 3cm (1⅛in) before the end to leave space to attach the lining.

continues on page 160...

Step by step notched collar with fusible interfacing (continued)

Step 6

Press open the seam allowance of both seams on the under and top collar.

Step 7

Turn to the right side and press the lapel seam and facing and collar corner.

Step 8

With wrong side out, fold back the facing to expose the collar and neckline seams. Pin the seam allowances of the garment neckline together and stitch parallel, as close as possible to the previous stitch line.

Step 9

Apply a final press from the right side of the garment.

Single-breasted tailored jacket with peak lapel. Prada, SS 2014.

Constructing stretch necklines

Necklines on a stretch or knitted fabric can be finished with ribbing, self-fabric, elasticated tape or stretch binding. When finishing necklines without openings use a stretchable finish to make sure the garment slips easily on and off – see pages 259–60. This method can also be used to construct a turtleneck collar.

Step by step T-shirt neckline with ribbing or self-fabric finish

Step 1
Measure the neckline of the garment and cut a strip of self-fabric or ribbing to a width that suits the garment design and the length of the circumference of the neckline. Fold the strip in half lengthwise and pin-mark the shoulder, centre front and centre back position.

Step 2
Close the right shoulder seam of the garment using a 4-thread overlocker.

Step 3
Pin the ribbing to the garment neckline, matching marking points and placing the shoulder seam allowance towards the back. The ribbing should be slightly short so it stretches onto the neckline – how much shorter depends on the stretch of the ribbing.

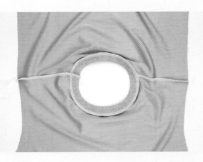

Step 4
Stitch the ribbing onto the neckline using a 4-thread overlocker. Close the left shoulder seam and binding in one go. Press the shoulder seam to the back and the neckline seam into the body.

Step 5
If you are using self-fabric, turn to the right side and retain stitch the facing seam allowance onto the garment before stitching the left shoulder seam.

Step 6
Continue constructing the T-shirt. This method can also be used to attach ribbing, self-fabric or elasticated tape to armhole openings or hemlines.

Step by step bomber-jacket neckline with ribbing

Ribbing is a popular finish on a fabric bomber-style jacket with either zip or press-stud fastening.

Step 1

Close the shoulders on the jacket. Cut the ribbing double the width of the final collar and slightly shorter than the neckline; the exact length depends on the stretch of the ribbing. Fold the ribbing in half lengthwise and pin onto the neckline, pulling the centre front downwards so the centre front point on either side aligns with the fold of the ribbing.

Step 2
Hand-tack in place and then stitch.

Step 3
Cut the excess ribbing away to a 1cm (⅜in) seam allowance at the front.

These garments are normally lined so the neckline seam does not need finishing. Apply the fastening.

Bomber jacket with ribbing finish on neckline, waistline and sleeve hemline. Jonathan Saunders, SS 2014.

Step by step all-in-one neckline facing

A neck facing gives a neat finish and can be applied with or without a collar. Facings can be cut from self-fabric or from a contrast or lightweight fabric, for decorative reasons or to reduce bulk. Facings can also be used to neaten other raw edges, such as hemlines and armholes (see page 142). The all-in-one facing neatens neckline and armhole in one. Some collars, such as the cowl, are part of a garment and need a facing. This can be cut and constructed as below.

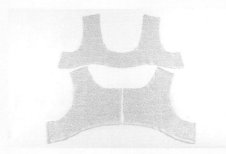

Step 1
Cut out the facing and garment front and back. When using a lightweight fabric, interface the whole facing and tape the neckline and armhole of the garment front and back. The interfacing and tape used should be tailored to the garment fabric.

Step 2
On the garment pieces, close all darts and stitch the side and shoulder seams together. Press the seams open.

Step 3
On the facing, stitch side and shoulder seams together and press open, but leave the centre back unstitched. Overlock and turn the hemline to the wrong side by 1cm (⅜in) and topstitch down. The hemline on the facing can also be bound. If the garment is lined, the hem of the facing does not need finishing.

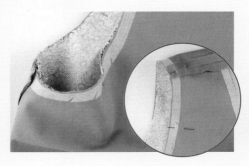

Step 4
With right sides together, pin the facing to the garment, lining up raw edges and matching shoulder and side seams, centre front and back.

Step 5
Stitch the neckline and layer the seam allowance. Clip the intersecting seam allowance to reduce bulk.

Step 6
Turn to the right side and fold the seam allowance towards the facing. Retain stitch the seam allowance to the facing to keep the facing inside the garment and make the seam lie flat.

continues on page 164...

Step by step all-in-one neckline facing (continued)

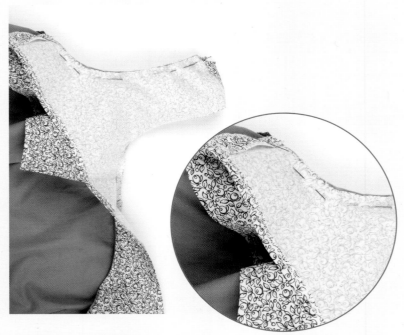

Step 7 (not pictured)

From the right side, match and pin the shoulder and side seams of the armholes together – this will help bring the right parts together once the garment is turned to the wrong side.

Step 8

Turn to the wrong side and match up the facing armhole with the garment armhole, then remove the marking pins. This may be tricky to pin and sew: pin first from the side seam up to the shoulder seam on the facing side, and stitch from side seam to shoulder. Then pin the other side from the side seam up to the shoulder, and stitch.

Step 9

Turn to the right side, fold the seam allowance of the armhole towards the facing and retain stitch as much as possible of the armhole facing. Press the neck and armhole area and proceed with the rest of the garment construction.

The Waistline

The waistline on skirts and trousers can be finished with different types of waistband or facing. A waistband can be cut straight if it sits on the natural waistline or shaped and cut in sections if placed on the hip or cut extra wide. It can open at any point but front, side or back openings are most common. The type of finish very much depends on the garment design and material choice.

There is a lot of stress on this part of the garment so the waistband or facing is stabilized with interfacing, which is matched to the material quality and garment design. Some waistlines are constructed for comfort and others for support or body shaping. In general, the waistband is attached after all garment seams have been constructed and the garment fastening has been installed.

Straight waistband

Straight waistbands can be cut as a one- or two-piece pattern. The one-piece waistband has a fold line in the middle and is usually cut to a finished width of 3cm (1⅛in). The waistband can be cut in two pieces for decorative reasons, for shape or with a lightweight facing to eliminate bulk.

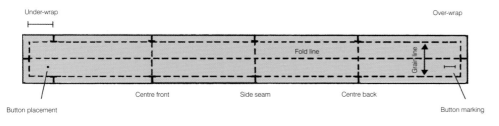

Under-wrap · Over-wrap · Fold line · Grain line · Centre front · Side seam · Centre back · Button placement · Button marking

A double waistband fastening. A heavy-duty hook-and-bar and zip fastening on the trouser part is covered by a second waistband with concealed button fastening, to look like a self-fabric belt.

***Step by step straight waistband
with topstitching***

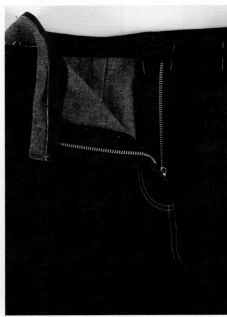

Step 1

Apply interfacing to the wrong side of the
waistband. Fold in half and fold wrong
sides together. Press the seam allowance
to the wrong side on the outer long edge
of the waistband. Pin the inner side of the
waistband with right side to wrong side
of the garment waist edge, matching up
all marking points. Stitch the waistband
in place, backstitching to start and finish.

Step 2

Apply belt loops if required – see page
168. Fold both ends of the waistband in
half, right sides together, and machine
stitch across the ends, securing with
backstitching. To reduce bulk, trim the
seam allowance and trim off the top
corners diagonally.

Step 3

Turn the waistband right side out,
slightly covering the stitching line with
the pressed edge. Pin in place, making
sure the waistband lies flat. If necessary
hand-tack in place and remove the pins.

Step 4

Starting at the under-wrap, topstitch
all edges of the waistband in one go
from the right side of the garment. The
topstitching pattern can vary depending
on the garment design.

STRAIGHT WAISTBAND WITHOUT TOPSTITCHING

The method is almost the same as the
topstitched version.

Step 1

Apply interfacing to the wrong side of the
waistband. Fold in half and press wrong
sides together. On the long edge of the
waistband press the seam allowance to the
wrong side on the inside of the waistband.

Step 2

Consider belt loops at this point and add to
the waistband if applicable.

Step 3

Pin the outer side of the waistband right
sides together to the waist edge, matching all
marking points. Stitch the waistband in place,
starting and ending with backstitching.

Step 4

Fold both ends of the waistband in half, right
sides together, and machine stitch across the
ends, securing with backstitching. To reduce
bulk, trim the seam allowance and trim the
top corners diagonally.

Step 5

Turn the waistband right side out, slightly
covering the stitching line with the pressed
edge. Pin in place, making sure the
waistband lies flat. If necessary, hand-tack
and remove the pins.

Step 5

From the right side of the garment sink stitch
along the line where the waistband meets
the garment, catching the inside of the
waistband at the same time. See page 133
for how to sink stitch.

Belt loops

Belt loops are applied to a garment to hold a belt in position and can be made of fabric, thread, cord or tape. Belt loop positioning can be adapted – on a trouser waistband there are generally two loops at the front on either side and three loops at the back, one at centre back and one either side. Some dresses and tops have thread loops attached to the side seam only. On coats and jackets, loops should be positioned with two on the front panel and at least two on the back panel. With fabric loops it is more slimming to move the loops a couple of centimetres from the side seam towards the centre front and back.

Making fabric loops

Consider the fabric weight when making loops – if it is too heavy use a contrast lightweight fabric to reduce bulk and interface the loop.

1 Cut a long enough strip of fabric for all loops. Measure the width of the belt, then add seam allowance plus 2cm (¾in) for ease, to make sure the loops are long enough for the belt to fit through.

2 Loop width depends on the fabric weight and design. For a light- to medium-weight fabric, cut a strip four times as wide as the finished size.

3 *For a bagged out loop*, fold with wrong sides together and stitch. Press the seam open. Turn to the right side and move the seam into the middle of the loop. Press the loop flat and edge stitch each long side.

For a folded loop, fold the long edges of the strip into the centre then fold in half so the raw edges are on the inside. Press and edge stitch both long edges.

4 Once the strip has been made, cut it into individual loops 2cm (¾in) longer than the belt width plus seam allowance.

Belt loops for medium- to heavyweight fabric

1 Cut a long strip of fabric 3cm (1⅛in) wide and overlock one long edge. Press in the other long raw edge by 1cm (⅜in), then press the overlocked edge over the raw edge by 1cm (⅜in) and edge stitch both long edges. Cut into individual strips.

2 Place onto the marking points on the waistline pointing downwards and attach the waistband. Fold the loop up over the waistband, leaving a 1cm (⅜in) fold to the bottom of the waistband for ease. Sew the loop, right side up, along the waistband edge.

3 If the waistband is already stitched to the garment, fold both loop ends under and topstitch through all layers at top and bottom of the waistband.

Wide tab-style belt loops on a dress by Julien Macdonald.

Step by step applying a fabric belt loop

The exact method of applying the loop depends on the waistline finish and garment design. The method described here is for a straight waistband on trousers or a skirt. Belt loops are applied after the facing side of the waistband has been stitched onto the garment – see the project beginning on page 170.

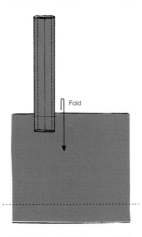

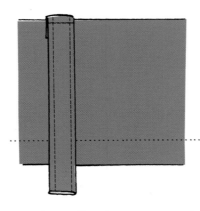

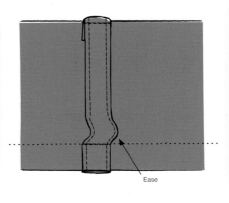

Step 1
Pin-mark the loop placement on the waistline. With right sides together, pin one end of the loop to the top of the waistband, extending upwards away from the waistband. Stitch back and forward a few times to hold the loop in place.

Step 2
Turn the loop down towards the garment, onto the waistband. Stitch across the top of the loop, going back and forward a couple of times.

Step 3
Place the loop end onto the seam line of the waistband, allowing 2cm (¾in) ease so the belt will sit comfortably in the loop without pulling. Stitch back and forward a couple of times to hold the loop in place.

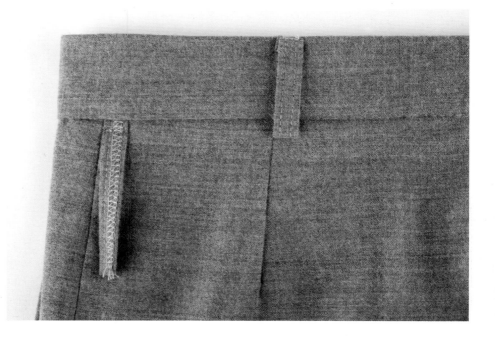

A belt loop attached to the waistline before the waistband is stitched on. Once the waistband is attached, the belt loop is secured with enough ease to allow for a belt.

Elasticated waistband

An elasticated waistband is used in active wear and casual wear. The elastic can be sewn directly to the garment or inserted into a casing. If sewing on the elastic use a wide waistband elastic, which is quite firm and less likely to fold or crease. A casing for elastic can be cut as an extension of the waistline or cut separately. The elasticated casing can be topstitched or the empty casing can be stitched in parallel rows and individual lengths of elastic threaded through each channel. Elastic can be adapted to any opening, such as at the neck, wrist or ankle.

Topstitched elastic casing

1 Cut a casing twice the width of the elastic plus 5mm (³⁄₁₆in) allowance, to make sure the elastic sits well within the casing, plus seam allowance. The length of the casing is the same measurement as the waistline plus seam allowance.

2 Cut the elastic band to size, making sure it slides over the hips and sits comfortably at the waist. The elastic will stretch a bit when topstitched, so cut a couple of centimetres short. The amount of stretch will depend on the quality of the elastic.

3 Neaten the long inside edge of the casing, either with a binding or overlocking, or turn under and topstitch. Put the short ends of the casing right sides together. Sew with a plain seam leaving an opening for the elastic to feed through on the inside centre back. Press open.

4 With right sides together, pin and stitch the raw edge of the casing onto the waist edge, matching marking points and matching the casing seam to the centre back seam of the garment. Make sure the opening for the elastic will be sitting inside the casing when it is folded over.

5 From the wrong side, fold over the casing and pin in place. From the right side either sink stitch or topstitch along the bottom of the casing.

6 Use a bodkin or attach a safety pin to one end of the elastic and feed the elastic through the casing – make sure to hold onto the other end in case it slips through.

7 Pull both ends of the elastic out of the casing and overlap as shown in the illustration. Stitch or zigzag the elastic ends together.

8 Arrange the gathers evenly and secure with pins at side seam, centre front and centre back. Hold the casing taut with both hands, stretching the elastic between pins, while feeding it through the sewing machine to make evenly spaced parallel rows of stitching through both casing and elastic.

9 It is not essential to topstitch the elastic, but if you do not it may turn within the casing when the garment is worn.

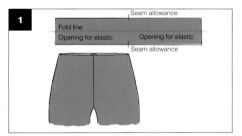

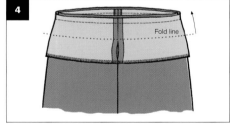

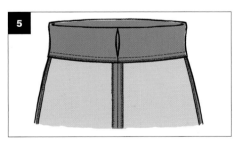

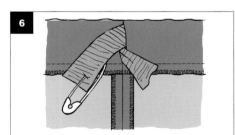

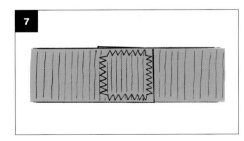

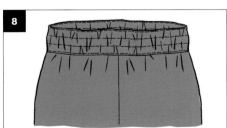

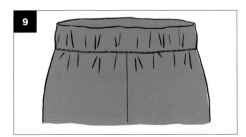

Tailored waistband with zip guard

The tailored waistband is for the more advanced sewer but its methods can be incorporated into a straight waistband. Quite often fashion designers apply techniques from a tailored waistband to improve the quality of a garment – for example, the waistband could be seamed at centre back to release the waist. Another option is that the under-wrap fly could be bagged out and fastened to the inside of the waistband while the rest of the construction is based on a conventional straight waistband.

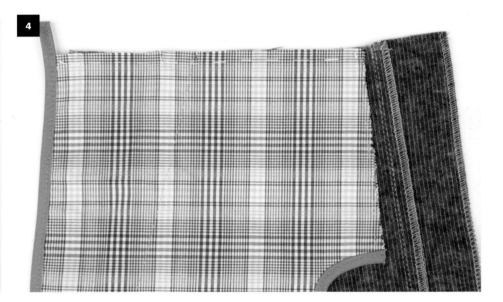

1 Construct the slanted side pocket first on both sides (see Slant pocket, page 188). Add a suitable finish and bind the pocket bag. Prepare the belt loops as described on page 167. Prepare the waistband facing or use a pre-finished tailored waistband tape for the facing – see Sew-in tapes, page 88. Here the waistband facing was made from two pieces, cut on the bias and seamed down the middle with a piece of binding sandwiched between the two pieces to provide stability. Press under the outer edge of the facing.

2 With right sides together, attach the facing of the over-wrap to the zip opening and stitch to the end of the zip opening.

3 Turn to the right side of the garment, fold the facing away from the trousers and retain stitch the seam onto the fly facing. Draw on the topstitching line of the over-wrap with vanishing chalk or pen.

4 Place the pocket bag towards the fly seam and hand-tack to the trouser waistline.

5 Fold and press the over-wrap facing towards the wrong side, overlapping the pocket bag.

6 Attach the zip guard facing (checked fabric) onto the shaped zip guard and bag out the shaped side, leaving a 1cm (⅜in) gap at the top edge of the fly.

7 With right side up, line up the zip onto the straight edge of the zip guard. Stitch in place from the top. Stop at end of zip teeth.

8 Place the trouser front opening with zip and guard right sides together, lined up on the straight edge, and match with the waistline. Pin in place and stitch together from the wrong side.

9 Turn the zip guard facing and zip guard to the right side. The zip is now sandwiched between the guard and trouser front.

10 Pin the over-wrap onto the under-wrap, placing the right and left trouser fronts on top of each other, right side up and overlapping by 1cm (⅜in).

11 Turn to the wrong side and pin the zip onto the over-wrap facing, then stitch in place, close to the zip teeth.

12 Lay the facing onto the waistband overlapping by 5mm (³⁄₁₆in) and topstitch along the edge. Alternatively zigzag stitch can be used to attach the facing to the waistband. On the over-wrap, stop the facing just before the notch at centre front.

13 Attach belt loops to the trouser front panel at the waistline edge, 3cm (1⅛in) from the pocket opening (described on page 168).

14 Attach the waistband extension to the over-wrap facing, right sides together, stopping at the seam line.

8

9

10

15

16

15 Pin the waistband onto the trousers, on the over-wrap side, right sides together. Stitch the waistband to the waistline, stopping at the facing seam. Bind the edge of the over-wrap facing and waistband extension.

16 Bag out the waistband extensions and waistband, cutting off the corners of each seam allowance to reduce bulk.

17 The over-wrap of the waistband is where the hook or buttonhole is placed. Turn it right side out and press.

17

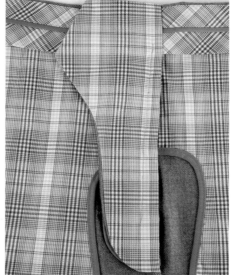

18 Attach the waistband to the under-wrap side of the front trouser waistline and zip guard.

19 Bag out the top part of the zip guard facing with the under-wrap waistband and turn right side out.

20 With the right side of the under-wrap facing up, pin the zip to the guard. Right side up, edge stitch through trousers, zip and guard to the bottom of the zip as far as possible.

21 With wrong side up, pin the zip tape and the zip guard onto the under-wrap.

22 Fold the zip guard away.

23 With the right side up, topstitch the over-wrap facing to the front along the marking line.

24 On the back of the trousers, place the back pocket with the pocket bag running up to the waistline. Bind the seam allowance of the crotch seam.

25 Stitch the inside leg and side seam of front and back with a plain seam.

26 Attach the belt loops to the back waistline and attach the waistband onto the back waistline. Sew the crotch seam from the top of the waistband to the front zip end. Start with a 3cm (1⅛in) seam allowance at centre back, gradually taking the allowance down to 1cm (⅜in) at the front. Press seam open.

27 With wrong side up, at the top of the waistband fold in the corners of the centre back seam allowance and pin.

28 Fold the waistband facing in place and pin the facing to the waistline from the wrong side. Sink stitch from the right side in the waistline seam of the waistband to attach the facing to the waistline.

29 Sew the belt loops onto the top of the waistband, leaving space for ease.

30 Press the waistband. Attach a hook-and-bar to the over- and under-wrap and a buttonhole and button to the zip guard of the under-wrap.

Drawstring waistband

The casing for a drawstring waistband can be cut as an extension of the waistline or separately. Drawstrings, such as cord and elasticated strings, can be purchased to suit the garment design or made of self-fabric. Consider a toggle or drawstring stopper to give a professional finish and to stop the drawstring from being pulled out of the waistband.

1 Prepare the pattern for an extended casing by adding double the measurement of the casing plus seam allowance to the edge. Mark the position of openings for the drawstring on the front of the garment and reinforce with interfacing. Choose an opening option – either construct two small buttonholes or insert eyelets (see the manufacturer's instructions for how to do this). Construct the garment, stitching the side seams, centre front and centre back together.

2 Fold and press the allowance over at the edge of the waistband casing. Turn the casing along the fold line to the wrong side of the garment, secure with pins at centre points and stitch in place from the wrong side of the garment. Turn to the right side and topstitch the top edge so the casing stays in shape.

3 Make the string with self-fabric, cut on the bias or straight grain, or use a decorative cord. Thread the drawstring through the holes. Secure the ends with either a knot, toggle or drawstring stopper.

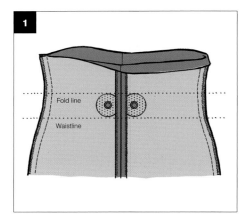

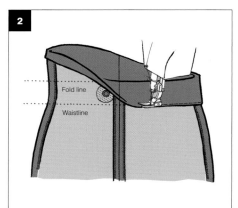

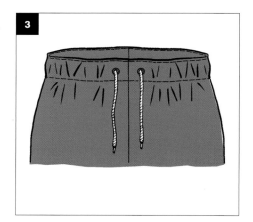

Vest top with drawstring detail in the waistline. A drawstring can be used in any part of the garment, wherever a tape can be stitched in place for the drawstring to go through. Sportmax, SS 2012.

Waistline facings

A faced waistband looks neat from the outside so will not distract from other design features. The facing can be cut in self-fabric or contrast fabric – use a lightweight fabric on garments in heavyweight material to reduce bulk. Alternatively, the facing can be replaced with a wide ribbon or tape stitched onto the waist edge and turned inside.

 Step by step applying a waistline facing

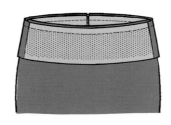

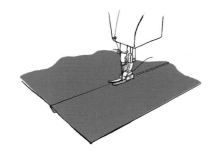

Step 1
Prepare a pattern for the facing by copying the top 5–8cm (2–3⅛in) of the garment pattern. Cut out the fabric and interface the wrong side of the facing pieces. Construct the garment and sew the zip in place.

Step 2
Sew the facing pieces together. With right sides together pin the facing onto the waist edge matching all marking points, then sew in place.

Step 3
Fold the facing away from the garment and fold the seam allowance towards the facing. Retain stitch the seam allowance onto the facing.

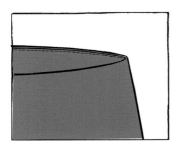

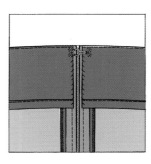

Step 4
Turn the facing into the garment and press the waist edge.

Step 5
The bottom edge of the facing can be overlocked or turned under and topstitched. For a high-end finish consider a binding. Hand stitch the facing onto the zip, or bag it onto the zip using machine stitching, or secure it to the seam allowances.

Step 6
Attach a hook-and-eye fastening on the inside above the zip.

Fastening options for waistbands

Waistbands can be fastened with a zip, button and buttonhole, snap fastener or hook-and-bar/eye. On most waistbands there is a combination, such as a zip plus a button. Here are some designer examples of waistband fastenings.

Trousers with tailored waistband facing, wrapped-over waistband with buttoned fly and two hooks-and-bars to fasten the waistband.

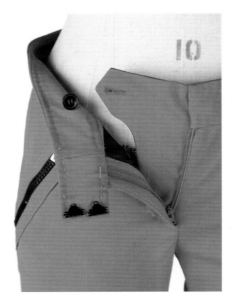

Trousers with waistband extension and self-fabric facing, fastened with a zip and two hooks-and-bars on the waistband, and a fly guard fastened with a button and buttonhole.

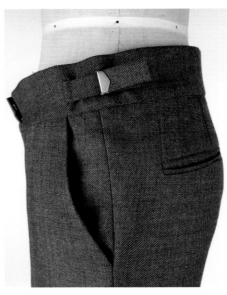

Trousers with wide waistband, zip and hook-and-bar fastening at centre front, and a tab fastened by a buckle with teeth over the side seam to regulate the width of the waistband. On the inside is a tailored facing and a fly guard with button and buttonhole.

Skirt with straight waistband, heavy-duty snap fastener and zip.

Skirt with invisible zip and hook-and-eye fastening on top of the waistband. The waistband facing is cut in self-fabric.

Pockets

Pockets are functional but can also be decorative. They may be on the outside or inside of a garment. They must be the right size and in the right place to be aesthetically pleasing and, depending on the style, can make the design look more tailored or casual. Pockets are divided into two categories: the set-in pocket, which is set into a seam line or slash; and the applied or patch pocket, which is sewn onto the outside of a garment.

The pocket bag

The purpose of a pocket bag is to hold things and to accommodate the hand comfortably, so it needs to be big and sturdy enough.

Pocket bag lining
This can be decorative or hardwearing but needs to suit the garment design and fabric quality.

- Use pocketing or cotton twill lining for pocket bags on coats, jackets and tailored trousers – it is durable and will extend the wear of a garment.
- For a garment in light- to medium-weight material the pocket bag can be cut from self-fabric or lining material of the same weight.
- Self-fabric pocket bags reduce the chance of shadowing.
- For some casual garments, such as fleeces or hoodies, comfort is key and a pocket bag can be cut from fleece or brushed cotton.
- Semi-transparent, white or light-coloured garments should have pocket bags in a nude colour to reduce the chance of shading.
- There is nothing worse than a pocket bag that is too small. Make sure it is big enough to contain all of the hand and part of the wrist.

Pocket bag shape
- Cut a pattern by tracing around your hand leaving an extra 2–3cm (¾–1⅛in) of space for comfort. Cut the bag deep enough for the hand to relax inside.
- Pin pocket bags together on a flat surface facing the right direction.
- Round off corners to avoid fluff becoming trapped.
- On trousers and skirts with centre front openings, run the pocket bag into the centre front for more stability and a neater look from the inside (bottom left).
- Extend the pocket bag of a back pocket into the waistband for a tailored look, better fit and to prevent the pocket sagging (bottom right).

Neatening the pocket bag
- Pocket bags should be invisible on the outside of a garment.
- If the garment is lined, the pocket bag will not need edge finishing because it is protected, lying as it does between the garment fabric and lining.
- The pocket bag on an unlined garment will need finished edges for a clean and professional look and to prevent fraying. Edges can be overlocked, which adds the least bulk, or bound, which gives a high-end finish. The pocket bag can also be bagged out with the seam allowance facing the inside.

Front pocket finish with the pocket bag running into the centre front for stability.

Back pocket finish with the pocket bag extending into the waistband. This prevents the pocket opening gaping.

Applied pocket variations

Applied pockets are placed on top
of the garment so can be any size
or shape and may be lined, unlined
or faced. They may be left open at
the top, or have a flap, and can be
fastened with a zip, button, Velcro
or snap fastener.

Step by step lined patch pocket

Step 1

Mark the position of the pocket onto
the garment. Cut out the patch pocket,
allowing 4cm (1⅝in) for the facing at the
top and 0.5–1cm (³⁄₁₆–³⁄₈in) seam allowance
around other edges. Cut out the lining
minus the facing allowance.

Step 2

Place the pocket bag and lining right
sides together, with the facing edge
aligned with the top of the lining. Stitch
together along the facing edge, leaving
a gap of 3cm (1⅛in) in the middle of the
seam to turn the pocket inside out after
it has been bagged out with the lining.
Press the seam open.

 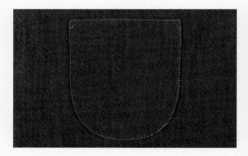

Step 3

Fold the pocket facing and attached
lining over, right sides together, lining up
side and bottom edges. Stitch together,
to bag out the pocket with the lining.
Carefully pull the pocket to the right side
through the opening in the facing seam.
Press the pocket.

Step 4

Slipstitch the opening in the facing seam
closed and edge stitch the facing edge.
Place the pocket onto the marking points
on the garment and topstitch in place.
Give the pocket a final press.

*Jacket showing patch pockets and side slant pockets,
both with flap detail. Junya Watanabe, Fall 2012.*

Step by step unlined patch pocket

Step 1

Mark the position of the pocket onto the garment. Cut out the patch pocket, allowing 4cm (1⅝in) for the facing at the top and 0.5–1cm (³⁄₁₆–⅜in) seam allowance around other edges. Overlock the top edge or all edges if the fabric frays badly. Cut a cardboard template to the finished pocket size to help shape the pocket evenly – cardboard templates are useful to achieve a clean shape on many other garment details before stitching.

Step 2

If the patch pocket has round corners, stitch a gathering stitch within the seam allowance. With wrong side up, pull the gathering thread from the right side so the seam allowance folds onto the wrong side to shape the round corners. Slide the template under the seam allowance and press to shape, then remove the template.

Step 3

Turn the facing to the wrong side and bag out both sides of the pocket.

Step 4

Turn the facing to the right side and press. The facing can be topstitched down in various ways, such as edge stitching across the top edge and topstitching on the bottom – consider using a contrast colour topstitching thread.

Step 5

Pin the pocket onto the marking points on the garment and hand-tack in place if necessary.

Step 6

Topstitch the pocket in place and give it a final press.

Step by step bellows pocket

Step 1

Mark the pocket position onto the garment and cut out the pocket pattern. Mark all fold lines onto the wrong side of the fabric and press the top edge of the facing to the wrong side.

Step 2

Fold the facing along the fold line, right sides together, and stitch at each side. Layer the seam allowance if necessary to reduce bulk.

Step 3

Turn the facing to the right side and topstitch the bottom edge of the facing onto the pocket. Press in all fold lines and seam allowance on the outer edge. Be accurate, as the pocket will only fit in place when precisely folded.

Step 4

Fold the mitres of the pocket, right sides together, and stitch. Clip into the corners to the seam line.

Step 5

Turn the mitres out to the right side and press.

Step 6

Edge stitch the outer folded edges from the right side to make sure the pocket retains its shape. Pin the pocket to the marking points on the garment and edge stitch the seam allowance of the folded edge to the garment through all layers.

Set-in pocket variations

Set-in pockets can be sewn into a seam or behind a slashed pocket opening and have a pocket bag inside the garment. The in-seam or side seam pocket is strictly functional and invisible on the outside, while a set-in pocket behind a slashed opening has a jet or welt on the outside. Alternatively, it can be worked with a zip instead of the welt or bagged out with a facing, as in a slanted pocket.

Coat by Julien Macdonald with patent leather detail and deep set-in welt pockets. The welt is inserted into the garment instead of being stitched on top. See Making a welt pocket, page 185.

TIP

Interfacing the pocket and pocket opening will provide body and support to the clipped and slashed areas, preventing them from pulling out of shape and providing a crisp edge to corners and fold lines. Always match the stabilizer to the fabric quality and sample before inserting the pocket into the final garment.

- If the pocket is worked into the garment, interface the pocket opening with a stabilizer. To cover the area well, apply the stabilizer 2cm (¾in) longer than the pocket opening on each side and 4cm (1⅝in) wide.
- To prevent interfacing outlines from showing through to the right side, cut the interfacing with rounded edges or pink the edges.
- Interface pocket parts such as jets, welt and flaps for more stability.

Jet pocket

Jet pockets are found on tailored jackets, coats and trousers but can also be used on skirts or less formal wear. The jet pocket illustrated is worked into an unlined garment so has a decorative pocket bag with bound edges. See page 182 for Step by step making a jet pocket.

Trousers by Julien Macdonald with jet pockets and jet pocket with flap.

Step by step making a jet pocket

Step 1

Mark the pocket opening on the right side of the garment. Apply interfacing to cover the pocket opening on the wrong side.

Step 2

Cut two jets 4cm (1⅝in) wide by the width of the pocket opening plus 1cm (⅜in) seam allowance; they can be cut on the same grain as the garment or on the bias. Add interfacing (left) to the wrong side of the jet and press in half lengthwise, wrong sides together (centre). Cut a piece of self-fabric (right) for the facing and overlock one long edge.

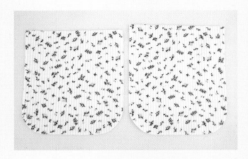

Step 3

Cut the pocket bag pieces the width of the pocket opening plus 1cm (⅜in) seam allowance and to a good length. Cut the under pocket piece 1cm (⅜in) longer than the top pocket piece.

Step 4

With right side up, place the facing on top of the wrong side of the under pocket piece with raw edges aligned. Stitch the facing onto the pocket bag piece at either side.

Step 5

With the raw edges butting each other, pin the jets to the right side of the garment along the marked pocket opening line. Using a 2mm stitch length, stitch each jet through the middle from start to end of the pocket opening.

Step 6

With wrong side up, cut along the centre line of the marked pocket opening, stopping 1cm (⅜in) before each end and snipping into each corner up to the stitching line.

across the base of the triangle to attach it to the jets then fold the garment material back in place. Repeat at the other end and then press.

Step 8 (right)
Place the top pocket bag piece (right side up) onto the bottom jet with raw edges aligned and stitch through the jet stitching line.

Step 9
Fold the top pocket piece away from the opening and press. Apply a retain stitch along the top of the bag piece onto the jet to keep the pocket bag from coming through to the right side, but do not sew through the garment layer.

Step 7
Push the jets through the opening to the wrong side and align the folded edges. Hand-tack the folded edges of the jets together to keep them correctly aligned. With the right side up fold the garment material back to access the triangular corner at one end. Stitch

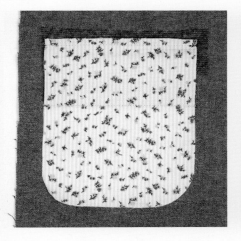

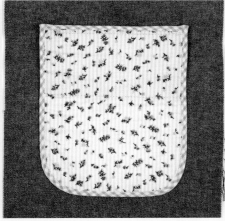

Step 10
Place the under pocket bag piece with the facing side down onto the top jet, with top raw edges aligned, and stitch through the jet stitching line.

Step 11
Pin the pocket bag pieces to each other and stitch around the edges. The raw edges of the bag can be overlocked, or bound as shown here.

Step 12
The finished pocket.

Jet pocket with flap

A flap can be added to a jet pocket –
the construction is the same as for
the jet pocket on the previous pages,
with a couple of steps amended. The
facing on the under pocket piece is
not necessary in this case because the
flap covers the opening.

*Blazer with three jet pockets with flap. The jet pockets
are the focal point. Antonio Berardi, SS 2014.*

Making a jet pocket with flap

1 Mark the pocket opening on the right
side of the garment. Apply interfacing to
cover the pocket opening on the wrong
side of the garment. Cut two jets 4cm
(1⅝in) wide by the width of the pocket
opening plus 1cm (⅜in) seam allowance;
they can be cut on the same grain as the
garment or on the bias. Add interfacing
to the wrong side of each jet and press
in half lengthwise wrong sides together
(see steps 1 and 2, page 182). Cut the flap
pieces but interface only one of them,
unless the fabric frays badly or is
loosely woven.

2 Place the flap pieces right sides together
and stitch around the sides and bottom
edge only. Layer the seam allowance and
cut away the corner to reduce bulk.

3 Turn the flap to the right side and press.
Topstitch the edges with a single or double
line. Align the raw edges of one jet along
the top of the marked pocket line on the
right side of the garment. Hand-tack in
place through the centre of the jet. Place
the flap, wrong side up, on top of the jet,
raw edges aligned. Pin or hand-tack along
the same line as for the jet. Stitch through
all layers from one side of the pocket
opening to the other. Place the second jet
beneath the marked pocket line with raw
edges butting up to the raw edges of the
first jet and flap. Stitch as for the first jet.

4 With wrong side up, cut along the
centre line of the marked pocket opening,
stopping 1cm (⅜in) before each end and
snipping into each corner up to the
stitching line (see step 6 on page 182).
Push the jets through the opening to the
wrong side, leaving the flap on the right
side of the garment.

5 With right side up, fold the garment
material back to access the triangular
corner at one end. Stitch across the base
of the triangle to attach it to the jets then
fold the garment material back in place.
Repeat at the other end and then press.

6 Continue to apply the pocket bag
pieces as in steps 8–11 on page 183,
remembering there is no facing attached
to the under pocket bag piece.

Step by step making a welt pocket

Welt pockets can be seen on most garment types. The welt can be any depth from 1–4cm (⅜–1⅝in) – if deeper, it should be constructed like a single jet pocket.

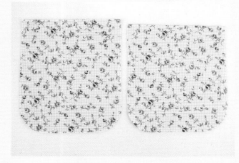

Step 1

Mark the pocket opening on the right side of the garment. On the wrong side, apply interfacing to cover the pocket opening.

Step 2

Cut a welt piece the width of the pocket opening, plus 1cm (⅜in) seam allowance, by twice the finished welt depth. It can be cut on the same grain as the garment or on the bias. Add interfacing to the wrong side of the welt and fold in half lengthwise, right sides together. Stitch across the short edges and then layer the seam allowance and cut the corner diagonally to reduce bulk. Turn to the right side and press. Edge stitch along the fold line.

Step 3

Cut the pocket bag pieces the width of the pocket opening plus 1cm (⅜in) seam allowance and to a good length. Cut the under pocket piece 1cm (⅜in) longer than the top pocket piece.

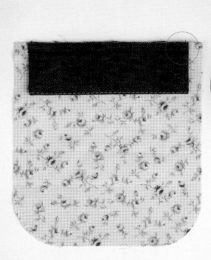

Step 4

Place the welt on the wrong side of the top pocket piece with the raw edge aligned to the top edge. Stitch the welt to the pocket piece, starting and ending 1cm (⅜in) in from the edges.

continues on page 186...

Step by step making a welt pocket (continued)

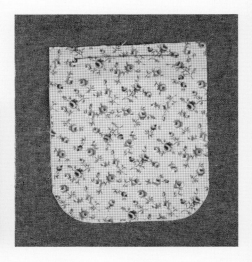

Step 5

Place the top pocket bag piece with the welt facing the garment's right side and the raw edge aligned along the bottom marked line of the pocket opening. Stitch through all layers from start to end of the opening, on the previous stitching line. Place the under pocket piece with the raw edge butting up to the first pocket bag. Stitch a line 1cm (⅜in) shorter at each end than on the first pocket bag.

Step 6

With wrong side up, cut along the centre line of the marked pocket opening, stopping 1cm (⅜in) before the ends of the shorter stitch line, then snip into the corners up to the stitches.

Step 7

Push the pocket bag pieces through to the right side. The welt will fall into place on the right side, covering the opening. Press in place.

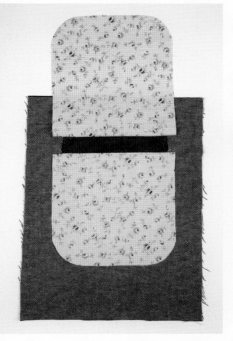

Step 8

With wrong side up, lift the under pocket bag piece to expose the top bag piece. Retain stitch the top bag piece onto the jet to stop the pocket bag coming through to the right side. Do not sew through the garment layer.

Step 9

Right side up, fold the garment material back to access the triangular corner at one end. Stitch across the base of the triangle to attach it to the pocket bag then fold the garment material back in place. Repeat at the other end and then press.

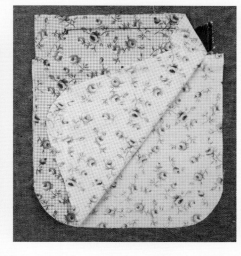

Step 10

Push the pocket bag out of the way on the wrong side of the garment.

Step 11

With right side up, topstitch both short sides of the welt to the garment.

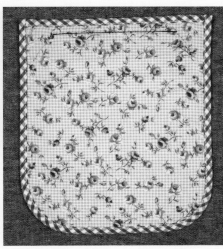

Step 12

Pin the pocket bag pieces to each other and stitch around the bag. Overlock the raw edges of the bag, or bind as shown.

Slant pocket

Slant pockets are popular on trousers and skirts, placed at hip level on either side. The opening can be diagonal, square or curved but the pocket needs to be a comfortable size to fit a hand.

 Step by step making a slant pocket

Tape

Lining

Fabric

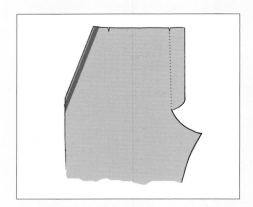

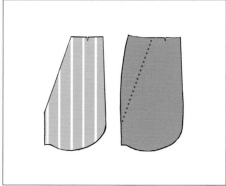

Step 1
Prepare the garment pattern with the opening for the pocket. Cut out in fabric and add a strip of stabilizing tape to the pocket opening on the wrong side.

Step 2
Cut the pocket facing in lining and the under pocket from self-fabric – note that the under pocket includes the cut away part of the garment.

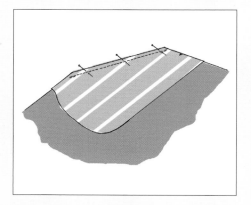

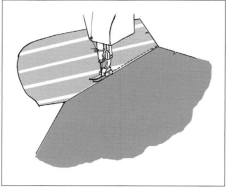

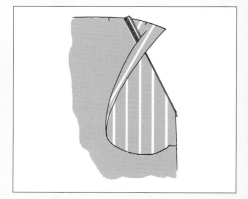

Step 3
Place the pocket facing onto the garment, right sides together, matching the pocket opening. Pin in place and stitch from top to bottom.

Step 4
Retain stitch the seam allowance to the pocket facing from the right side of the facing.

Step 5
Turn the pocket to the wrong side and press. Topstitch the edge from the garment side if required.

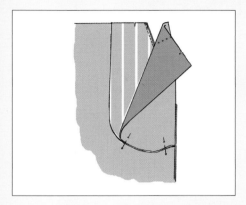

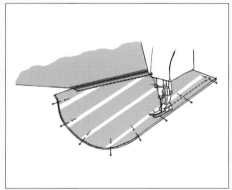

Step 6
Pin the under pocket to the facing, matching up the marking points and edges. Pin only the pocket bag layers and not into the garment.

Step 7
Stitch the pocket bags together from the facing side and overlock or bind the raw edges.

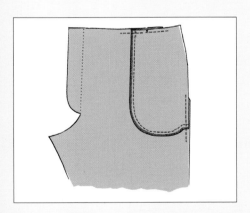

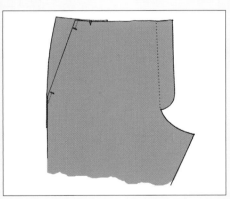

Step 8
Turn to the wrong side and, with the pocket bag in the correct place, stitch the bag to the waistline and side seam.

Step 9
Topstitch the pocket opening for 2cm (¾in) from top and bottom to stabilize and avoid ripping at the side seam. Apply final pressing.

Under pocket in lining with self-fabric facing

In the tailored version (below), the under pocket is cut in lining with a self-fabric facing covering the opening.

Prepare the under pocket in lining fabric. Overlock the facing for the under pocket and pin its wrong side to the right side of the under pocket. Topstitch in place around the edges, then follow the instructions for Slant pocket on page 188.

Side seam pocket

A side seam pocket is sewn into a seam and is invisible from the outside. This type of pocket is functional, with no impact on the garment design.

Right: Printed silk satin dress by Julien Macdonald, with detail of the side seam pockets (below).

Step by step making a side seam pocket

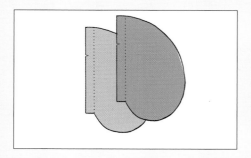

Step 1
Mark the opening of the pocket onto the front and back side seams, allowing for 2cm (¾in) seam allowance on both seams. Cut two pocket bag pieces from self-fabric or lining, both the same size with a 1cm (⅜in) seam allowance on all edges.

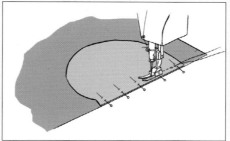

Step 2
Place one pocket bag piece onto the garment front, right sides together, matching up the marking position. Stitch the bag onto the garment side seam, 1cm (⅜in) in at both ends, with a 1cm (⅜in) seam allowance.

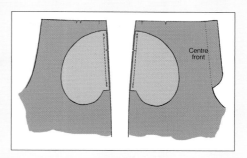

Step 3
Repeat on the garment back with the other pocket bag piece.

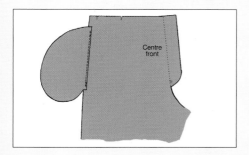

Step 4
Retain stitch the seam allowance to the pocket bag from the right side. Remember to leave a 1cm (⅜in) gap at both ends.

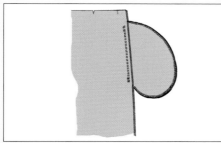

Step 5
Place the front and back of the garment right sides together with side seams and pocket bags aligned. Pin the pocket bags together and sew. Overlock or bind the pocket bag edges – the 1cm (⅜in) at both ends left in step 4 will allow the pocket bag to be completely edge finished.

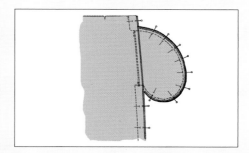

Step 6
With right sides together, pin the side seams of the garment together. Start sewing from the top with a medium stitch length and a 2cm (¾in) seam allowance. Backstitch at the first marking point for the pocket opening, then with the needle down pivot and sew around the pocket bag a second time in the previous stitching line. At the end of the bag pivot again, backstitch and finish the 2cm (¾in) seam allowance to the hem.

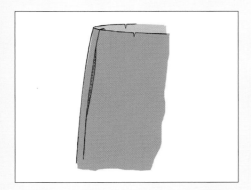

Step 7
Press the side seam to the side with the pocket facing to the front. The pocket opening can be topstitched if required. The pocket bag can also be topstitched to the front panel or left without topstitching to be invisible.

The Sleeve

A sleeve can be set into an armhole, as in a set-in or a shirtsleeve, or be an extension of the garment body, as in raglan and kimono/batwing sleeves. All sleeves can be made using the construction techniques used for these sleeves. The type of sleeve defines the garment design and the choice of sleeve hemline should suit the style. Options include a wide range of cuffs, elasticated or taped hems, with or without drawstrings, openings with button or zip, vents or slit openings, or a simple turned-up hemline with topstitching. See Hemlines on page 204 for more ideas on how to finish a sleeve hem.

TIP

A set-in sleeve pattern is cut with extra fullness, or ease, in the sleeve head, to create a good fit and a cup to fit over the top of the shoulder. The amount of ease added depends on the fabric weight. The extra fullness is eased in across the sleeve head – see Ease stitching on page 131, and the step-by-step project on pages 194–95.

Sleeve types

Each sleeve design requires a different method of construction.

Set-in sleeve: This is sewn together before it is attached into the armhole. See the step-by-step instructions on page 194 for more information.

Shirtsleeve: This is attached into a dropped shoulder armhole, with very little to no ease in the sleeve head.

Raglan sleeve: With a diagonal seam running from underarm into the neckline at front and back of the garment, this sleeve design creates a soft shoulder and a casual look. A raglan sleeve can be cut with a shoulder seam or shoulder dart, or, on knitted fabric, may have neither.

Kimono/batwing sleeve: Part of the garment front and back pieces, this sleeve can have shoulder and side seams or be cut with no shoulder seam. For a design without a shoulder seam consider a front or back opening, the fabric width available and the grain direction, because the pattern might have to be placed onto a crosswise grain.

Constructing a shirtsleeve

1 The sleeve has been prepared with the placket in place (see Plackets and sleeve openings, page 196).

2 The front and back shoulder/yoke seams are stitched together.

3 The sleeve is attached into the armhole position, with both the underarm seam of the sleeve and side seam of the garment remaining open.

4 Complete the sleeve and garment by stitching the underarm seam and side seam together in one go.

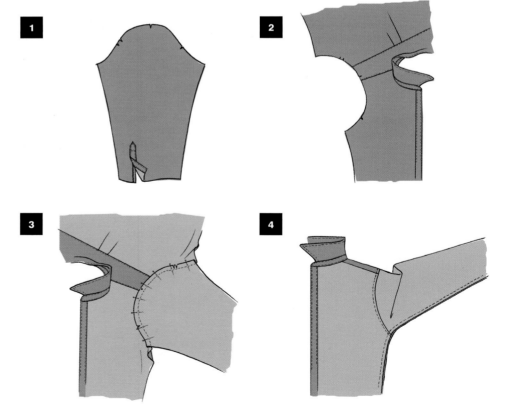

Constructing a raglan sleeve

1 Pin (a) and then sew (b) the shoulder seam of the front and back sleeve together.

2 If the pattern has a dart instead of a seam, sew the shoulder dart.

3 Attach the back of the garment to the back raglan seams and the front to the front raglan seams.

4 Complete the sleeve and garment by stitching the underarm seam and side seam together in one go.

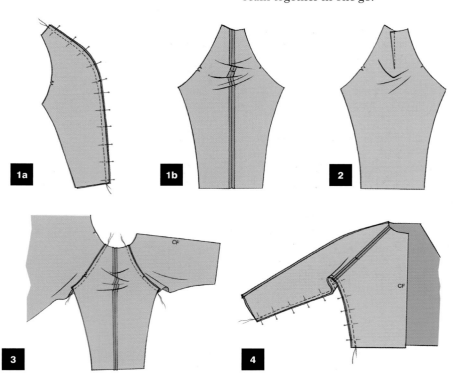

Raglan sleeves give this dress a sporty look. Versus, SS 2012.

Constructing a kimono/batwing sleeve with shoulder seam

Place the front panel onto the back panel and match up any marking points, such as the shoulder notch of front and back.

Stitch the shoulder seam/top-arm seam and the underarm/side seam together.

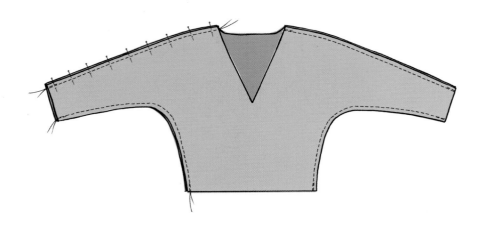

Man's top with short batwing sleeves. Lanvin, AW 2013.

The perfect set-in sleeve

A set-in sleeve is always cut with ease, which makes it larger in circumference than the armhole. For a good fit the sleeve head must be prepared and the sleeve must be pitched into the right position before it is sewn into the armhole.

1 Close the shoulder and side seams of the garment and assemble the sleeve. Reinforce the armhole with tape to prevent it stretching. Complete the hem finish on the sleeve, including any vent or cuff.

2 Change to a long stitch length on the machine. Working from the wrong side and leaving long thread ends, make two lines of stitching within the seam allowance round the sleeve head from front to back notch.

3 Still working from the wrong side, pick up a thread end on one side and pull to ease the head to fit the armhole, then do the same on the other side (a). The ease should be distributed more across the head and back to accommodate the shoulder blade. The sleeve head should not be gathered but rolled slightly in towards the wrong side to create a cup (b). Do not ease more than allowed for in the pattern – if unsure, measure the armhole and make the sleeve fit the same length.

4 Using a tailor's ham or sleeve board and steam iron, shrink the ripples at the sleeve head and mould into a cup shape. Be careful not to steam press too far into the sleeve head.

5 Place the garment on the stand and pin the shoulder pad underneath, if required. Place the sleeve to the armhole and check the pitch. The straight grain should be straight down through the sleeve and the sleeve should slightly swing to the front.

6 If the sleeve swings to the back, the pitch is not correct – stand in front of a mirror and see how your own arm hangs in a relaxed position.

7 When the pitch is correct, remove the garment from the stand. Pin the sleeve edge to the armhole edge from the inside of the sleeve, right sides together. After pinning, place the garment back onto the stand and check the pitch again before stitching. If necessary, hand-tack before stitching.

8 Start stitching from the sleeve side at the back sleeve seam or back notch position. Use fingers in front of the foot to help the ease go in. Stitch round to the starting point and carry on stitching in the same stitch line up to the front notch position so the underarm is stitched double for extra strength. Take off the machine and lightly press the seam allowance only.

9 On a tailored jacket, a shoulder roll and/or shoulder pad can be added into the sleeve head to support the sleeve cup.

10 Pin the sleeve roll onto the armhole seam across the shoulder with the wider part facing the sleeve head. Pin from front to back notches then machine or hand stitch in place with a large stitch.

11 Pin the shoulder pad in position (a). Attach to the shoulder seam and armhole seams with large machine or hand stitches (b). The garment is now ready to be lined, if necessary – see Lining, page 212.

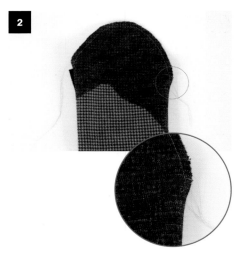

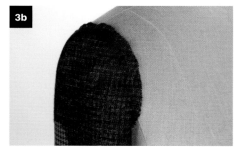

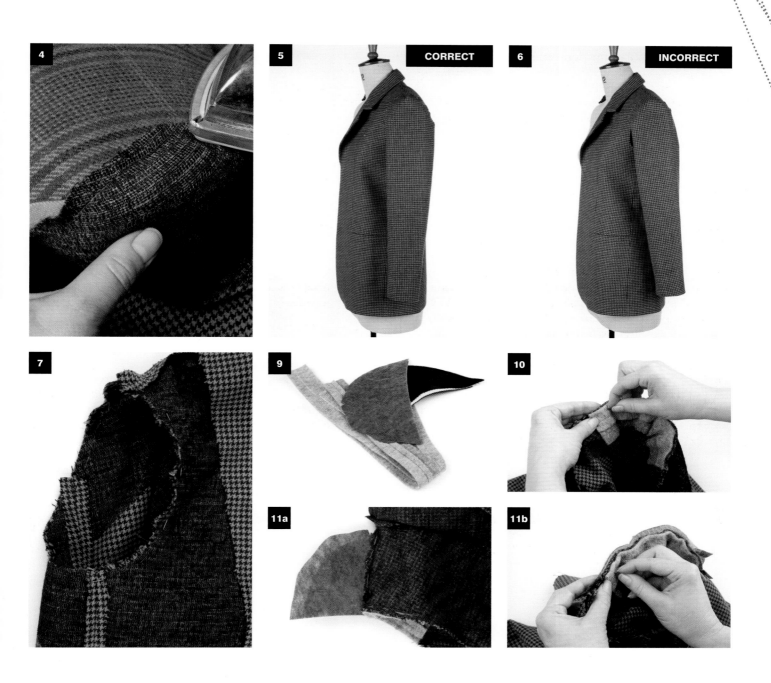

4

5 CORRECT

6 INCORRECT

7

9

10

11a

11b

Plackets and sleeve openings

A cuff that opens may need an opening in the sleeve on the hemline. The opening is placed at the back of the sleeve in line with the elbow and can be finished as a placket, or turned and hemmed, to suit the garment style. Either way, the opening is finished before the underarm seam is sewn and the sleeve is inserted into the armhole. All the different plackets illustrated in this section can also be used at other garment opening points, such as the neckline or centre back.

Continuous bound placket

The continuous bound opening can have a binding of self-fabric or contrast fabric, but avoid fabric that frays. When the cuff is closed the opening is hidden, creating a neat finish.

1 Mark the line of the placket and sew reinforcement stitches along either side. Start 6mm (¼in) from the line at the bottom edge, narrowing to 3mm (⅛in) at at the tip, then pivot the needle to stitch down the other side, widening back out to 6mm (¼in) again at the bottom.

2 Cut along the marked line. Cut a strip of fabric for the placket 4cm (1⅝in) wide and the length of the opening. Press the seam allowance of the binding to the wrong side on each side and press the binding in half again. For pre-folded and pressed binding, just press the binding with the seam allowances facing into the binding.

3 Place the sleeve on a flat surface right side up. Open out the cut into a straight line. Pin the right side of the binding to the wrong side of the opening. Place a pin at the centre opening.

4 Stitch the binding to the opening just behind the reinforcement stitches, using a 2mm stitch length and starting with a 6mm (¼in) seam allowance but narrowing towards the centre point – the seam allowance of the binding stays the same.

5 Fold the binding over to the right side of the sleeve to slightly cover the stitching line. Topstitch the binding along the folded edge.

6 Align the edges of the binding. From the wrong side, press the binding away and stitch the top of the binding at an angle.

7 Turn to the right side and place the binding into the right position. Press the binding towards the front of the sleeve; the back of the binding will form the under-wrap. The sleeve is now ready to add pleats or gathers and attach the cuff.

2

3
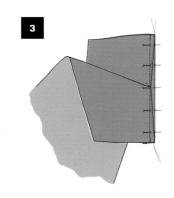

5
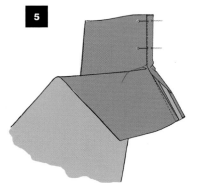

6
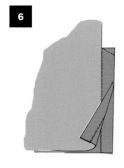

Hemmed sleeve opening

This is the simplest and quickest method to finish a sleeve opening; the opening is hemmed with the top of the opening finished with a short dart. Avoid fabric that frays for this method.

1 Mark and cut the opening. On the wrong side of the sleeve, turn over the opening twice to enclose the raw edge and press – begin with a 3mm (⅛in) turn, narrowing towards the centre point. Start stitching from the wrist to the top, lower the needle at the centre point and pivot to stitch the remaining side.

2 Align the edges of the hemmed opening, right sides together (a). Start stitching a small curved dart, beginning 2cm (¾in) above the opening and finishing 1cm (⅜in) into the hemmed opening, to reinforce the end (b).

3 Press the dart towards the back sleeve. To finish, add pleats or gathers and attach a cuff with extension.

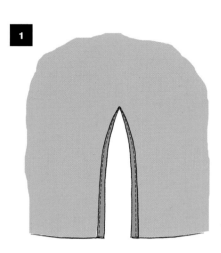

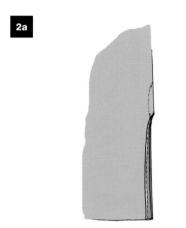

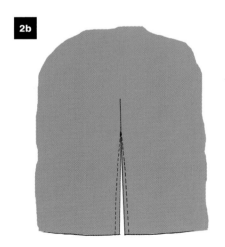

Making a statement with extra-large cuffs. Maison Martin Margiela, Fall 2013.

Step by step shirt placket
The shirt or tailored placket is the most time-consuming to make but also gives the most durable and professional-looking result. It can be constructed from one or two pieces – the one-piece placket illustrated here is the easier of the two.

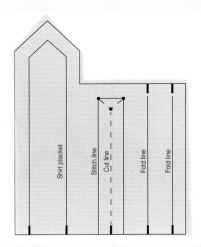

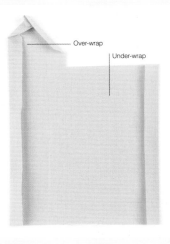

Step 1
Mark the opening of the placket onto the wrong side of the sleeve. Cut out the placket pattern.

Step 2
On the placket pattern, mark all fold lines onto the wrong side of the fabric.

Step 3
Wrong side up, fold and press the right and left edges in and fold the top corner to make a triangle. The placket can also be constructed with the top corner folded to make a square.

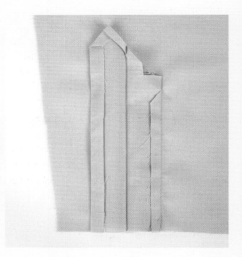

Step 4
Place the placket wrong side up on top of the wrong side of the sleeve and line up the cutting line with the marked opening. Pin in place. Stitch around the stitching line with a 2mm stitch length.

Step 5
Cut along the cutting line and into the corners.

Step 6
Turn the placket through to the right side of the sleeve and press the fold lines of the under- and over-wrap.

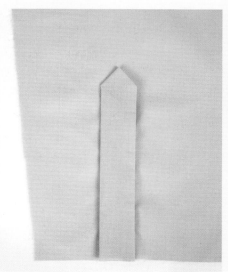

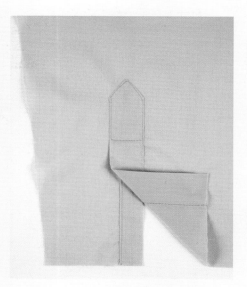

Step 7
Line up the fold line of the under-wrap placket to slightly cover the stitching line. Topstitch the placket edge from top to bottom.

Step 8
Press the over-wrap of the placket over the under-wrap.

Step 9
Secure with pins and topstitch around the edges and across the top end of the opening. To finish the sleeve, add pleats and attach a cuff with extension.

Preparing the sleeve end for the cuff

A sleeve is cut with extra room to sit comfortably around the arm and this extra fullness is taken in at the wrist to fit the cuff measurement using pleats or gathers (see Gathers, Pleats, Tucks and Darts on page 146). This is done after the sleeve opening is constructed and before the cuff is attached. Traditionally, pleats are used with a shirt or a continuous bound placket – usually two or three pleats folded towards the placket – and gathers are distributed around the wrist with a hemmed sleeve opening. However, designers can try different techniques, such as darts.

Shirt placket with pleats.

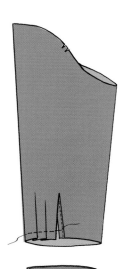

Bound placket with pleats.

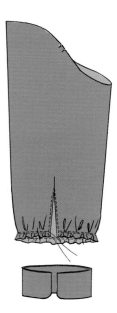
Hemmed sleeve opening with gathers.

TIP

On a double cuff secured with cufflinks, the cuff opening lies together rather than being overlapped, so the placket is folded to the inside towards the shirt before the cuff is attached.

Cuff variations

Cuffs can be open or closed: an open cuff requires fastening while a closed cuff has the two ends stitched together. Cuffs can be cut in one piece and folded in the middle or cut as two pieces, an outer cuff and a cuff facing, that are stitched together. A two-piece cuff is used for shaped cuffs or for a contrast fabric facing. To achieve a sharp edge and for stability the outer cuff is interfaced, although both sides of the cuff can be interfaced if more body is required.

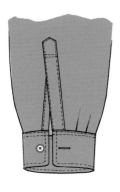 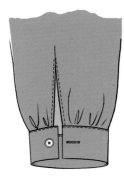 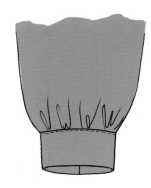

From left to right: A two-piece, open cuff with a shirt placket opening and pleats; a one-piece cuff with a hemmed sleeve opening and gathers; and a closed cuff with gathering.

Trouser cuffs

Although cuffs are traditionally placed at the end of a sleeve, cuff construction methods can be used on other openings and they can also be worked into a trouser hem. Here are some examples. See Step by step cuffed trousers, page 207.

Turn-up cuff with Velcro fastening on a trouser hem.

Cuff with buckle fastening on a trouser hem.

> **TIP**
>
> To make sure a sleeve cuff fits comfortably, wrap a tape measure around the widest point of the hand – not around the wrist – making sure the tape slides comfortably past the hand. This measurement plus extension and seam allowance is the length for an open cuff. For a closed cuff use the measurement and add another 1–2cm (⅜–¾in) ease for comfort plus seam allowance – an extension is not needed.

Open cuff

Open cuffs come in different styles and traditionally fasten with a button and buttonhole. The one- or two-piece cuff can be constructed with rounded or slanted corners. Use the two-piece cuff as a shaped cuff. A double cuff is cut double the cuff width and folded back in the middle; it can be worn with cufflinks or cut to create a turn-up cuff.

Two-piece open cuff with contrast cuff facing.

Double cuff with shirt placket.

Continuous bound placket with a slim cuff finish.

Traditional one-piece cuff with continuous bound placket opening and two pleats

1 Prepare the sleeve with a continuous bound placket (see page 196). Add two pleats on the wrist line, pointing in the same direction as the over-wrap, and sew the underarm sleeve seam.

2 Add interfacing to the wrong side of the outside cuff to 1cm (⅜in) past the fold line.

3 Fold the cuff in half with right sides together and then stitch across each end. Layer the seam allowance to reduce bulk.

4 Turn the cuff to the right side and press, making sure the corners are turned out properly.

5 With the cuff right side out, pin the cuff facing to the wrong side of the sleeve matching up the placket and cuff ends. Pin on the sleeve side.

6 With sleeve side up, stitch the cuff facing to the sleeve hem.

7 Turn the sleeve to the right side and pin the outside cuff to the sleeve, slightly covering the stitching line.

8 Edge stitch through all layers along the entire folded edge of the outer cuff. The cuff can also be edge stitched or double stitched. Press to finish off.

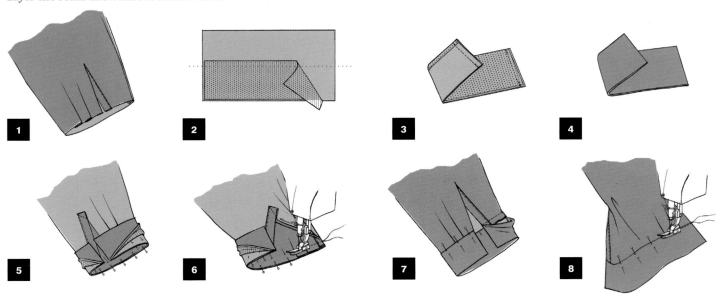

Closed cuff

Closed cuffs do not open so make sure they are big enough to pass the hand through. They are mostly cut in one piece but can be cut as a two-piece with contrast fabric on the facing.

1 Prepare the sleeve hem, adding pleats or gathers around the wrist line.

2 Add interfacing to the wrong side of the outside cuff to 1cm (⅜in) past the fold line.

3 With the right sides together, pin the outside cuff to the sleeve, lining up the seam allowance of sleeve and cuff. Make sure the gathers are evenly distributed.

4 Stitch the cuff to the sleeve.

5 With wrong side up, press the seam allowance towards the cuff but avoid pressing the gathers. Next press the lengthwise seam allowance towards the wrong side of the cuff.

6 With right sides together, pin and sew the underarm seam and cuff seam together in one go.

7 Fold over and pin the cuff facing to the sleeve, slightly covering the stitching line.

8 From the right side, edge stitch along the entire folded edge of the cuff facing through all layers. The cuff can also be edge stitched on the folded bottom edge. Press to finish off.

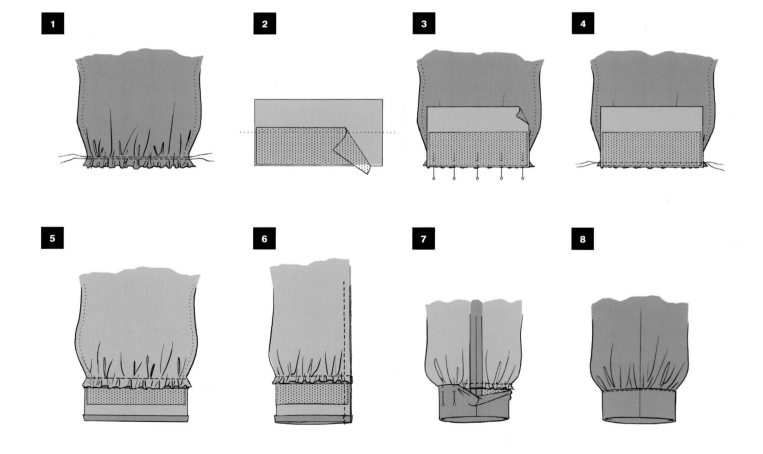

Underarm gusset

A gusset can be added into a sleeve to provide extra movement for a sleeve that is cut as an extension of the garment. The gusset is sewn into a slash in the underarm and can be cut as a one-piece diamond or two triangles.

1 Mark all points and cut-lines onto the wrong side of the garment and gusset. On the wrong side of the garment, reinforce the ends of the cut-lines on the front and back panel with a dot of interfacing or a piece of lightweight fabric such as lining (a). Sew reinforcement stitches all around each marking line, starting and ending 6mm (¼in) to each side of the marking line at the side seam and narrowing the stitching to 3mm (⅛in) at each point (b).

2 Slash the cut-lines from side seam to point on both front and back to create the opening for the gusset. Close the underarm and side seam to the cut-line where the gusset will be inserted.

3 Fold the seam allowance around the opening over to the wrong side and press. With right sides together, pin one side of the gusset to the seam allowance and sew in place just behind the reinforcing stitches. At the centre point lower the needle and pivot to stitch the second side of the gusset. Repeat on the other side.

4 Clean up the seam allowance by facing the gusset, overlocking the gusset seam allowance or topstitching the gusset seams. To topstitch the gusset, press the seam allowance away from the gusset and, from the right side, edge stitch around the gusset catching the seam allowance.

1a

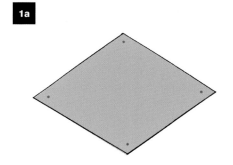

1b

2

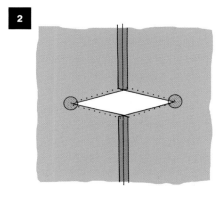

3

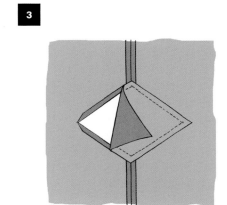

4

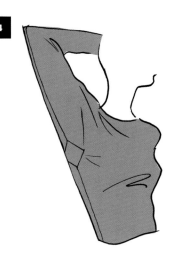

Hemlines

The hem defines the end of a garment and provides a neat bottom edge. The allowance for a hem will vary with the garment style; see Seam Allowance and Hem Allowance on pages 39 and 40. The hem can be finished by hand, machine or with bonding materials and may be invisible – such as a turned-under hem hand sewn with blind stitch – or decorative, such as a wrong-side-out hem. Match the hem finish to the garment design and material quality – find fabric-specific hem-finishing suggestions in Chapter 5.

Preparing for a turned-under hem

A hem is applied after the seams leading to it have been closed. When a hem is turned under over a seam, two layers of seam allowance sit together, which can create bulk. The seam allowance will need layering and clipping by one of several methods.

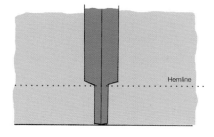

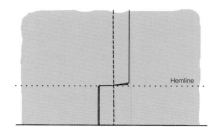

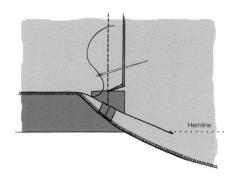

1 Press the seam open and cut away the allowance by half on either side up to the hemline.

2 Reduce bulk on a seam pressed to one side by clipping into the seam allowance on the hemline and pressing the allowance below the hemline in opposite directions.

3 Another option for a seam pressed to one side is to clip into the seam allowance on the hemline and press the seam allowance open below the hemline. The bulk can be reduced further by cutting the seam allowance in the bottom part of the hem down by half.

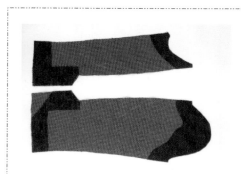

TIP

Some hemlines, such as on jackets and coats, are interfaced to add body, stability and a crisp edge finish. When interfacing is applied, make sure the entire hem is fused to 1cm (⅜in) past the fold to achieve a sharp edge. The fold lines are indicated with dotted white lines.

Topstitched hem

For a less formal look, on most garments a machine-stitched hem can be finished with topstitching. Topstitching is usually done with a larger stitch length and a contrast colour thread – if the garment already has topstitching, match the stitch length and thread colour for the hem. For a less obvious finish, use a matching colour thread.

Double-turn hem

On light- to medium-weight fabric the hem can be turned under twice. Add twice the hem allowance to the pattern piece. Fold the hem allowance twice to the wrong side of the garment, pin in place and topstitch from the edge, then press.

For a different look, a wrong-side-out hem can be used with two-tone or double-face fabric to create a decorative finish. Add the hem allowance plus 1cm (⅜in) to turn under. Fold twice to the right side, first by 1cm (⅜in) and then by the hem allowance, and topstitch on the folded edge.

Single-turn hem

On most fabric weights the hem allowance can be turned once and the raw edge neatened with overlocking or binding. Binding may not be suitable on heavier fabrics since it adds bulk and the binding might show on the right side.

Add the hem allowance once to the hemline. Overlock or bind the raw edge before turning the hem allowance to the wrong side. Topstitch from the wrong side along the edge.

Faced hemline

A facing may be used on the hem to reduce bulk, on a shaped hem, or to add a decorative finish. To reduce bulk, use a lighter fabric or lining for the facing. To deal with a shaped hem, cut a facing following the shape of the hem or use a bias-cut strip. For a decorative finish, cut the facing from contrast fabric or use decorative tape.

Step by step faced hemline with tape

Step 1
Add 1cm (⅜in) seam allowance to the hemline. Place the wrong side of the tape to the right side of the hem to overlap the 1cm (⅜in) seam allowance and pin in position.

Step 2
From the right side, machine stitch along the top edge of the tape.

Step 3
Fold and press the tape part onto the wrong side of the garment and either topstitch or hand stitch in place.

Bias-cut facing
Cut the bias strip to a hem allowance depth of between 2–4cm (¾–1⅝in) to suit the garment and long enough to go around the hem. Pin the facing and garment right sides together, being careful not to stretch the facing. Join the ends of the bias facing and stitch it to the hemline. Press the seam allowance towards the facing and retain stitch it to the facing. Fold the facing towards the wrong side of the garment and press the hemline edge. Pin the facing in place and topstitch or hand stitch.

Pin hem

A pin or rolled hem is applied to shaped hemlines or garments made of sheer or lightweight fabrics. A special rolled hem foot allows the hem to be rolled and stitched in one process, but this type of hem can also be constructed with a normal machine foot.

A pin hem can also be rolled and finished by hand, for example in haute couture. An example is shown on page 267.

Add 1.5cm (⁹⁄₁₆in) seam allowance to the hemline. With wrong side up, turn 7mm (⁹⁄₃₂in) to the wrong side and edge stitch as close as possible to the folding edge to achieve a fine pin hem. Trim the excess seam allowance as close as possible to the stitching using small scissors.

With wrong side up, turn the hem again by 7mm (⁹⁄₃₂in) and edge stitch on top of the last stitching, then press the hem.

Trouser cuffs

For a tailored look, add a cuff or turn-up to a trouser hem. For more about trouser hem allowances, see pages 41 and 200.

Step by step cuffed trousers

Step 1
Add to the hemline twice the depth of the cuff, plus a hem allowance of 2–3cm (¾–1⅛in). Overlock or bind the raw edge of the hem allowance.

Step 2
Fold one cuff depth and the hem allowance to the wrong side and machine or hand stitch in place.

Step 3
Fold and press the cuff to the right side.

Step 4
Secure the cuff to the side seams of the trousers with invisible hand stitches.

Step 5
Apply trouser creases, if required, and a final press.

The giant cuffs on these trousers are one of the main features of their design. Duckie Brown, 2013.

Hand-sewn hem

A hand-sewn hem finish is applied for an invisible finish and at parts of the garment where a machine stitch cannot be applied.

Turned-up hem

Add 2–5cm (¾–2in) hem allowance to the hemline and overlock or bind the raw edge. Turn the hem to the wrong side and press. Pin in place and hand sew with hemming stitch for woven fabric or herringbone stitch for knitted/stretch materials (see pages 116 and 117). In the manufacturing industry, a blind hemstitch can also be applied with a specialized machine using a single thread chain-stitch.

Rolled hem

A fine rolled hem can be hand stitched on sheer and fine fabrics. Add 1cm (⅜in) to the hem edge and use prick stitch or slipstitch to hand sew the hemline (see pages 115 and 116).

Baby-locked hem finish

An unturned, fine edge finish can be created using a superlock or baby lock machine (see page 24). An overlocker can also be set up to sew a baby lock finish. This hem finish is used for shaped hemlines and fine and sheer fabrics and is a quick way of finishing hemlines on garments with layers and tiers. No seam allowance is necessary: place the raw edge under the machine and baby lock the edge.

Bound hem finish

A binding can be applied at the hem for decorative reasons, to add body and on shaped hemlines. Use a bias-cut binding for shaped hemlines and a straight grain tape for straight hemlines.

No seam or hem allowance is necessary at the hemline. Some bindings are pre-folded; for Step by step cutting and preparing bias binding, see page 122. Encase the raw hem edge with the folded binding and edge stitch the binding to the hem. A tape or lace finish can be applied to a raw edge if binding would add too much bulk.

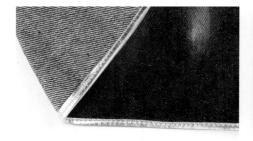

Above: Silver leather pre-folded binding encasing a denim hem. The binding is attached by machine using edge stitch.

Right: Trench coat with contrast binding used as a hem finish. Martin Grant, SS 2012.

Mitred hem

A mitre is applied where a vent or slit joins a hemline and also at square corners on the hemline, such as on a scarf.

Hem with mitred vent and bound seam and hem allowance.

Step by step mitred hem

Step 1
Add the hem allowance to both edges, turn back the hems and fold one over the other. Mark or notch at both raw edges where the hem allowances meet.

Step 2
Unfold both hems and, with right sides together, bring the marking points together folding the hem allowance diagonally through the corner. Stitch diagonally from the corner to the marking points.

Step 3
Trim away excess fabric to a 1cm (⅜in) seam allowance.

Step 4
Press the seam open.

Step 5
Turn the hem to the inside of the garment and continue attaching the hem allowance to the garment with machine or hand sewing.

Shirt hem

Shirt hemlines are traditionally double-turned and topstitched. The button stand marks the beginning and end of the hem because turning the hem twice at this point creates bulk – although mass-production finished shirts do have

a double-turn at the button stand. However, on a one-off design a tailored and less bulky method can be applied. This technique can also be used on leisurewear jackets and coats with an increased hem allowance.

Step by step shirt hemline

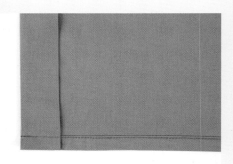

Step 1

Add 2cm (¾in) seam allowance to the hemline for a 1cm (⅜in) double-turned hem finish. Prepare the button stand as explained on page 226. Fold the button stand under-wrap on the fold line over to the right-side of the garment. Stitch across the button stand 2cm (¾in) from the bottom.

Step 2

Clip along the outer fold line of the button stand to the stitching. Fold half the hem allowance (1cm/⅜in) up and edge stitch all along the fold line, being careful not to stitch through the stand.

Step 3

Trim the button stand allowance to reduce bulk and turn it through to the right side, at the same time folding the hem up by another 1cm (⅜in) along the length. Make sure the corner is square and press. Stitch the hemline through all layers next to the top fold and right across the button stand and then press.

Fused hemlines

Some very tightly woven fabrics can be difficult to hand sew, but if an invisible hem finish is required consider a fused hem. Two methods can be used – sample both with the final fabric before applying it to the garment. Add the hem allowance to the hemline and overlock the raw edge of the garment before beginning.

Step by step applying fusible web

Step 1
Cut a 1–2cm (⅜–¾in) wide strip of paper-backed fusible web – the exact width depends on the depth of the hem, the bigger the hem the wider the strip needed to hold the weight. Following the manufacturer's instructions, apply the fusible web onto the wrong side of the hem allowance 5mm (³⁄₁₆in) in from the raw edge. Remove the paper backing.

Step 2
Fold the hem allowance up into the correct position and fuse the hem allowance to the garment – use a pressing cloth over the fusing area.

Step 3
The finished hemline.

Fused hand-sewn hemline
If the fusible web is not working try reinforced or woven fusing with hand stitching.

1 Cut a strip of fusing 2–3cm (¾–1⅛in) wide, depending on the hem allowance. Apply the fusing to the wrong side of the garment, making sure it will be covered once the hem allowance is folded into position.

2 Fuse in place, following the manufacturer's instructions. Once the fusing is cold, hand sew the hem allowance onto the fusing strip, not the garment fabric.

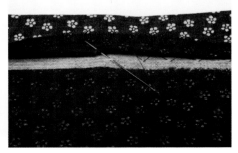

Lining

The inside of a garment should be considered as much as the outside – a lining is part of the design process and can be both functional and decorative. It is constructed separately and applied to the inside to protect seams and hem allowance from fraying, add comfort and help a garment retain its shape. Match the lining texture and quality to the outer fabric and consider the garment's function. Lining fabrics are discussed on pages 76–77. A garment can be fully or partially lined and lining can be closed or open – a closed lining is attached to the hemline so seams and hem allowance are encased completely. With an open lining the seams and hem allowance are partly exposed so need to be finished. Most skirts and trousers are open lined to allow for movement in the hem.

Lining patterns

The lining pattern is taken from the original garment pattern with slight adjustments – for instance, pleats in a lining pattern allow for comfort and movement.

- Copy the garment pattern without including any facing sections and eliminating any seams not required for shaping.
- Do not make the lining pattern bigger, because it sits inside the garment as a second skin – only add ease in length and pleats or gathers as detailed below.
- Mark the pattern pieces clearly and transfer all pattern markings to the lining.
- The lining is usually made in a lighter fabric than the outer garment. When a lightweight fabric is stitched onto a heavy one the lighter fabric may pull, so cut the lining slightly longer to be eased onto the outer fabric for a smooth fit.

- The hemline for a closed lining is cut 1cm (⅜in) longer than the finished garment hemline to allow for a pleat at the hem after the lining is attached – this allows for movement and prevents the lining from pulling on the hem.

Jackets and coats
- On linings with sleeves add 1cm (⅜in) to the underarm seam of both sleeve and body to allow the lining sleeve to fit over the underarm seam allowance of the garment.
- Add a pleat at centre back to allow for movement across the shoulder blades.
- The ease on the garment sleeve head may be too bulky on the lining. Turn the ease into pleats or a dart.
- Cut the garment bigger when adding a quilted lining, to allow extra room for the lining.

Skirts and dresses

- Allow 1–2cm (⅜–¾in) extra length to ease a lining onto a vent to prevent the lining from pulling up the vent. Add allowance by cutting into the lining pattern.
- Designs with voluminous areas should not be restricted by lining. If necessary, partially line such garments.
- On garments with many pleats or gathers fold out some of the fullness on the garment pattern to eliminate bulk, especially round the waistline, when preparing the lining pattern. Do not take out too much fullness, which might affect the hip or bust measurement.
- Single-pointed darts can be pleated instead of stitched to allow extra ease.
- On dresses consider whether the lining is attached to the hem or left loose.
- Add a pleat at centre back of a dress lining to allow for movement across the shoulder blades.

Trousers

- Trouser linings can be added into the front only, down to the knee or the trousers can be fully lined.
- On knee-length lining the selvedge is used as the hemline finish, or add a pinked finish. Do not turn the hem under and topstitch because this adds too much bulk that will show on the outside.

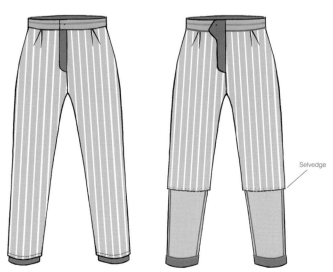

Selvedge

Full lining

With a full lining the entire inner surface of a garment is covered. Use this technique for garments in fabric that needs insulation, frays badly or is uncomfortable next to the skin and on designs with many seam and pocket details, or to add body. A full lining can be closed or open depending on the garment shape. Match the lining to the outer material in quality and texture. The following designer garments show different ideas for full lining.

This page: A fully lined dress. At the front and back the lining is cut up to the collar facing and is edge-to-edge at the armhole. The hem is open with a double-turned hemline and the lining is bagged onto the zip at centre back. The vent is also bagged out.

Above: A skirt fully lined up to the waistband. The zip guard at the centre front zip opening is bagged out with the lining. The lining runs up to the decorative zips in the front panel and is bagged onto the zip, exposing only the zip teeth, then retain stitched to each side of the zip to avoid it being caught in the zip teeth. The lining hemline is open, double-turned and topstitched.

Left: A man's jacket with full lining in contrasting colours.

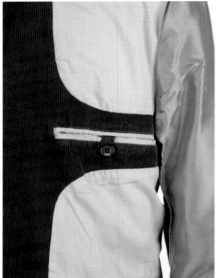

TIP

Inside pockets are common in jacket and coat linings, some with a button fastening below the pocket opening to secure the contents. To make sure the button does not damage the garment underneath, cut a square from lining fabric and fold in half, then fold towards the centre to form a triangle. Add a buttonhole to the unfolded side, then insert the triangle into the top of the pocket opening (above). Alternatively, insert a tab loop in the same place (left and far left).

Left: Fully lined man's jacket with contrast lining on the sleeves and for the front piping.
Below: Detail of the contrast piping.

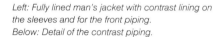

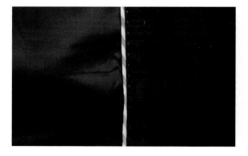

TIP

Consider adding a hanger into the back neckline of a jacket, either by sandwiching the hanger between the lining and back neckline or attaching it to a back neck facing after the lining has been inserted. A hanger can be purchased or a strip made from self-fabric.

Lining a jacket

A tailored jacket is usually fully lined and closed at hemlines and vents. The lining is stitched into the garment after the garment has been constructed with the pockets, facing/lapel, sleeves and collar in place.

Step by step lining a jacket

Step 1
Stitch the lining together. Leave a gap in the left sleeve, halfway along the seam, big enough to pull the jacket through when attaching the lining.

Step 2
With right sides together, pin and stitch the lining to the facing from hem to shoulder seam.

Step 3
Retain stitch the lining to the facing from hem to shoulder seam.

continues on page 218...

Step by step lining a jacket (continued)

Step 4

Stitch the shoulder seams of the facing to the back shoulder lining and press open.

Step 5

Pin and stitch the back neckline of the lining to the garment top collar, lining up shoulder and centre back seams.

Stitch the top collar and under collar seam allowance together from shoulder to shoulder.

Step 6

Align the lining and garment hemlines, matching all seams. Pin and stitch in place.

Step 7

Turn the jacket to the right side and press the lining down to the hem edge to form a pleat.

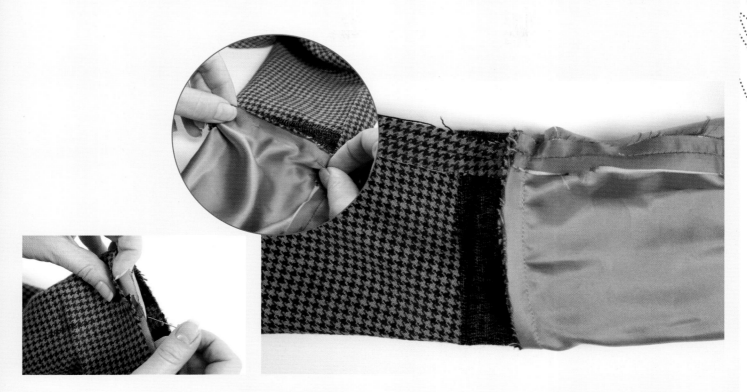

Step 8
Place the sleeve lining into the garment sleeve, aligning the seams on the hemline. Pin in place to make sure the lining will not twist when turning the garment to the wrong side.

Step 9
Turn the jacket to the wrong side through the gap left in the left sleeve (see step 1). Re-pin the lining and garment sleeve hem right sides together and stitch.

Step 10
Hand-tack the armhole seam allowance of the lining to the garment armhole seam allowance at shoulder and underarm seam, to make sure the lining stays in place. Turn the jacket right side out through the gap in the left sleeve and press the lining of the sleeve down to the hem edge to form a pleat.

Step 11
Close the gap in the left sleeve lining by edge stitching from the right side of the lining. Finish by applying a final press.

Vents

Vents are placed where a garment needs to open for comfort when walking, sitting or stretching, for example at garment or sleeve hemlines.

Step by step lined vent with mitred corners

Step 3
Stitch the lining parts together. Stitch the seam in the lining up to the vent opening and press the seam open. Double-turn the hem allowance on the lining and topstitch the hemline.

Step 4
Lay the garment on a flat surface. With wrong side up, fold and press the under-wrap facing over on the fold line and pin onto the over-wrap only – do not pin through to the garment side. Stitch across the extension, starting 1cm (⅜in) in from the raw edge.

Step 1
On the garment, mark the end of the vent to the seam and add a facing to the left seam, and a facing and extension to the right seam for the under-wrap. The vent and hemline can be interfaced if necessary (shown above).

Step 2
Construct the garment, closing the seam with the vent to the vent opening – the vent and hem finish will be the last part of construction. Overlock or bind the hem allowance on the garment.

Step 5
Construct the mitres on the over- and under-wrap – see page 209, Step by step mitred hem.

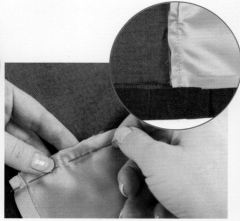

Step 6
Pin and stitch the lining to the under-wrap raw edge, up to the marking, stopping 1cm (⅜in) before the end.

Step 7

Pin and stitch the lining to the under-wrap across the top of the vent to the marking point, stopping 1cm (⅜in) before the end – be sure to fold the garment out of the way so it is not caught in the stitching.

Step 8

Stop at the marking point. With the needle in the fabric at the marking point, clip into the corner of the lining up to the needle/marking point.

Step 9

Pivot and stitch the rest of the lining to the over-wrap facing (see also next photograph).

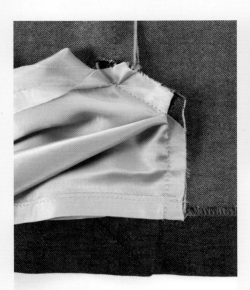

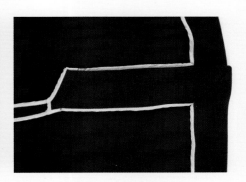

Step 10

Press the lining around the vent and finish the hemline of the garment.

Unlined garments

In an unlined garment, bind or overlock the edges of the under- and over-wrap.

Partial lining

Partial lining is used for lightweight jackets and coats to create interest inside without adding bulk, and for fully shaped or pleated designs where a full lining would detract from the beauty of the garment or restrict its movement. To reduce bulk, a lightweight lining can also be stitched to the underside of garment pieces, such as the collar, yoke or pocket flap, instead of using self-fabric. A partial lining can be open or closed depending on the garment shape.

An outerwear garment can also be constructed without a lining – instead, the inside is designed with deep facings and all seam allowance and raw edges are self-finished or bound.

Inside finishing a partially lined garment

If the lining and facings only cover part of the garment, the finishing of pockets, seams and hemlines must be considered. The lining and facing can be cut in different ways, but always make sure that stabilized areas are concealed. Raw edges on pockets, seams and hemlines can be bound or stitched with a self-finishing seam. When using a partial lining choose a design with limited seam lines and applied pockets, if possible, to avoid a lot of extra finishing work. When choosing finishing methods, consider the garment fabric's texture and quality, as well as the overall garment design and end use.

- Seams can be stitched with a flat fell, welt, French, lapped or bound seam.
- Hemlines can be turned and topstitched or bound.
- Pockets can be bound or the pocket bag can be finished with the seam allowance facing inside the bag. Alternatively, use applied pockets.

A coat with a partial lining and facing. The facing at the front is cut wide, reaching up to the seam, halfway through the front panel continuing to the back to cover the shoulder. The sleeves are lined with a satin lining so they are easy to slide on and off. The hemline, pocket bags and seams are finished with binding.

A jacket with the front completely lined in self-fabric and the back lined with a wide bias-cut strip worked into the neck, shoulder and armhole. Using a crossover lining at the back allows for extra movement. The sleeves are completely lined.

A corduroy men's jacket with cotton lining at the front and the upper part of the back. The sleeves are lined in slippery viscose lining so they are easy to slide on and off.

Fastenings

Fastenings can be the focus of a garment or remain inconspicuous, and different types of fastening can be used together. Choose the fastening before cutting pattern pieces, because some may need pattern adjustments. The opening of a garment can be symmetrical or asymmetrical and may be edge-to-edge or overlapped, and an overlapped design can be single- or double-breasted or have concealed fastenings. Women's garments fasten right over left, men's garments fasten left over right.

> **TIP**
>
> To choose a suitable button size, place different-sized paper circles onto the paper pattern or sample garment to analyse which size will fit the garment proportions. This will also help to decide on button placement.

Buttons and buttonholes

Buttonholes and buttons should be placed at key points – at the bust-line, waistline, hipline and neck-point – that are subject to stress due to body movement. This type of fastening needs an extension added to both sides of the opening; the extension on top to hold the buttonhole is called the over-wrap and that underneath holding the buttons is called the under-wrap. The extension is added to the centreline at front or back and will be wider for a double-breasted design, which has at least two rows of buttons. A horizontal buttonhole on a

single-breasted design should extend 2mm (³⁄₃₂in) past the centreline to make sure the button sits at the centreline. A vertical buttonhole is placed along the centreline.

Positioning can be marked with pins, chalk or thread marking as shown in the illustration, depending on the garment material.

After the buttonholes have been constructed use them to mark the button positions. Pin the garment

shut, matching up the centreline of the over-wrap and the under-wrap. On a horizontal buttonhole insert the pin at the end of the buttonhole towards the opening edge, and on a vertical buttonhole insert the pin in the centre of the buttonhole (see below). Push the pin through into the under-wrap, then unpin the opening and carefully lift off the over-wrap. Sew the button on at the pin-mark position. If the garment material cannot be pinned use a disappearing pen or chalk pencil for marking.

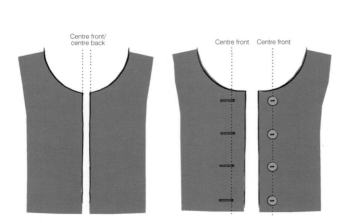

Left: The centre front position.

Right: The over-wrap and under-wrap or button stand with buttonholes.

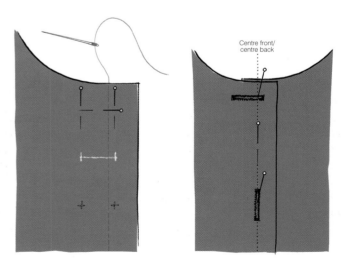

Left: Three different methods of marking buttonholes, using pins, chalk or thread. The red thread marks the centre line.

Right: Marking the position of horizontal and vertical buttonholes.

Buttonhole size

The size of the button will determine the size of the buttonhole and the width of over- or under-wrap needed. When measuring a button consider not only the width and length but also the height – see page 81 to learn more about button shapes.

Place the button onto a ruler or tape measure and measure the diameter. Add ease to the measurement, which allows the button to slip easily in and out of the buttonhole.

- For a flat button add 2–3mm (³⁄₃₂–⅛in) to the diameter for ease.
- For a shank button add the height of the button to the diameter for ease.
- For a ball-shape button wrap a strip of paper or the tape measure firmly around the diameter of the button and then add 2–3mm (³⁄₃₂–⅛in) for ease.

TIP

Do not construct a buttonhole fastening for oversized buttons because a very large buttonhole will look unattractive. Sew the button onto the outside and sew a snap fastener underneath to fasten the opening.

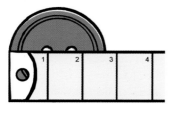

Flat button

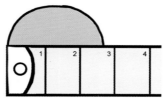

Button with shank

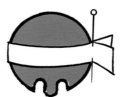

Round button

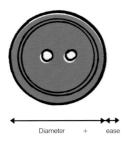

Diameter + ease

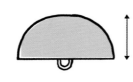

Shank + height

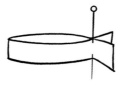

Strip of paper around button

Button stand

The extension for a button stand or placket can be added onto the paper pattern once the size of button has been established. Make sure the stand or placket will be wide enough so the button is positioned within the over-/under-wrap area. In general the stand is the measurement of the button diameter, so for example a 1.5cm (⁹⁄₁₆in) button diameter will need a 1.5cm (⁹⁄₁₆in) button stand added on either side of the centreline. A fancy button design must be sampled, because the general rule might not apply.

Once the fabric has been cut out add interfacing to the button stand or placket to stabilize the area, matching the interfacing quality to the fabric texture and weight. The interfacing will prevent the buttonhole from stretching and provides a firm base for the button. Cut a strip of interfacing to the finished size of the stand or placket and add it to the wrong side of the fabric. Position the interfacing on the inner side, not on the face side, so it will not change the quality and appearance of the fabric.

Button stand variations

A button stand may be part of the garment piece or a placket sewn on separately, and the button can be visible or concealed.

Integral or grown-on button stand for a shirt

This is the simplest and fastest way to make a button stand and can be applied to any garment style and material weight.

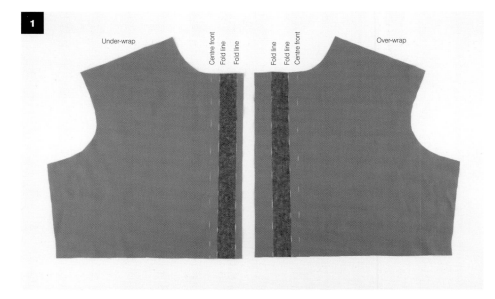

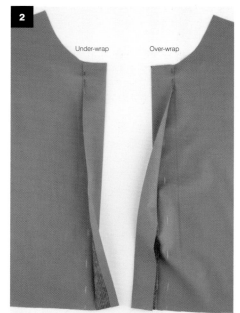

1 *Over-wrap pattern:* To the centreline add half the width of the stand plus twice the width of the stand.

Under-wrap pattern: To the centreline add half the width of the stand plus one width of the stand plus 1cm (⅜in) to turn under.

When working with heavyweight material, use the under-wrap pattern for the over-wrap.

2 *Over-wrap construction:* Fold the stand width towards the inside of the shirt and press. Fold the stand width towards the inside of the shirt again and press.

Under-wrap construction: Fold 1cm (⅜in) towards the inside of the shirt and press. Fold the stand width towards the inside of the shirt and press.

3 *Finishing:* Topstitch the folded edge of both the over- and under-wrap to hold in place. The outer edge of the over-wrap can also be topstitched if required.

The buttonhole is applied to the centre of the stand lengthwise.

Sewn-on placket for a shirt

This design is ideal for adding a contrast fabric as a button stand and can be used for garments in knitted fabric, cutting the stand in woven fabric for extra stability. Avoid using on heavyweight materials because of extra bulk.

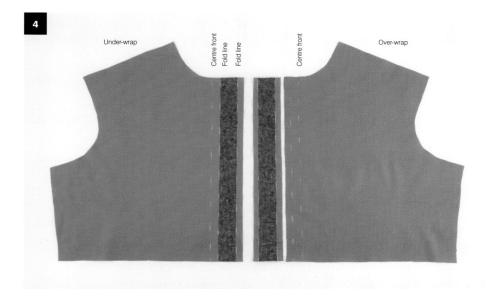

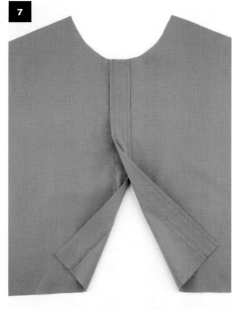

4 *Over-wrap pattern:* Cut a separate pattern piece the width of the final placket plus 1cm (⅜in) seam allowance on each side. Make the placket the length of the opening. Add half the width of the placket plus 1cm (⅜in) to the centreline of the shirt pattern.

Under-wrap pattern: To the centreline add half the width of the stand plus one width of the stand plus 1cm (⅜in) to turn under.

5 *Over-wrap construction:* Place the placket wrong sides together to the shirt front and stitch a plain seam with 1cm (⅜in) seam allowance. Press the seam allowance towards the placket. Fold and press the placket along the stitching line over to the right side of the shirt.

6 *Under-wrap construction:* Fold and press 1cm (⅜in) towards the inside of the shirt. Fold the stand width towards the inside of the shirt and press again.

7 *Finishing:* Topstitch the folded edge to hold the placket in place. Traditionally, the topstitching is done 5mm (³⁄₁₆in) on both edges of the placket. Topstitch the folded edge of the stand to hold it in place.

With a sewn-on placket the buttonhole is applied to the over-wrap lengthwise in the centre of the placket.

Hidden button stand for a shirt

The hidden button stand offers a clean finish because the buttons are concealed. This fastening option can be applied to any garment, but avoid using on heavyweight materials because of the extra bulk.

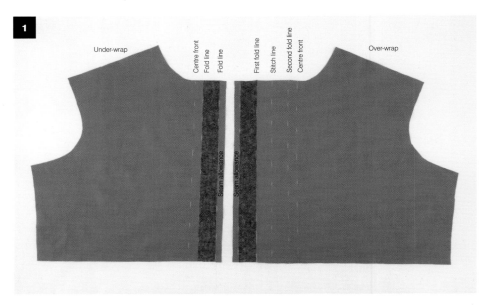

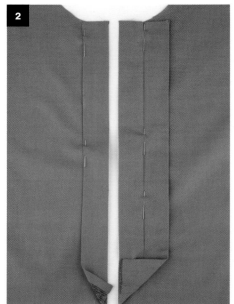

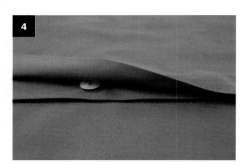

1 *Over-wrap pattern:* To the centreline add half the width of the stand plus three times the width of the stand plus 1cm (⅜in) to turn under.

Under-wrap pattern: To the centreline add half the width of the stand plus one width of the stand plus 1cm (⅜in) to turn under.

2 *Over-wrap construction:* Fold and press along the first fold line towards the inside of the shirt (see photo). Fold along the second fold line towards the inside of the shirt and press again (see photo).

Under-wrap construction: Fold and press 1cm (⅜in) towards the inside of the shirt. Fold the stand width towards the inside of the shirt and press again.

3 *Finishing the over-wrap:* Stitch through the centre of the stand – the 1cm (⅜in) seam allowance is caught at the same time. Press the stand back along the stitching line until both edge folds meet, making the top layer slightly wider than the concealed under layer.

Finishing the under-wrap: Topstitch along the folded edge to hold the stand in place.

4 With a hidden button stand the buttonhole is applied in the centre of the concealed under layer of the over-wrap.

Here is a beautiful example of a hidden button stand in which the collar stand button is also hidden. The buttonhole has been worked into the under-wrap of the collar stand and the button is sewn on the inside of the over-wrap.

Sewing on buttons

Buttons may be sew-through or have a shank on the reverse. When sewing on buttons use the thread double and wax it to prevent it from breaking and knotting.

Right: Sew-through buttons can have two or four holes. A four-hole button can be sewn on in three different ways (shown left to right): cross, fan and parallel.

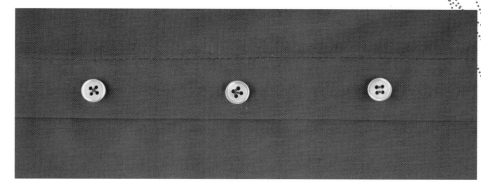

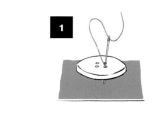

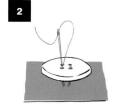

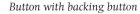

Sew-through buttons
When sewing on a sew-through button make a thread shank so the button will sit properly in the buttonhole.

1 Secure the thread with a knot. Insert the needle from wrong side to right side at the marking position. Take the needle up through one of the button holes and back down through the next, leaving a space between fabric and button to create a thread shank.

2 Make several stitches, going through the fabric and button holes in your chosen stitching design.

3 For the last stitch, bring the needle out between the fabric and button. Wind the thread around the threads under the button a few times to create a shank. Take the needle through the fabric to the wrong side and secure the thread with a couple of stitches – try to stay within one area and keep it neat.

Button with backing button
A backing button is applied to the inside of a garment behind the fastening button to prevent material such as leather, fur or loosely woven fabrics from ripping under strain. It is mostly used on coats and jackets.

1 Use a small, two-hole, flat button. Sew on the buttons as for the sew-through button, but stitching through the backing button, fabric and outside button.

2 Keep the backing button close to the fabric underneath and make the thread shank for the outer button as normal.

Buttons with shank
These buttons have a shank underneath, usually a metal loop, so the thread should be waxed to prevent it breaking.

1 Secure the thread with a knot. Insert the needle from wrong side to right side at the marking position. Take the needle through the shank. Pull the button tight to the fabric layer – there is no need to leave space between fabric and button because the shank provides room to accommodate the buttonhole.

2 Make several stitches through the fabric and button shank. Take the needle through the fabric to the wrong side and secure the thread with a couple of stitches – try to stay within one area and keep it neat.

Buttonhole types

There are several types of buttonholes to choose from. Machine-sewn buttonholes are the quickest and simplest to produce. Other types are hand stitched, bound and in-seam buttonholes and button loops. Match the buttonhole type to the garment style and material texture and weight.

Machine stitched buttonholes can be made using the automatic buttonhole function, in the shirt (right) or keyhole (far right) shape, or a simple version can be made using a tight zigzag stitch.

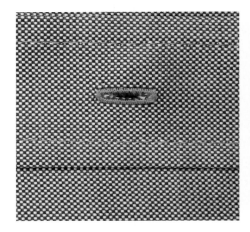 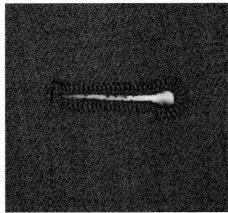

Step by step hand-sewn buttonhole

Hand-sewn buttonholes are time-consuming and take a certain amount of hand-sewing skill, but add the finishing touch to high-end garments. They are ideal for lightweight fabrics that may be damaged by close machine stitching, or if you want to stitch the buttonhole in an unusual thread.

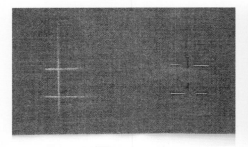 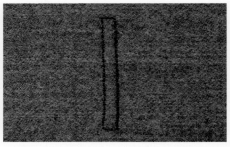

Step 1
Mark the position of the buttonhole with chalk or pins on the wrong side.

Step 2
On the wrong side machine stitch a 2mm (3⁄32in) wide rectangular box along the marking lines using a 1mm stitch length.

 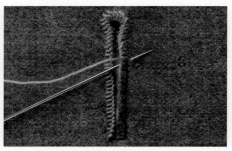 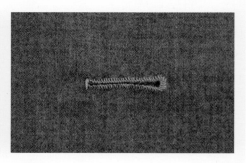

Step 3
Cut open down the centre of the box.

Step 4
From the right side, sew around the edges using buttonhole stitch (see page 118).

Step 5
For a keyhole buttonhole, cut into the corners at the end of the buttonhole where the button sits, or punch a hole, and sew a circular shape.

Step by step bound buttonhole

Bound buttonholes have strips of fabric, called jets, to neaten the edges so are made in areas of the garment with a facing to conceal the jets inside. They are ideal for leather, suede, or any other material that would be weakened by the needle holes required to produce a machine buttonhole. Depending on the style of garment, the buttonhole can be constructed with matching or contrast material.

Step 1
Mark the buttonhole position on the right side with chalk. On the wrong side, fuse with interfacing behind the buttonholes for extra support.

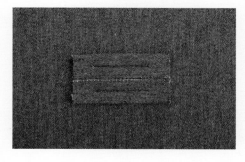

Step 3
Pin the jets onto the right side with raw edges meeting. Using a 1.5mm stitch length, sew down the centre of each jet from start to end of the marking point and secure with backstitching.

Step 2
Cut two strips of material in straight or bias grain 2cm (¾in) wide and the length of the buttonhole plus 2cm (¾in) for allowance. Fuse on the wrong side with interfacing and press in half, wrong sides together.

Step 4
On the wrong side, cut an opening through the centre of the buttonhole stopping 5mm (³⁄₁₆in) before the end of the stitching lines and snipping into each corner up to the stitching line.

Step 5
Push the jets through to the wrong side and align the folded edges together.

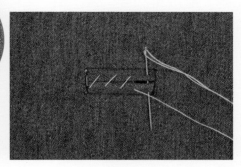

Step 6
Hand-tack the jets together to keep them correctly aligned.

continues on page 232...

Step by step bound buttonhole (continued)

Step 7
With wrong side up, fold the material back to access each triangular corner. Using a 1.5mm stitch length, stitch across the base of each triangle to attach it to the jets.

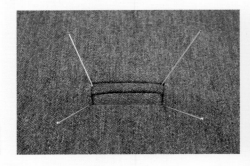

Step 8
Press the buttonhole and pin garment and facing together. From the right side, pin-mark each corner of the buttonhole to the facing side by pushing the pin vertically through.

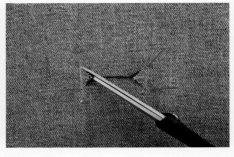

Step 9
From the facing side, cut down the centre of the buttonhole, stopping 5mm (³⁄₁₆in) before the end, then cut into the corners up to the pin marks.

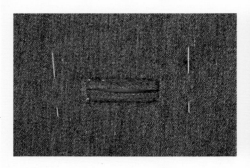

Step 10
Pin the facing in place, fold under the edges of the facing buttonhole and hand stitch to the jets with a small, invisible slipstitch.

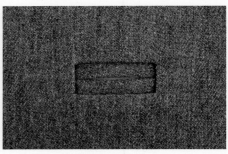

Step 11
Remove the tacking from the right side and press the buttonhole from the wrong side.

In-seam buttonhole

In some cases a buttonhole can be distracting or interrupt a fabric pattern or style line. An alternative option is to leave an opening in a seam as an in-seam buttonhole, which will be concealed. If the garment is lined or faced, this layer will need a matching buttonhole.

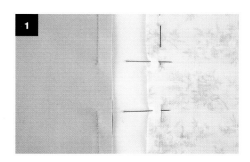

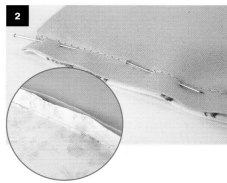

1 Make sure the seam is correctly aligned and pin-mark the buttonhole position on the wrong side of the seam allowance of garment and lining. Stitch a plain seam, backstitching at the start and end of the buttonhole opening.

2 Pin the seam allowance of garment and lining with right sides together, matching the buttonhole opening. Stitch together the seam allowance of the garment and lining as close as possible to the first stitching line.

3 Turn to the right side and press.

Loop fastenings

Rouleau loops and tabs are decorative fastenings that are attached to the edge of a garment between fabric and facing. Loop fastenings can be worked edge-to-edge or with an under-wrap as shown. See also Thread loop on page 269.

Rouleau loops

Rouleau loops are most often seen on formal blouses and dresses. The loops are made of bias tubing, although for a different look consider using decorative elastic, ribbon or cord. The loops can be round, straight or oval and are usually combined with a round, domed or shank button.

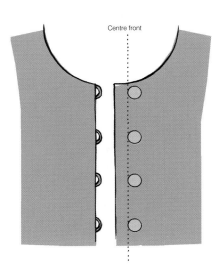

Centre front

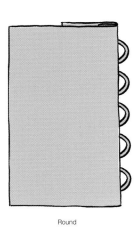

Round

Straight

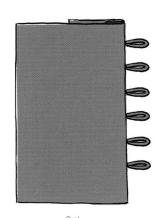

Oval

Step by step making rouleau loops

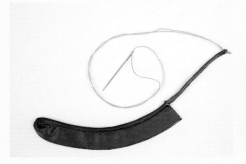

Step 1

Cut a bias strip of fabric and fold in half lengthwise, right sides together. Stitch close to the folded edge using a 1.5mm stitch length. Using a strong double thread and blunt-end embroidery hand-sewing needle, make a secure stitch at one end of the tube. Feed the needle, eye first, through the tube. Gradually push the fabric through by pulling the needle and thread, turning the bias strip inside out.

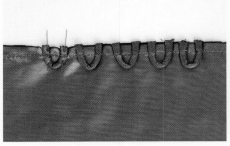

Step 2

Cut the tube into short lengths for the loops. Pin the loops to the right side edge of the facing as shown and stitch in place within the seam allowance.

Step 3

Pin the facing onto the garment, right sides together. Stitch the seam allowance together.

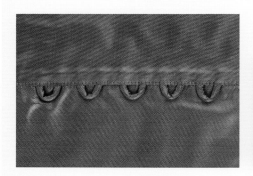

Step 4

Fold the seam allowance to the facing side and retain stitch the seam allowance to the facing side from the right side.

Step 5

Bring the facing and garment piece together and press lightly on the edge. Take care not to flatten the loops.

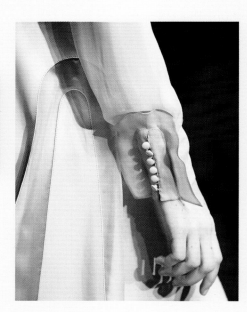

Sleeve hem with rouleau loops and self-fabric-covered shank buttons, adding an elegant finish. Valentino, SS 2013.

Tabs

Tabs are used to enhance a garment design and can be cut to any size and several shapes. They can be used with sew-through or shank buttons. Two different examples of tabs are shown here: tab loops, which are strips of fabric cut on the straight grain, and flat tabs, which can be cut in any size and end in a triangular, round or square shape.

Tab loops

1 Cut a fabric strip 3cm (1⅛in) wide, which includes 5mm (³⁄₁₆in) seam allowance, and fold right sides together. Bag out the tab by stitching a 5mm (³⁄₁₆in) seam allowance. Turn the tab to the right side and press, positioning the seam on one edge. Edge stitch both edges.

2 Fold as shown in the illustration to make a triangular end. Stitch across the ends to secure.

3 Attach the tab loops between garment and facing.

Flat tabs

1 Cut two pieces of fabric to the tab shape and interface one piece. Place the pieces right sides together and bag out. Clip the corners to reduce bulk.

2 Turn the tab to the right side and topstitch round the edge. Apply a buttonhole to suit the button size.

3 Insert the tab between garment and facing. Tabs can also be topstitched onto the garment instead.

Frog fastening lends a garment a military or oriental look, depending on the design. Valentino Haute Couture, AW 2011.

1

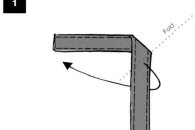

Fold

2

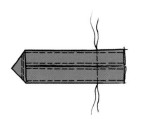

3

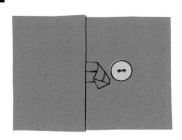

Tab loop

1

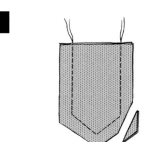

Cut the corner

2

3

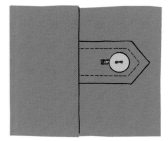

Flat tab

Snap fasteners

Snap fasteners, or press studs, are used where a lightweight flat closure is needed; they are available in metal and plastic and in a variety of sizes and colours. They can be sew-on or a non-sew version, which is attached with a special tool or hammer. For more on snap fastenings, see page 83.

Hand-sewn snap fastening

1 Use a single thread and secure the end with a knot. The half with the stud sits on the underside of the over-wrap, and the half with the socket on the face of the under-wrap.

2 Mark the position of the stud on the over-wrap first. Attach the thread to the wrong side of the fabric at the marking point and bring the needle through to the right side.

3 Sew the stud onto the over-wrap by sewing a few buttonhole stitches over each hole and through the fabric behind without stitching through to the right side. Secure the end of the thread with a few stitches.

4 Close the opening and pin-mark the position of the socket. Sew on the socket as for the stud.

The large snap fasteners on this neoprene coat by Julien Macdonald are made into a design feature by choosing a contrast colour to match the trim.

Magnetic fastenings

The magnetic fastening is common in accessories and has moved into fashion. It offers a concealed finish with a modern touch. For more on magnetic fastenings, see page 84.

1 Mark the centre of the magnet onto the right side of the facing. Place the magnets between garment and facing and pin into position. It sometimes helps to hand-tack around the magnet to hold it securely before stitching.

2 Change the machine foot to a zip foot so the stitching will fit closely around the magnet. Topstitch the magnet in place from the right side – experiment with topstitching patterns to suit your design. Make sure to use paired magnets for over- and under-wrap.

1

2

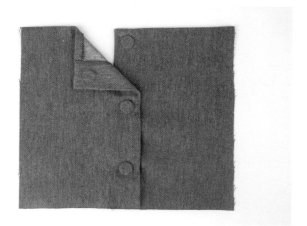

Velcro fastening

Velcro comes in different sizes and colours and is purchased by the metre. It is used on casual or active wear to provide a quick fastening, mostly in combination with other fastenings, such as zips or snap fasteners. See also Velcro on page 83.

1 Mark the position onto the over- and under-wrap and cut the Velcro to the required size. Pin the hook strip of Velcro to the face of the under-wrap and the loop strip on the underside of the over-wrap.

2 Topstitch the Velcro strips in place, either around the edges only or add a topstitched cross from corner to corner.

This Velcro strip fastening allows a cuff to be adjusted to fit.

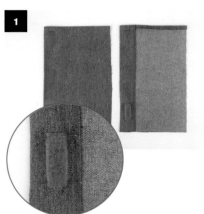

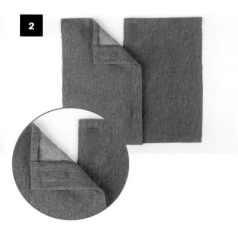

Hooks-and-eyes

These are two-part fasteners that are usually combined with another fastener, such as at the top of a zip. For more on hooks-and-eyes, see page 84.

The hook
Turn the garment inside out. Use a double thread or a single topstitching thread and secure the end with a knot and a couple of backstitches to the inside of the facing. Bring the needle through to the right side of the facing. Place the hook in position slightly inside the edge of one side and work buttonhole stitches around the circular rings. Stitch closely together to cover the metal.

Slip the needle between garment and facing to the other end of the hook and secure the hook part with a few stitches over the neck of the hook. Finish off by securing the thread between garment and facing.

The eye
The eye is positioned slightly over the edge on the other side. For a perfect fit, move the edges to meet after the hook has been attached and position the eye to mark the correct position so that the edges will be as close together as possible. Secure the thread end and position the eye on the marking point. Bring the thread through to the right side of the facing and work buttonhole stitches around the circular rings. Stitch closely together to cover the metal.

Slip the needle between garment and facing to the centre of the eye and secure with a few stitches over the eye on each side. Finish off by securing the thread between garment and facing.

The hook-and-bar
A hook-and-bar is used on skirt and trouser waistbands and is applied the same way as a hook-and-eye. The hook goes just inside the edge underneath the over-wrap, with the bar positioned to match on top of the under-wrap.

The eye   *The hook*

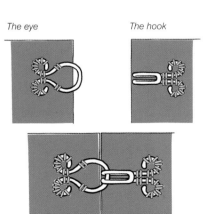

The hook-and-bar

Zips

A zip can either be conventional (opening at the top and closed at the bottom) or open-ended, and can be coil or chain (see page 82). A zip can be installed as a centred, lapped, exposed, concealed or fly zip. There are also a few points to consider when installing an open-ended zip.

Far right: Leather biker suit. The jacket fastens with an open-ended zip and has zipped pockets. A zip runs the whole length of the trouser legs, opening from both sides. Versace, AW 2013.

Above: Jersey and mesh dress by Julien Macdonald with zip fastening and zip decorations.

Shortening a zip

Any zip can be shortened, although an open-ended zip can only be shortened from the top. A coil zip can be cut to size at top or bottom using an old pair of shears. After cutting the top secure with a couple of overcast stitches, or if cut at the bottom apply a zigzag machine stitch to secure – this will stop the zip-pull from coming out. A chain zip has individual metal teeth, so remove teeth one at a time with a pair of pliers to the required size, then secure the end as described for the coil zip or try to replace the metal caps.

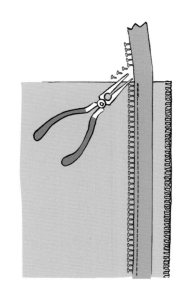

Preparing the zip opening

When designing a garment with a zip opening consider the sizes available first, or have a zip custom-made. The measurement of a zip starts and ends with the teeth – the extra tape at top and bottom is to help secure the zip in the garment. The tape at the top is caught in the waistband or facing and at the bottom is caught in the fly or attached to the seam allowance.

There are different ways to create an opening for a zip, and some installation methods need the seam to be pre-stitched while with others it is stitched afterwards. Mark the zip length on the seam allowance on the wrong side with a notch, pin or chalk mark. If the seam needs to be pre-stitched, choose from the following options.

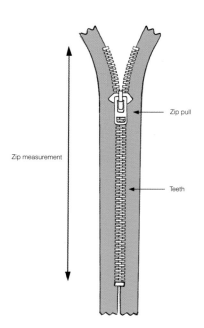

Zip pull

Zip measurement

Teeth

Option 1
Construct a plain seam, stitching the length of the zip opening with a 4–5mm stitch length and backstitching just past the zip-end mark, then continue with a smaller stitch to complete the seam allowance. Press the seam allowance open and let the fabric cool down. Unpick the large stitches along the zip opening.

Option 2
Construct a plain seam but do not stitch the zip opening. Press open.

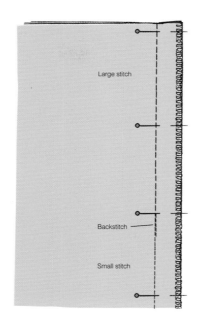

Large stitch

Backstitch

Small stitch

Centred zip
This method is used for a conventional zip, which will be centred behind a seam with the teeth covered by two flaps of fabric and a line of stitching showing either side. The zip can be placed centrally or off-centre on the garment, but avoid the side seam where it is likely to gape. A centred zip can be topstitched by machine with topstitching or by hand with prick stitch (see page 115).

Machine-stitched centred zip:
1 Prepare for the zip opening using option 1.

2 With the garment right side up, place the zip centred under the zip opening with the tape lined up on the top edge of the garment. Pin the zip into place, making sure the zip teeth are well covered. For beginners, hand-tack the zip into place and remove the pins. Change the machine foot to a zip foot.

3 Open the zip halfway to start and place the garment right side up under the machine with the needle close to the teeth at the top of the zip. Secure at the start with backstitching and continue

topstitching the zip close to the teeth, 5–6mm (³⁄₁₆–¼in) from the seam edge.

4 Stop just before halfway down then, leaving the needle in the fabric, lift the foot and close the zip to the top. Carry on topstitching to the end of the opening, then swivel on the needle and stitch across the zip end. Do not stitch over the teeth but over the tape just beyond the teeth.

5 Stitch halfway up the other side then, leaving the needle in the fabric, lift the foot and open the zip past the stitching. Topstitch the rest of the zip, backstitching at the top.

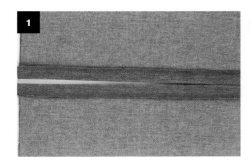

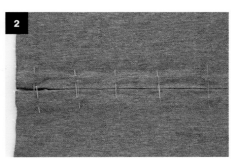

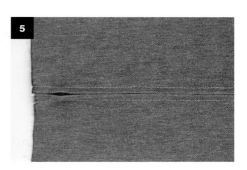

Fly zip

The fly zip is mainly used on trousers and skirts and is constructed with an under-wrap or fly facing to prevent a tucked-in shirt being caught in the zip and so the zip does not touch the skin. For women the fly closes right over left and for men left over right.

Step by step constructing a fly zip

Step 1
Cut the facings and overlock the over-wrap facing on one long side and one short side. Fold the under-wrap facing in half, wrong sides together, and overlock along one long and one short side. Alternatively, the under-wrap facing can be bagged out.

Step 2
Place the front trouser panels right sides together and stitch the crotch seam to the zip opening, backstitching both ends. With right sides together pin the over-wrap facing to the zip opening, stitch to the end of the zip opening and fold the seam allowance towards the facing.

Step 3
Turn the garment to the right side, fold the facing away from the trousers and retain stitch the seam.

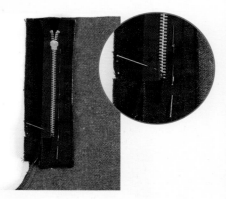

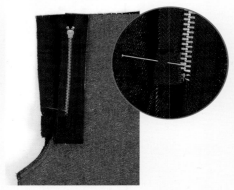

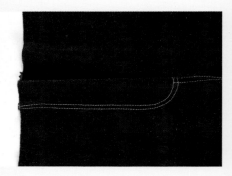

Step 4
Fold the over-wrap facing onto the trousers and place the zip, wrong side up, lining up the left side of the zip tape with the left side of the facing seam. Pin to the facing only on the right side of the zip tape. At the bottom of the zip, pin up the excess left tape as shown to avoid catching it when topstitching the over-wrap.

Step 5
Open the zip halfway down. Using a zip foot, stitch the right side of the tape onto the facing as close as possible to the teeth, pausing halfway to slide the zip-pull past the needle without lifting the needle from the fabric. Close the zip.

Step 6
Mark the topstitching line of the over-wrap onto the right side. Topstitch the over-wrap through all layers from the right side using single or double lines to suit the garment design. Traditionally, the bottom is curved in.

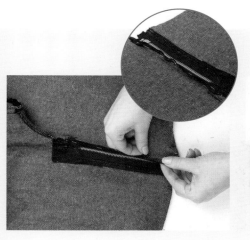

Step 7

Remove the pin holding the bottom of the zip tape out of the way. Pin the under-wrap of the trousers to the zip tape, lining up seam allowance and tape edge. Stitch in place as close as possible to the teeth.

Step 8

Pin the under-wrap fly facing to the under-wrap side of the trousers so the zip is sitting between the fly facing and trousers. Pin within the seam allowance as shown.

Step 9

Turn the trousers right side out. With zip open, edge stitch the seam close to the teeth, attaching the under-wrap fly facing at the same time. Pause to slide the zip-pull past the needle without lifting it.

Step 10

Turn to the wrong side and secure both facings at the bottom with machine stitching, going back and forward a couple of times and being careful only to attach the facings.

Step 11

Continue constructing the trousers by attaching a waistband or facing – see The Waistline, page 165, for instructions on how to attach a waistband and on how to construct a tailored waistband and fly with guard facing.

The fly opening on a trouser can also be worked with a button fastening instead of a zip.

Lapped zip

A lapped zip covers the teeth with one flap of fabric, with only one line of stitching showing. This type can be used at side seams with the lap facing from front to back.

1. Prepare the pattern with a 2cm (¾in) seam allowance at the zip opening. Prepare for the zip opening using option 2 (see page 239). With the garment right side up, place the zip under the zip opening with the tape lined up on the top edge of the garment. With right side up, pin the right edge next to the zip teeth. Hand-tack if necessary, then edge stitch in place using a zip foot.

2. Place the left side over the zip teeth so that the zip and edge stitching is slightly covered. Pin in place and hand-tack 1cm (⅜in) in from the edge if necessary. Mark the topstitching line with a disappearing pen or follow the hand-tacking line for guidance.

3. With right side up, open the zip and beginning with a short length of backstitching, stitch from the top, stopping to slide the zip-pull past the needle without taking the needle out of the fabric.

4. At the end of the zip, swivel and stitch across in a curve or square – do not stitch over the teeth but over the tape just beyond the teeth. Finish with backstitching.

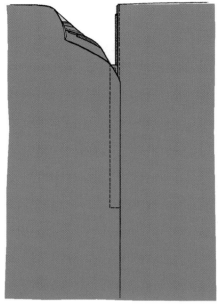

A lapped zip.

Exposed zip

An exposed zip can be inserted in any area because it does not need a seam. The zip teeth are visible as a feature.

Right: Detail of an exposed zip on a red taffeta jacket by Julien Macdonald.

Far right: Detail of a skirt by Julien Macdonald featuring an exposed zip on the pocket, which is covered by a flap with snap fasteners.

Step by step inserting an exposed zip

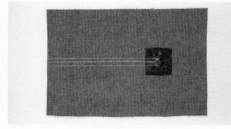

Step 1
With wrong side up, mark the length and width of the zip opening – the width of the opening depends on the zip type and size. Reinforce the end with a piece of interfacing.

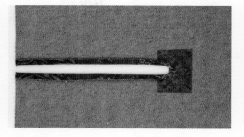

Step 2
Cut through the centre of the marked rectangle, stopping 1cm (⅜in) before the end and cutting into the lower corners. Wrong side up, fold the edges over by 5mm (³⁄₁₆in) – the exact width of fold depends on how much of the zip is exposed.

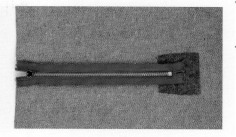

Step 3
Turn the zip wrong side up and pin the tape to the fold lines, centring the zip in the opening. Changing to a zip foot, stitch both sides from the top to the lower corner. Backstitch at both ends to secure.

Step 4
On the bottom corner, fold the zip tape back to access the triangular corner. Stitch across the base of the triangle into the tape to close off the bottom opening.

Step 5
The zip can be finished with topstitching and the inside neatened with a facing, lining or binding.

Concealed zip

The concealed zip is invisible in a seam with no stitching showing on the outside and works with most fabric types. Buy a zip 2cm (¾in) longer than the finished length. The zip can be inserted before or after the seam has been constructed – use an invisible zip foot to allow the needle to get as close as possible to the teeth.

 Step by step inserting the zip before stitching the seam

Step 1
Open the zip. Starting on the left-hand garment piece, place the zip wrong side up onto the right side of the garment and pin the zip tape along the seam allowance with the centre of the zip on the seam line.

Step 2
Using an invisible zip foot, machine stitch the zip in place until the foot hits the zip pull. Close the zip. Pin the other side of the zip to the garment, open the zip and stitch in place.

Step 3
If the seam is constructed after the zip has been inserted, change to a traditional zip foot. Close the zip and stitch the rest of the seam, starting at the end of the zip.

Step 4
Secure the ends of the zip tape to each side of the seam allowance by going back and forward a couple of times.

Open-ended zip

Open-ended zips can be inserted exposed or covered. They are mainly used on coats and jackets because the zip opens completely. On some materials the opening may need reinforcement with tape or interfacing.

1 Measure the zip and match the opening of the garment to the exact zip measurement. Stitch the garment opening closed with a plain seam using a large stitch length. Press the seam open.

2 Centre the zip wrong side up onto the seam allowance and pin or hand-tack in place. Unpick the stitches holding the opening closed.

3 Change to a zip foot. From the right side topstitch the zip in place on each side. The topstitching can be anything from an edge stitch to 1cm (⅜in) from the edge.

An open-ended zip.

The Finishing Touch

Once the garment has been completed, final tweaking, checking over all seams and a final press will ensure a quality result. Place the garment on a hanger or model-stand and stand back to have a good look at it from all sides. Remove all the tacking stitches and apply final hand stitching such as buttons, hooks-and-eyes or press-studs. Check that every detail has been completed and that the lining is not pulling. Check all seams for loose threads and cut them off.

Under-pressing and final press

The very last process is the final press – take enough time to carefully press the whole garment. See Pressing Equipment on page 28.

1 Cover the floor around the ironing board with paper to protect long or heavy garments if they should touch the floor. Clean the iron base before the final press and wait until the iron reaches the correct temperature for the fabric.

2 Before turning the garment to the right side, under-press darts, seams and hem allowances. Place a piece of paper under the allowance and press from the wrong side to prevent construction elements marking the right side of the garment.

3 The final press is applied from the right side of the garment, so use a pressing cloth to protect the material.

4 If over-pressing has left unwanted creases or shine, sprinkle spearmint water (see page 29) on a lint-free pressing cloth and lightly stream or iron. If the fabric cannot be ironed, use a clothes brush sprinkled with spearmint water.

5 Curves and shaped areas are pressed over a tailor's ham, pressing mitt or sleeve board. Sleeves are pressed on a sleeve board, sleeve roll or pressing mitt.

6 Buttons, snap fasteners, magnetic and Velcro fastenings should be open and zips closed. Protect with a pressing cloth.

7 Press the garment in the grain direction. Tops, shirts, blouses and dresses are pressed from the neck down.

8 Trouser creases are pressed last. The crease line normally sits at centre front and back of the trouser leg. If there is a pleat at the front, then the crease line runs on from the pleat.

9 Once the garment has been pressed place it on a hanger or model-stand to cool down. Some garments benefit from being lightly steamed on the model-stand.

10 Use a clothes brush to remove any threads or fluff after final pressing and store the garment in a garment bag.

Under-pressing a seam allowance.

Under-pressing a dart allowance.

5 Fabric- and Cut-Specific Techniques

Working with Fabrics

The fabrics and materials discussed in this chapter have different characteristics and structures and often require special handling and specific construction methods. Designers, pattern cutters and sample machinists often come to know certain fabric types better than others and sometimes specialize and refine their skill in just one or two areas. This part of the book introduces the different ways to work with specific fabric and material types, illustrated with designer examples. Remember when exploring alternative ways of garment construction, always to make up a sample in the final fabric.

For each fabric group listed below, the section explains the structure or weave of the fabric and its treatment and finish; it considers what to look out for when buying the material; and offers tips on drafting the pattern and cutting it out. Special attention is given to the specific equipment required for cutting, pressing and sewing the fabric. Interfacing/interlining and lining options, seam types and finishes, and hem and edge finishes relevant to the fabric are explained, often with step-by-step instructions. Finally, fastening ideas are offered for the garments typically made with each fabric.

Denim.. page 248
Knitted and Stretch-Woven Fabrics.. page 254
Transparent and Semi-Transparent Fabrics .... page 262
Lace, Sequined and Beaded Fabrics .... page 270
Napped and Pile Fabrics .... page 276
Leather and Fur .... page 282
Felted and Non-Woven Fabrics.. page 290
Latex, Neoprene and Plastic Materials... page 294
Patterned Fabrics.. page 300
Mixing Fabrics... page 306
Bias-Cut Fabrics...page 310

Denim

Denim was apparently named after a sturdy fabric called serge made in Nîmes, France – the name *serge de Nîmes* became shortened to *denim* – although a similar twill-weave fabric called jean originated in 16th-century Italy. Denim was woven using one coloured and one white thread, while jean was made of two threads the same colour – denim was known as the stronger and therefore more expensive fabric. By the 18th century both denim and jean were being imported to England for work trousers because of their durability and ease of care.

Garments

Leading designer companies specializing in denim include Levi's, Wrangler, Diesel, Mustang and Lee and it is also used by leading fashion labels for both casual wear and stylish designer items. Most people own at least one denim garment, either the classic jeans or a shirt or jacket. Although the text in this section refers mainly to jeans, the treatments and construction methods also apply to other denim garments and accessories.

Weave, treatment and finish

Denim is a tightly woven twill fabric that is strong and stiff and comes in a variety of weights; it is usually 100% cotton but can be cotton mixed with man-made fibres such as viscose or polyester. To produce stretch denim, elastane fibres are included. Traditionally the warp yarns are dyed indigo blue and the weft yarns left natural off-white; on one side the blue yarn dominates (normally used as the right side) while on the other the white yarn is prominent.

Over time and washes the strong indigo blue fades to a streaky pale blue, which is considered desirable – fashion has introduced pre-faded jeans, often with treated patches to imitate natural wear. Treatments can be separated into two categories, physical or chemical.

Washed denim all-in-one and bleached and unbleached denim patchwork bomber jacket with large dogtooth or houndstooth and check pattern. Pierre Balmain, SS 2014.

What to consider when buying

- Choose the right weight for your garment.
- Check the treatment or finish; denim might be unwashed or not pre-shrunk.
- Use stretch denim for narrow leg or skinny jeans.
- For casual fitting jeans use non-stretch denim to avoid the garment stretching out of shape.
- Finishing treatments for denim garments are available – if these cause shrinkage, allow extra fabric when cutting.

Stonewashing An industrial tumble-washer with pumice stone is used to abrade the surface for a worn appearance and to soften the fabric.

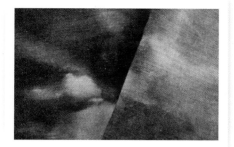

Bleaching The denim can be bought pre-bleached, or bleached after purchase to make the whole garment paler, show off a detail or introduce pattern.

Sanding and **Brushing** The surface is rubbed with sandpaper or a stiff brush for a distressed look or for a velvety, suede-like finish.

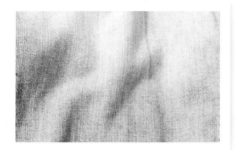

Enzyme Treatment and **Acid-Washing** These destroy the surface, producing a soft, smooth hand, although also reducing the fabric's weight and strength.

Coating Treatments Spraying, painting or adding resin-coated glitter offer a metallic or high-shine look. Plastic coating gives a glossy wet-look effect.

Teflon Coating This adds strength and warmth for outdoor garments.

Colour Printing or **Laser Printing** adds pattern, while techniques such as flock printing add texture.

Distressing is achieved by abrading the fabric surface, for example by hand sanding with sandpaper to produce a worn look.

Pattern Cutting

Use any suitable trouser pattern as a basic block to adjust – an old pair of well-fitting jeans can be used as a guide; take measurements to modify the block pattern. Analyse the area around the crotch, especially if the jeans are meant to fit well around the bottom. For a current look or specific style check Internet shopping sites for measurements such as rise, inside leg/inseam and leg opening width – most have a 'click to zoom' option, which allows you to study details.

Cutting Out

Preparation

- Pre-shrink the fabric or include a shrinkage allowance for post-construction treatment.
- Check care instructions and consider washing the fabric before cutting – or wash a sample to establish the shrinkage percentage.
- Washing softens the fabric but removes excess dye; add white vinegar to the water to minimize fading.
- Press the fabric before laying the pattern out. This also helps to fix the colour.

Layout

- The diagonal lines on twill weave give it a direction – use a one-way layout.
- Cut single or double layer; if cutting double, cut right sides together.

Marking

- Mark onto the wrong side with chalk.
- Notch marking points on the pattern edge; denim does not fray excessively.
- For placement points use a hole punch or a chalk pencil.

Shears

- Use bent-handled shears for better control.

Sewing

Machine needles

- Seams will be bulky: use a 16/100 or a jeans/denim needle with a strong, thick shaft and a sharp point to stitch through multiple layers of heavy fabric without breaking.
- For topstitching, use a topstitching needle with bigger eye to accommodate heavier thread.

Stitch size

- Analyse stitch length on ready-to-wear denim. Topstitching is usually 3.5–4.5mm.
- Test topstitching thread with different stitch lengths before applying.

Thread

- Topstitching is usually done with heavy polyester thread in contrasting yellow-orange to strengthen seams and add visual impact.

Flat fell seam topstitched with two different colours of thread to create a subtle design feature.

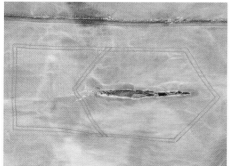

Distressed pocket with a raw edge pocket opening and twin topstitching.

Construction

Seams

Bulky seams are common on denim. Applying the waistband to jeans means dealing with several layers and domestic machines may not be powerful enough for some tasks, such as applying belt loops. Try moving the needle manually using the hand wheel and consider changing to a walking foot to help transport the fabric through the machine. At places like pocket corners, try hammering the seam to flatten it before machining. Most seams, especially on the waistband, need trimming and may need finishing because denim does fray to some extent. The garment design may suit a taped or bound seam or a facing, using either contrast or self-fabric.

Topstitching

Most seams on denim garments are topstitched for extra support and the right topstitching is essential for an authentic look. For instructions see page 132. A flat fell seam will show a double line of topstitching on the right side of the garment so measure the distance between the lines and reproduce it when double topstitching similar seams. The pocket opening and fly on the front and the patch pockets in the back are usually double topstitched – refer to ready-to-wear jeans to establish suitable stitching widths. Some areas can be tricky to topstitch – try different sewing machine feet, such as a compensation foot, zip foot, roller, even feed or walking foot.

Hemming

The best method is to use a double-folded, topstitched hem. If the garment is to be washed after construction, a raw edge finish will create a distressed look.

The flat fell seam is often found on the inside leg seam, centre back seam and back yoke of denim garments. For Step by step flat fell seam see page 128.

The side and inside leg seams may be stitched with a plain seam pressed open or to one side, towards the back, with seam allowances overlocked together.

Some designs have edge stitching on the inside leg/inseam, with the side seam/outside leg partly edge stitched and ending with a bar tack. For this look, edge stitch down from the waist, past the pocket opening and stop on the hip.

Jeans usually have a double-turned hemline, topstitched down with a topstitching thread. A distressed look is typical in denimwear, especially at the hem edge.

Fastenings

Sturdy fastenings suit most denim garments; metal zips, press-studs and buttons and machine-made buttonholes. The waistband fastening is traditionally a metal jeans button, consisting of a button and a tack in silver, copper or bronze, and in either antique finish or polished. There are different designs – ready-to-wear jeans buttons often feature the designer's logo. Buttons on women's jeans may sit on the right like those on men's jeans.

To attach the waistband button, mark the button position and make a hole. Insert the tack from the back and the button from the front, plug together, then hammer from the tack side with the button resting on a soft surface. The keyhole-shape buttonhole is positioned horizontally in the centre of the waistband.

Denimwear is designed to be hardwearing.

DESIGNING A DENIM COLLECTION

It is essential to research traditional denim garments to achieve a convincing result. Some elements should be copied exactly, but others can be altered – such as copying the back pocket shape, but redesigning the topstitching. Changes can be more daring – even adjusting overall shape. A denim garment will keep its identity as long as iconic styling and key parts are retained.

It is difficult to make authentic-looking jeans because of the specialized machinery and finishing treatments used in the industry but you can achieve good results with the right styling and correct accessories. Analyse ready-to-wear jeans – look at the waistband, fastening, pockets, topstitching and cut.

CONSTRUCTION ORDER

Construct the front and back pockets, stitch the fly, then sew the inside leg seam/inseam together and topstitch before closing the outside leg/side seam. Finally add the waistband.

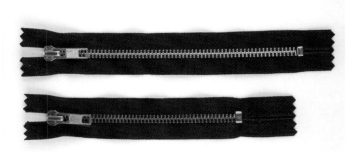

Traditional jeans fastenings of two-part metal buttons (above) and metallic chain zips (right) counterbalance the sturdy material.

Fabric-Specific Elements

Waistband

The jeans waistband is cut in one piece without a centre back seam; it can be cut in one piece on a lengthwise fold or in two pieces and stitched together. The centre back is cut on the straight grain with the centre front coming off grain, which helps shape the waistband onto the body. The finished waistband is usually 4cm (1⅝in) wide – copy the measurement of your favourite jeans.

Jeans fly

This can be constructed with a zip or as a button fly. The zip fly has a metal chain zip that opens at the top only, while the button fly has a hidden button stand and tack buttons. Copy the style of ready-to-wear jeans because the topstitching, bar-tacks and construction can vary. See pages 240–41 for how to construct a zip fastening on a trouser fly.

Pockets

Most jeans have five pockets; two spade-shaped rear patch pockets, two slant pockets at the front and one small pocket on the right side. The pocket bags are cotton, preferably with self-finished seams, although an overlocked seam is acceptable. The pocket corner is secured with rivets or bar-tacks. Topstitching can be quite elaborate on designer jeans, but traditionally the pocket has double topstitching, further apart at the top, with bar-tacks at the corner.

The topstitching on the waistband may be a single edge stitch all around or have double stitching along the bottom. Match the overall look you want to achieve.

Front fly with a hidden button stand and tack buttons in the waistband and button stand.

Bar-tacks

A bar-tack is a tight, narrow line of zigzag machine stitching, run back and forth, used to reinforce weak points. On designer jeans, bar-tacks may be stitched in different colours as decorative features.

Rivets

Metal rivets in a range of designs are used to strengthen the pocket corners and the bottom of the fly. Match to other metal accessories, such as the zip and buttons.

Top: The origin of the small pocket is unknown: it may have been intended as a fob pocket for a watch on a chain.

Above: The spade-shaped back pocket is one area where the designer can include different stitching designs.

On jeans, bar-tacks are found on each corner of the pocket opening, to secure belt loops, and on the end of the fly at the bottom and just above, to hold the fly facing in place.

Two-part metal rivets add an authentic look.

Knitted and Stretch-Woven Fabrics

These fabrics have greater stretch and recovery (ability to return to the original shape and size) than traditionally woven fabrics, allowing snug-fitting garments with few seam lines that are able to expand and contract with body movement. Stretch-woven fabrics also tend to wrinkle less and are more resilient. The degree of stretch and recovery is influenced by the combination of fibres, yarn structure and fabric construction. Knitted fabrics include boiled wool, jersey single knit, double knit, interlock knits, raschel knit, sweatshirt, mesh, tricot, Milanese knit, ribbing, sweater knit, stretch terry and velour, athletic knit, power-net and polar fleece.

Garments

Stretch fabric garments include items designed to allow unrestricted body movement (sportswear, athletic wear, high-performance clothing), items for comfort (casual wear, leisurewear) and body-fitting items (lingerie, corsetry).

The development of elastic fibres and fabrics has also allowed designers to make traditional garments fit well without compromising on comfort – for instance, stretch suiting has transformed tailored suits.

Long T-shirt jumper worn with a cropped sweatshirt top and softly draped sweatshirt trousers. Louise Goldin, SS 2013 Ready-to-Wear.

DESIGNING WITH KNITS

- Jerseys are soft and drape, pleat and gather well for a soft, relaxed design.
- Double knits are crisp with little stretch so suit simple tailored garments.
- Raschel knit varies in weight; choose easy-fitted shapes, simple collarless necklines, in-seam pockets, dropped shoulders.
- Sweatshirt and fleece are brushed; ideal for casual wear with simple collarless shapes, elasticated waistbands and raglan, batwing or kimono sleeves.
- Mesh works as an insert or for simple pull-on garments.
- Tricot is used for lingerie and nightwear, and for active wear or linings.
- Sweater knit resembles hand knits. Choose unstructured, simple designs with loose fitted sleeves, simple necklines, in-seam pockets.

- Ribbing is used for tubular garments or to finish neck- or hemlines.
- Stretch terry and velour are soft nap fabrics, ideal for casual wear with a loose fit, dropped shoulders, and raglan, batwing or kimono sleeves.
- Athletic knit is two- or four-way stretch, ideal for tight-fitting high-performance sportswear.
- Power-net provides support and controls shape in body-conforming garments, but allows movement so is ideal for bras and corsetry or as body-shaping panels.
- Polar fleece provides warmth without bulk or weight, ideal for insulating linings or unlined casual wear.

Weave, construction, treatment and finish

Stretch fabrics are split into 'comfort stretch' such as jerseys and stretch denim, used for everyday garments, and 'power stretch' such as power mesh, used to compress and control the body.

Stretch-woven fabrics

These are made in standard weaves as a one- or two-way stretch using natural or synthetic fibres combined with stretch synthetic elastomeric yarns such as rubber, elastane or spandex. The same effect can also be achieved by weaving with core-spun yarns or high-twist yarns. They offer the comfort and fit of knitted fabrics and can give a modern twist to traditional fabrics such as denim or lace.

Knitted and jersey fabrics

Knitted fabrics may be one-, two- or four-way stretch, made in natural fibres, artificial or synthetic fibres, or a blend of both. Some knitted fabrics contain elastomeric yarns, for enhanced stretch to achieve a tighter fit while retaining shape with good recovery. For more information see Knitted and Jersey Fabrics, page 74.

What to consider when buying

- Design the garment to establish the level of stretch and stretch direction required before selecting fabric.
- Avoid any stretch fabric that is off grain – not many can be straightened.

- Check recovery by stretching and then checking if it returns to its original shape.

Knitted fabrics

- Designs on printed knits may break up or distort when stretched – pull the fabric to see the effect.
- Choose a double knit for a raw edge finish as the cut edge will not roll.
- Tubular or pre-cut ribbing strips vary in stretch, recovery quality and care. Match care requirements to the garment fabric if used as neck or hem finish.

Dress by Julien Macdonald constructed with double jersey on the body and stretch netting on the sleeves.

Pattern Cutting

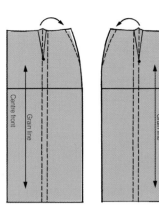

Most patterns designed for woven fabrics can be altered for stretch fabrics, but use simple shapes without elaborate details. Take out estimated stretch allowance, minimize seam lines and eliminate darts. The stretch allowance can vary and should be tailored to the stretch ability of the intended fabric. Make a test garment using fabric with the same stretch characteristics, try out seam and fastening ideas and then adjust the pattern.

Knitted fabrics

- Avoid darts; use ease, pleats or gathers.
- Avoid tailored waistbands; use elasticated, drawstring or faced waistbands.
- Sharp corners or angled seams are difficult to achieve.
- For skiwear or dancewear place the stretch lengthways, otherwise place across the body.
- With athletic knit prepare patterns with no ease, or minus ease by deducting 5–15cm (2–5⅞in) across the body width measurement. Make a test

garment to check sleeve and leg length and neckline and armhole depth. Use side and centre back seams.

Stretch-woven fabrics

- Use collar shapes or pockets with crisp lines.
- Avoid gathers and pleating; use darts and seams.

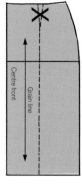

Adjust a basic block by transferring the darts to the side seam and taking in the pattern along the straight grain (right, top). Do not simply remove the darts (right, bottom).

Cutting Out

Preparation

- Pre-shrink fabric if necessary.
- Before cutting out allow the fabric to relax on the table, overnight if possible.
- Press or steam out the crease line or adjust the pattern layout to avoid it.
- Avoid stretching the fabric when transferring pattern pieces or cutting.

> **TIP**
>
> To check if the fabric needs pre-shrinking, cut a 10cm (3⅞in) square and wash as normal. Dry the sample, measure to check shrinkage and compare to the unwashed fabric.

Layout

- Avoid allowing the fabric to hang over the table edge.
- Some knitted fabrics have an irregular selvedge: use a vertical rib to establish a straight grain.
- Check for colour irregularity and pattern design.
- Cut along one fold of tubular fabric to open it out.
- Determine right from wrong side. The edge of jersey will curl to the right side when stretched.
- Place the pattern onto the wrong side unless the fabric has a pattern design – in which case place right side up to match motifs.
- Use a one-way layout single layer for patterned or nap fabrics or fabric with colour irregularities.
- Some knits and stretch-woven fabrics can be cut on a double layer right sides together; if in doubt use a single layer.

Marking

- Mark on the wrong side of the fabric.
- Pin or weigh down pattern pieces before marking. Use new pins with a ballpoint to avoid knits running and pin in the seam allowance.
- Use a marking pen, chalk or thread marking but avoid stretching the fabric.
- For bulky knits and mesh with big holes use pearl-head pins, safety pins or thread tacking.
- Do not use tracing paper on knits because the tracing wheel may damage the fibres.
- Notch or clip marking points on the pattern edge – except on knits, which may run.
- For placement points on knits use thread marking – an awl can damage the yarn.
- For placement points on stretch-woven fabrics use chalk or thread marking.

Shears

- Use well-sharpened, bent-handled shears matched to the fabric weight.

Pressing

- Test on a scrap to find the correct method of steaming, finger-pressing or pressing and the right amount of pressure and heat.
- Do not apply much pressure on knitted fabrics because it can cause stretching.
- Avoid flattening the surface on napped fabrics – use a towel or needle board.
- When pressing from the right side, cover with a piece of self-fabric or a pressing cloth.
- To remove creases use a 50/50 vinegar and water solution or spearmint water.
- Press after each stage.

> **TIP**
>
> When using a single layer, duplicate pattern pieces to be cut twice so all pieces can be positioned before cutting starts. This will avoid any being forgotten.

Sewing

Hand-sewing needle

- Choose a ballpoint size 5–9, depending on fabric weight.

Machine needles

- A ballpoint needle slides between yarn strands to avoid damage.
- Use a twin ballpoint needle on a domestic sewing machine to imitate the look of cover stitching – but only on areas without stress, because the stitching will not stretch.

Stitching size

- For lightweight fabric such as jersey, raschel, tricot and interlock knits use 2–2.5mm.
- For medium- to heavyweight knits such as sweatshirt and sweater knit, use 2.5–3.5mm.

Avoiding stitching problems

- Test stitching on a scrap of the same fabric.
- Reduce pressure on the presser foot to avoid stretching. Consider changing to a roller or even feed (walking) foot.
- If stitches skip, adjust needle-thread tension and check the needle is a ballpoint.

- Stay-stitch the neckline, waistline and hem edges.
- Stretch the fabric moderately when using straight stitch on a flatbed sewing or domestic sewing machine, but not too much or seams will look wavy.
- Do not stretch the fabric when using zigzag stitch, or on an overlocker or cover stitch machine.

Thread

- Cotton-wrapped polyester, long-staple polyester thread or soft threads with elasticity such as textured polyester-multifilament.

Construction

Seams

Seams need to stretch to match the fabric otherwise they will snap; make seam samples before constructing the final garment. Some of these fabrics have very limited stretch so a plain seam stitched with straight stitch – or a slight zigzag, which allows more thread in each stitch – is fine.

Some knitted fabrics do not fray, but cut edges may curl and a finish such as overlocking will prevent this. Moderate to heavy stretch material should be sewn with a 4-thread overlocker or cover stitch machine for a professional seam finish.

Prepare the seam allowance to the size of the overlocking or cover stitch finish – in most cases about 7mm (9⁄32in). Use threads with elasticity if working on a domestic sewing machine. Check knitted fabrics to see if they run – stretch on both sides to analyse the direction of run. Use a fray stopper on the edge that runs or overlock/cover stitch straight after cutting out. Make sure the fabric stretch will not be compromised if considering decorative seam finishing such as piped, lapped or welt seams.

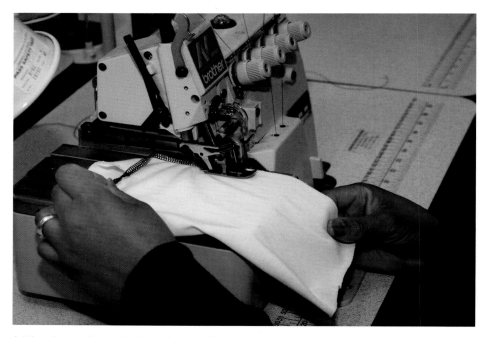

A 4-thread overlocking machine is used to sew knitted fabrics together.

SWEATSHIRT AND T-SHIRT SEAMS

The iconic white T-shirt has come a long way since Marlon Brando wore one in *A Streetcar Named Desire*, turning it from underwear into fashionable outerwear. The iconic shape, cut tight to the body in cotton jersey with crew neck and short sleeve, is still a firm favourite. Traditionally side, underarm and shoulder seams are closed with a 4-thread overlocking machine while sleeve and hemline are turned under and cover stitched, showing a double row of stitching on the right side. The neckline can be finished with ribbing, self-fabric or binding.

Hemming

Let the garment hang for 24 hours before hemming. Hems can be stitched by hand with herringbone stitch or by machine using cover stitching, topstitching, a twin needle machine or zigzag stitching. Alternative hem finishes include a facing, a wrong-side-out hem or a raw edge; some designs suit an elasticated hem finish. Consider the stretch in the material and where it is used when the garment is worn – some hemlines hang loose, so can be finished with a non-stretch method.

Edge finish

Match the edge finish to the garment style. For lightweight knits, eveningwear, nightwear and lingerie use lace or decorative elastic trims, woven or elastic tapes, ribbing, facing or binding to finish any edge. Bindings can be purchased pre-cut in stretch or non-stretch, or cut on the bias or straight grain in self-fabric or a contrast fabric. For medium- to heavyweight knits choose from binding, ribbing, trims, elastic or woven tapes and facings. Facings can be all-in-one, shaped, decorative or bias-cut and may be in self-fabric or a contrast to enhance the design. When finishing necklines and waistlines without fastenings use a stretchable finish to allow the garment to slip on easily.

Jersey-drape dress by Julien Macdonald with a twisted tape finish on the neckline.

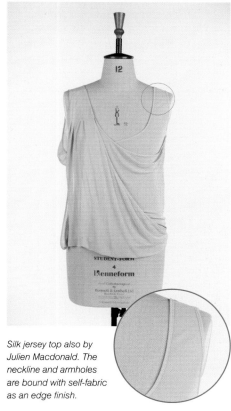

Silk jersey top also by Julien Macdonald. The neckline and armholes are bound with self-fabric as an edge finish.

TIP

If using bindings, tapes or trims on hem or edge, match the weight, fibre and care requirements to the garment material.

Ribbing

The most common edge finish is ribbing. Check the fit and size before cutting the ribbing and make sure that it is not too tight or loose – it is usually cut smaller than the garment edge, to hug the body. Make sure the ribbing is relaxed, not stretched, before cutting and cut slightly longer than the measured length. Pin together and try it on before attaching to the garment edge with overlocking or cover stitching.

Waistlines

Waistlines without an opening should be finished with an elasticated waistband, which can be a casing holding elastic or elastic applied directly to the waist edge. Use braided elastic in a casing and decorative elastic if directly applied, cutting the elastic shorter than the waist so the garment is drawn onto the body. A casing with a drawstring can be applied to a waistline wide enough to go over the hips. See also The Waistline, page 165.

Vintage T-shirt vest with ribbing detail from the neckline draped over the body. Jean Paul Gaultier, Jeans Collection No. 0010.

Interfacing and lining

Stretch fabric
Garments made from stretch fabric are designed to stretch, so they are not likely to be lined or interfaced. However, some areas may need support and some garments might require lining.
- Match care requirements to the garment fabric.
- Stabilizing tape prevents openings, shoulder seams or necklines from stretching.
- Reinforce seams that must stretch with transparent (polyurethane) elastic.
- Attach the lining only to the waistline on skirts and trousers and only to the neckline on dresses.

Knitted fabrics
- Use a lightweight fusing or fusible knit interfacing; always test on a scrap of final fabric.
- Use a lightweight knit or bias-cut woven lining for skirts, trousers and dresses. Other stretch linings include lightweight tricot and mesh.
- Reinforce with non-stretch interfacing or stabilizing tape before applying buttons and buttonholes, press-studs and zips.

Stretch-woven fabrics
- Use stretch interfacing; but on waistbands, buttonhole areas, collars, cuffs, pockets and pocket openings use non-stretch interfacing.
- For outerwear garments use tricot, mesh or stretch lining. Cut woven linings on the bias or add extra fullness and deeper pleats if cutting on the straight grain.

Fastenings

Some garments will not require a fastening because the stretch allows them to be pulled on and off. Jackets, coats and cardigans traditionally have a button, press-stud or zip fastening, but for fine fabrics consider hooks-and-eyes, button loops, frogging and ties.

On knits, place buttonholes parallel to the ribs and with the stress in line with the buttonhole to avoid rippling. Consider making the fastening area in a non-stretch fabric so the buttonhole can be worked in any direction – a traditional combination with knits is leather or woollen fabrics.

The zip can be metal or plastic and applied as a lapped or exposed zip – for finer fabrics try a lightweight invisible zip. Reinforce the opening just inside the seam line with tape or a piece of selvedge from a woven fabric. Make the opening 1–2cm (⅜–¾in) longer than the zip and ease the extra length onto the zip to avoid rippling. Always hand-tack the zip in place, then steam lightly to ease excess before stitching the zip permanently.

A taped button fastening on a knitted cardigan by Noa Noa. Using tape stops the buttonhole and button from stretching.

A lightweight invisible zip at centre back for a concealed look. Julien Macdonald, SS 2010.

Light cardigan with central zip fastening set in a contrast band at centre front. Lanvin, SS 2011.

Transparent and Semi-Transparent Fabrics

The character of these fabrics ranges from fine with a fluid drape to stiffer types with a crisp hand. They are available in light- to heavyweight and in most fibres. Softer types are batiste, challis, chiffon, crepe chiffon, gauze, georgette, maline and tulle. Semi-crisp and crisp types are dimity, dotted Swiss, double sheer, eyelash voile, gazar, handkerchief linen, lawn, marquisette, mousseline, net, organdie, organza, tarlatan and voile.

Garments

Sheer fabrics are popular for eveningwear, daywear and lingerie. Soft fabrics drape very well around the body and work for simple designs with minimum seams and plenty of volume – garments with soft tucks or pleats, gathering and shirring look great. Crisp fabrics also look best with few seams and used generously, but their stiffer nature means they will stand away from the body. Layering on tiered skirts, collars and sleeves shows off sheer fabric to its advantage. Bias cutting is also very popular but avoid fitted garment shapes because seams are likely to rip – kaftan-like shapes, harem-style trousers and puff, batwing and kimono sleeves are ideal.

Organdie T-shirt dress with French seams. The sleeves and hem are pin hemmed and the neck is finished with a slim binding. All seam and hem finishes are the same depth. Richard Nicoll, SS 2014.

Weave, treatment and finish

Semi-transparent and transparent fabrics may be open-weave, mesh, net, or knitted or crocheted in an openwork pattern. Some fabrics are sheer because they are loosely woven, others are woven with super fine yarn that makes them semi-transparent. Partly transparent fabrics can be produced using chemical burnout or flock print, both of which create a slightly raised solid pattern on a translucent background. A chemical process can also be applied to stiffen transparent fabric, or it can be PVC-coated. Some sheer fabrics have a printed pattern, which will be seen on both sides with one side more dominant than the other.

What to consider when buying

- These fabrics can inspire a design through their drape on the stand, so you might buy the fabric before knowing what to do with it.
- Light colours are more transparent.
- Hold the fabric up to the light to check for printing or colouring imperfections, or small holes.
- Analyse the drape and volume – some fabrics collapse so you might need double the amount.
- Sheer fabrics in natural fibres such as silk chiffon and cotton organza are easier to handle and work with than synthetics so buy good-quality fabric – it will save time in manufacturing and the result will be more satisfying.

Chiffon dress with pin hem finish on neckline, armholes and hemline. Alberto Ferretti, Spring 2012.

Pattern Cutting

Eliminate as many seams as possible – seams, facing and hem will all show on the right side. When using a facing at centre front or back, delete the seam by adding the facing to the edge instead of cutting a separate facing pattern. Instead of darts, consider adding tucks, gathers or pleats over the bust, waist or hips to create volume and shaping. Add at least 1.5cm (⅝in) for the seam allowance because sheer fabric tends to fray and consider openings and fastening options.

Underlay or layer-up the fabric for a less revealing look – layering-up will also create a rich effect – and add pocket details, pleating or gathering over the bust for modesty.

Cutting Out

Preparation

- Press the fabric before cutting out. Use a dry iron for soft and very lightweight transparent fabrics and move quickly and lightly.
- Cover the table with a piece of flannel or brushed cotton. Place a layer of tissue paper on top, then spread a single layer of fabric, right side up, on top of the tissue.
- Straighten out the fabric and snip into the selvedge if necessary so it lies flat.
- Weigh the fabric down or pin with a very fine pin, such as a lace pin.
- Lay out the pattern pieces and weigh down – only use pins in the seam allowance to avoid leaving a mark.
- Alternatively, mark pattern pieces on a second piece of tissue. Place on top of the fabric (see right). Pin or weigh down, then cut out through the two layers of paper. This keeps the grain of the pattern pieces secure.

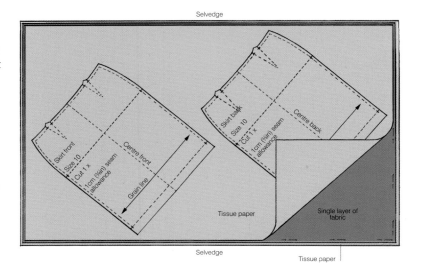

Cutting plan for fine or lightweight fabric. Lay a single layer of fabric between two single layers of tissue paper. Draft pattern pieces on the top layer of tissue.

When laying out chiffon for cutting, first cover the table with a piece of flannel or brushed cotton and then a layer of tissue paper.

Layout

- Some fabrics have a shine or look darker from one direction so will need a single layer one-way layout. One-way print designs need a one-way layout.
- Use a single two-way layout on plain fabrics without shading and patterned fabrics with a non-directional design – it is more cost-effective.
- For a single layer bias layout place the pattern pieces onto the fabric at a 45-degree angle to the selvedge. A 'true' bias-cut garment always hangs better.
- For more information on layout see pages 48–51.

Marking

- Delicate fabrics need extra care – thread marking is the safest option, using a fine hand-sewing needle and contrasting thread.
- Avoid notching marking points on the fabric edge because sheer fabrics can fray badly.
- Test chalk making on the edge before using because it can show through to the right side.

Shears

- Use serrated shears for narrow and round areas; make sure they are well sharpened.
- Use a rotary cutter for straight lines so the fabric stays flat on the table; protect the worktop with a cutting mat.

Sewing

Hand-sewing needle

- Use a fine sharps needle.

Machine needles

- Use a thin universal size 60/8 to 70/10.
- Insert a new needle at the start and check regularly for catches or faults – a damaged needle can cause permanent holes or pulled threads.

Stitching size

- A small stitch length of 1.5–2.5mm is best; make sure the tension is not too tight.

Avoiding stitching problems

- Seam slippage occurs with some transparent materials, especially on fitted garments. Try using an under-layer or baby seam finish (see page 266).
- For skipped stitches and puckered seams, see page 27.
- Some fabrics are very slippery; secure layers with pins or thread tacking before stitching.
- Very delicate fabrics are easily ripped by handling or by the machine presser foot. Take care and avoid multiple sewing processes.
- As you begin stitching, hold the threads to prevent the fabric being drawn into the machine. Alternatively, place tissue paper under the material when stitching and remove it afterwards.

Thread

- Use fine cotton-wrapped polyester thread or mercerized cotton. Match the colour and quality to the fabric.
- Avoid thick threads.

Construction

Seams

Prepare well before attempting to manufacture a sheer garment; research iconic garments and apply a delicate hand or approach. Seams on transparent or semi-transparent fabric must be carefully considered because they will show through; in general they should be narrow and unnoticeable, so sample ideas with the final fabric to find the right seam. If you are working on a budget,

with a plain seam, neaten the edges with a clean finish, binding or overlocking. For instructions on seams and seam finishing see Chapter 3.

A French seam is a self-finished seam for sheer fabrics that requires some practising to achieve the finest result. For Step by step French seam and French seam turned around a corner see pages 126–27.

Baby seam

A delicate but sturdy seam often used as an alternative to a French seam because it requires very little seam allowance. The baby seam is sewn from the wrong side of the fabric and is easy to use on curved seams.

Flat fell seam

The flat fell seam can also be applied to sheer fabrics for a more sporty finish. For step by step instructions see page 128.

 Step by step baby seam

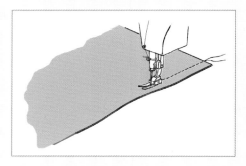

Step 1
Stitch the fabric with wrong sides together.

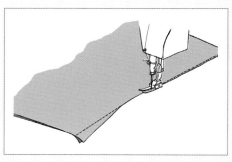

Step 2
Fold and press the seam allowance back along the stitching line and edge stitch along the fold.

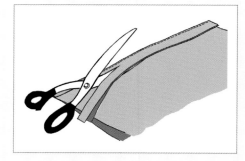

Step 3
Trim as close as possible to the edge stitching.

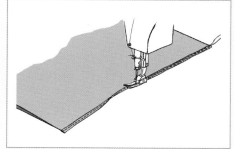

Step 4
Fold the seam again to enclose the raw edge and edge stitch again on the last row of stitching. Press to one side.

Hemming

A narrow hem works well for circular and flared hemlines and a double-turned or wider hem on straight hemlines. For a more luxurious look use deep, double-folded hems or a deep facing.

Baby-lock or superlock
This is the most cost-effective hem finish and it will save time, especially on layered garments or endless hemlines. See Baby-locked hem finish on page 208.

Hand roll hem
A great invisible hem finish, this is slipstitched so no stitching shows on either the right side or the wrong side.

Binding
A fine binding to finish a hemline will add weight and structure. Cut bias binding from the same material or use a contrast colour or pattern as a design feature. Pre-cut bindings are also available.

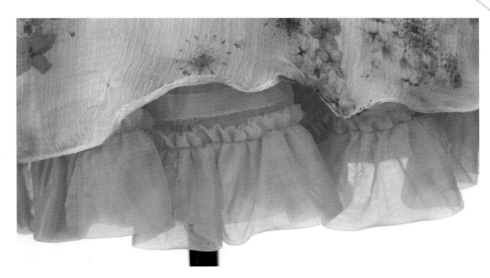

A pin hem is a nice finish for all types of sheer fabrics and can be found on both high-end designer garments and high street items. For instructions see page 206.

Edge finish

The edge finish on a sheer fabric should suit the style of the garment and possibilities include binding, lace, trim and tapes, decorative facings, raw edge finishing techniques and edge-to-edge linings. Using unusual edging materials, such as jersey rib or leather binding, on a sheer garment may create an original look.

Chiffon top by NoaNoa. The jersey rib edge defines the neckline but also creates a softly draped finish.

Underlining and interfacing

Transparent fabrics can be underlaid with underlining or multiple layers of self-fabric to add support and for an opaque look – which also means some of the structure and edge finishes can be hidden. Underlining can be used everywhere or only partially – for example the body of a dress may be underlined and the sleeves left sheer. Some understructures are used as a base to contour the body and support a draped design. Fabrics for underlining transparent materials include netting, tulle or mesh, organza or organdie depending on the crispness of the top fabric; satin fabrics work well with softer sheers. Try underlining with darker colours or a contrast colour and/or pattern to create a new and unique look. To support the top fabric without changing the colour, use flesh-coloured tulle, mesh or lightweight organza. Avoid fusible interfacing because the glue will show through on the right side of a transparent fabric – if support is needed look into alternatives.

Fastening

Try to avoid buttonholes – use fastenings such as rouleau loops, hooks-and-eyes, frogging, poppers or lightweight zips such as the concealed/invisible zip. Research garments made of sheer materials and analyse their fastening ideas.

The keyhole opening, or hemmed/bound slit, fastened with rouleau loops is traditionally used at centre front and back openings but can also be placed on other parts of the garment such as the shoulders.

Thread loop

This is a hand-sewn loop fastening.

1 Wax the thread to strengthen and stop it tangling. Anchor the thread at two points and sew three to six strands on top of each other.

2 Work blanket or buttonhole stitch over the strands, keeping the stitches close together.

3 Work the first and last blanket stitch through the fabric.

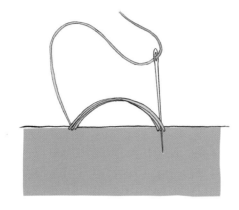

1

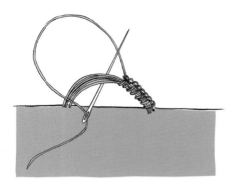

2

Ties

A tie can be a fun finishing.

1 Cut a bias strip double the width of the tie. Fold in half lengthwise and stitch the width of the tie from the fold. End the stitching slanted outwards.

2 Turn the bias strip either with a loop turner or with needle and thread. When using needle and thread, attach a double thread to the slanted end of the tube.

3 Insert the needle with the eye end into the tube and push the needle and fabric gently through.

The top layer of this dress is printed chiffon with a tie detail on the side. The ties are made of bagged out printed self-fabric. Julien Macdonald, SS 2011.

Lace, Sequined and Beaded Fabrics

These deluxe fabrics ooze glamour; once worn exclusively for special occasions and eveningwear, they are now frequently used for daywear. They are also now found in the high street although the quality varies and so does the price. Using lace and embellished fabrics requires advance planning, time and practice for successful results, but they are well worth the effort.

Garments

These fabrics can be used for a whole garment or as appliqué, placement design or trimming on specific areas. They are suitable for most types of garment although they are not popular for sports or outerwear for practical reasons – if they are used at all on such garments it is usually for a section or as a placement design.

Weave, treatment and finish

Lace

Lace is manufactured by hand or machine; handmade techniques include bobbin, needlepoint and knotted lace, crochet and embroidery. Many laces originally handmade are now machine-made using twisting, knitting or embroidery techniques. Raschel lace is a low-cost version in wider fabric widths, which is lightweight, strong and available in a variety of patterns and colours. It uses man-made, simple multifilament yarns such as polyester-Lycra blends, so it stretches well with good recovery. Also available is a simulated lace achieved by embroidering a base fabric with a thread resistant to heat or chemicals, then using a burnout method to remove the base fabric.

Sequined and beaded fabrics

Most of these fabrics have a thin woven or knitted base, in any type of fibre or yarn, which is embellished with beads, sequins, decorative threads, pearls or crystal stones that are sewn, glued or fused in place by hand or machine, either individually or in strips. Designs can be dense all-over patterns, random individual motifs or a border. All-over sequin and bead designs are usually applied by machine using a chain stitch, while individual motifs and borders can be hand or machine applied. Many techniques can be employed to enhance individual motifs, such as embellishing over existing embroidery or following outlines on a printed pattern.

TIP

To create a one-off garment in an unusual fabric, consider vintage tablecloths, curtains, doilies, lace, or duvets or pillow covers. Alternatively, consider recycling sections from second-hand garments or make your own lace fabric by joining strips of lace together. To create a unique fabric on a budget, add further embellishment to a lesser quality embellished fabric by working into the existing patterns.

Above: Vivid deep pink sequined tuxedo jacket with contrast black silk lapels. Dolce & Gabbana, AW 2011.

Below: Leather all-in-one embroidered with a life-size sparkling skeleton design, by Christina Ruby Walton.

What to consider when buying

- Most such fabrics feature one-way designs or motifs that require more fabric – plan the pattern layout before purchasing fabric.
- The fabric width tends to be narrow, which can influence pattern layout and garment design.

- The pattern may run horizontally or vertically – make sure the direction fits your design and the repeat is wide enough for your pattern pieces.

Lace

- Good-quality lace uses fine thread and small stitches creating textures and depth. Cheap lace has a flat and dull look and may have hanging thread ends on motifs.

- Silk and linen fibres are used for fine lace, which is more expensive. The low-cost equivalent is made of nylon and polyester.

- Lace is see-through so usually needs underlining – purchase this at the same time as the lace.

Allover Lace is a wide fabric with a repeating pattern, ideal for a whole garment but which can be used for only part.

Bordered Lace is finished on both lengthwise edges, usually with scallops, which can be used as a decorative edge finish. Bordered lace can be used for a whole garment or for only part.

Edging Lace has one straight edge and one decorative edge, often a scalloped or picot border – picots are small decorative edge loops.

Galloon Lace has scalloped patterns along both lengthwise edges and is for making ruffles, insertions and banding or for appliqué.

Motif and **Medallion Lace** are individual lace designs that can be used for parts such as collars and cuffs or as an appliqué.

Insertion Lace is plain along both lengthwise edges; it is ideal as a decorative strip between two fabric edges.

Pattern Cutting

Let the fabric guide the design. Some lace fabrics have self-finished edges, which determine garment length. Individual motifs on some beaded fabrics may need careful placement.

- For directional patterns prepare pattern pieces for a one-way or nap pattern layout by clearly marking the grain direction.

Lace

- Any shape garment can be used but consider the fabric width in relation to pattern pieces.
- Decide on the seam finish before cutting the pattern; different types need different allowances.
- Eliminate hemlines from pattern pieces when using the edge finish of a bordered lace as a decorative hemline.
- Straighten hem and neckline when using a scalloped or picot edge finish.

- Keep seams and darts to a minimum to avoid interrupting all-over fabric designs.
- Place motifs and pattern placement to show off the fabric to best advantage – mark onto the pattern before cutting out.

Sequined and beaded fabrics

- Simple designs without gathers, pleats, darts and pockets work best for all-over embellished designs.
- Collars, pockets or button stands will not be easy – make in a different material to complement the garment design. Alternatively, use a faced neckline, side seam pockets and fastening options without an over- and under-wrap, such as a concealed zip.
- Sequined and beaded fabrics scratch the skin, so avoid designs with tight-fitting or set-in armholes – use batwing, raglan and kimono sleeves or a dropped shoulder, or substitute a softer fabric around the armhole.

 ## Cutting Out

Preparation

- Make a toile to resolve fitting problems and test design ideas and placement of fabric motifs.
- Some lace shrinks; most is washable so pre-shrink by hand-washing in warm water and air-drying. Alternatively steam from the wrong side – place a towel or other padding underneath to avoid crushing a raised pattern.
- Embellished fabrics do not need pressing prior to cutting.
- Store lace and embellished fabrics rolled up, not folded.

TIP

Keep all lace and embellished fabric scraps – they can be used for other projects or as appliqué.

Evening dress decorated with a variety of black lace, partly draped and hand sewn after the dress was constructed. Julien Macdonald, SS 2011.

Layout

- Mark essential matching points on pattern pieces before placing them onto the fabric.
- Make sure any fabric pattern matches across adjoining pieces at centre front and centre back, the hemline, parts of the armhole and sleeve.
- Place a central motif/pattern repeat at centre front and centre back.
- Lay out all pattern pieces before cutting out.
- Weigh down pattern pieces or use pins in the seam allowance.

Lace
- Identify the right side and mark the fabric – lace is smoother on the wrong side.
- One-way designs need to be cut out in a single layer as a one-way or nap pattern layout.
- If there is no straight edge or selvedge use lengthwise motifs to establish the grain line.

Sequined and beaded fabrics
- Sequined fabrics have a shading or sheen like a napped fabric.
- The sequins should lie flat and feel smooth when running your hand down the lengthwise grain.
- Cut out as a single layer with the right side up using a one-way or nap pattern layout.

Marking

- Use tailor's tacks, thread marking, safety pins, pearl-head or T-head pins.
- Sequined or beaded fabrics can also be chalk marked on the wrong side.

Shears

- For lace use sharp shears matched to the fabric weight.
- For sequined or beaded fabric use old, well-sharpened, medium to heavy shears – do not use the best shears because the fabric may damage the blades.

Pressing

- Test press on a scrap.
- Cover or underlay with a towelling fabric to avoid flattening raised motifs.
- Press lace from the wrong side; if it cannot be pressed, steam by holding the iron 2cm (¾in) above the surface, then finger press the seams.
- Most sequined and beaded fabrics are easily damaged by steam and heat; cover with a towel or pressing cloth to avoid damage or flattening the embellishment.

 # Sewing

Hand-sewing needle

- Use a fine sharps needle for general sewing tasks.
- Use a beading needle for beading and fine embellishment work.
- For embroidery or embellishment work use a chenille or embroidery needle.

Machine needles

- Match needle size to the fabric weight and structure.
- For lace use a universal needle, size 60/8 to 90/14.
- Use a universal jeans/denim needle size 70/90/100 for sequined or beaded fabric.
- Have plenty of machine needles to hand when working with sequined fabrics because they are likely to break or dull.

Stitching size

- A suitable stitch size is 2–3mm to suit the fabric weight and structure.
- Use a smaller stitch length on open-weave lace.

Avoiding stitching problems

- On very fine or open patterned lace hold both threads when starting to stitch and place a piece of fabric between lace and machine foot to prevent the lace from being pulled down into the machine.
- To avoid seam puckering hold the fabric firm and stitch slowly. Using a stabilizer will help.

Thread

- For most sewing tasks use cotton-wrapped polyester or polyester thread.
- For delicate lace use extra fine cotton-wrapped polyester thread.

Construction

Seams

Lace

Seams should be unnoticeable on any unlined lace garment – for a quick and inexpensive finish stitch a plain seam with a narrow seam allowance, overlock seam allowances together then finger press to one side. On a lined lace garment use a plain seam pressed open. Tack seams before stitching, especially on open-weave lace.

Lace appliqué seam
For a high-end finish use lace appliqué seams, which will make the garment appear as if it is one piece of lace with no joins.

 Step by step lace appliqué seam

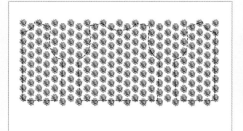

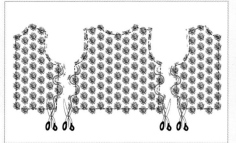

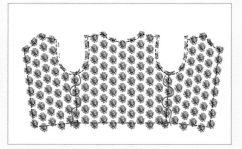

Step 1
Cut pattern pieces without seam allowance and place onto the right side of a single layer of fabric, leaving space between each piece. Align the pattern design on adjoining seams and place a centred motif at centre back and front. Pin or weigh down the pattern pieces.

Step 2
Thread trace the original stitching line of seams and darts onto the lace (black lines). Look at where motifs might overlap across the seams. Re-mark the seams avoiding the overlaps and allow 1cm (⅜in) around the motif edges (red lines). Cut out the pieces around the edges of motifs – the cutting line will be quite crooked.

Step 3
Lap sections right side up by matching the motif and seam lines, then tack around motif edges. Hand sew or machine zigzag sections together around the lace pattern and trim away excess lace.

Sequined or beaded fabrics

On woven embellished fabrics use a plain seam; on knitted fabrics use a 4- or 5-thread overlock finish. For a quick and inexpensive finish use a plain seam but always line the garment because the sequins left in the seam allowance can irritate the skin.

Sequin appliqué seam
This type of seam, which involves removing some sequins for comfort and a better look, gives a high-end finish.

1 Cut pattern pieces without seam allowance and place them onto the wrong side of a single layer of fabric, leaving space between each piece for a seam allowance.

2 If the fabric shows a pattern, align this on adjoining seams. Place a centred motif at centre front and back.

3 Pin or weigh down the pattern pieces. Mark seam lines with chalk, marking pen or thread tracing onto the wrong side of the fabric.

4 Mark a 2–3cm (¾–1⅛in) seam allowance around the pattern pieces, considering hemlines separately. Cut out the pattern pieces. Stay-stitch just inside the seam allowance to help secure the sequins or beads. On beaded fabrics you can also apply a thin line of fabric glue, but test thoroughly on the fabric first.

5 Pull the sequins off the seam allowance. Note that sequins and beads on an all-over design are usually applied with chain stitching, so take extra care because the whole row may unravel if you pull one end. Make sure no sequins

remain in the sewing line. Save sequins to fill in the seam later.

6 Secure the sequin threads by knotting, or thread the end into a hand-sewing needle and securely stitch in place.

7 Place pieces right sides together and pin or tack in place. Stitch a plain seam with a one-sided zip foot.

8 Seams can be left unfinished if the garment is lined. If it is unlined, finish seam allowances with overcast hand stitching or a binding. Seam allowances may be attached by hand at either side to lie flat so you can avoid pressing the seams.

9 On the right side replace damaged or missing sequins by re-stitching in place over the seam line and onto any bald spots.

10 On beaded fabrics remove beads from seam edges and allowances and from darts before stitching; place the fabric on a firm surface with the beads facing you and carefully smash with a hammer. Wear a pair of safety glasses to protect your eyes.

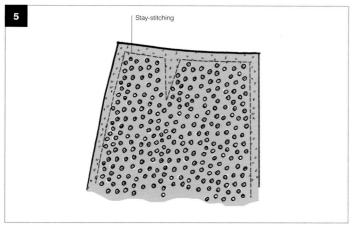

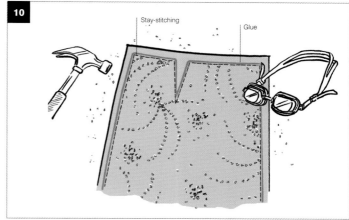

Hemming and edge finish

Lace: Try to lay out pattern pieces on bordered lace so the decorative edge finishes the hem and neckline, but if this is not possible the decorative edge can be cut off and reapplied to the finished garment. Alternatively, use edging lace or another trim. Some lace garments suit a bound edge finish, contrast facing or edge-to-edge lining.

Sequined or beaded fabrics: Depending on the fabric, hemlines can be turned under or faced with a complementary fabric and hand sewn with blind hemstitch. Edges can be bound or faced with contrast fabric or edge-to-edge lined. Consider beaded or lace trims for a decorative finish and ribbing or leather trims for a casual look.

Interfacing, underlining and lining

It is not common to use iron-on interfacing on either lace or embellished fabrics – on lace the adhesive will show through and the heat required to apply it will damage sequins and beads. Sew-in interfacing can sometimes be used on sequined and beaded fabrics. To support garment areas use tulle and organza or organdie, matching the weight and fibre contents to the fabric. If possible line lace garments to avoid stretching or ripping at stress points and line sequined or beaded garments to cover scratchy seams. If the lace or base fabric is a stretch material use a stretch lining for a comfortable fit.

Fastenings

Fastenings may support the traditional elegance of lace or embellished fabrics – using hooks-and-eyes, button loops, frogging, in-seam buttonholes and lightweight, invisible zips. To create a more sporty and modern look, consider contrasting with the fabric by using metal or plastic zips or press-studs.

Sequined bomber jacket, with a traditional rib collar and zip fastening at centre front to give an authentic look.

STABILIZING OPENINGS AND SEAMS

Stabilize neckline, shoulder seams, waistline seam and openings on lace with tape cut from lightweight lining or bias binding cut from nude silk organza or any sheer fabric. If an embellished fabric or knit is heavily beaded, tape shoulder seams, neck and openings.

Napped and Pile Fabrics

These fabrics can be woven or knitted, are soft to the touch and vary in weight; they are one-directional because the raised surface reflects light differently depending on the way they are viewed. The napping process was originally used to soften wool fabrics but now may be applied to cotton and man-made fibres; popular napped fabrics include melton, flannel and fleece. Pile fabrics are normally thick, warm and sometimes heavy and are made from man-made or natural fibres; popular cut pile fabrics include corduroy, plush, velour, velvet and velveteen. Loop pile fabrics include airloop, bouclette, chinchilla fabric, frotte, Montagnac and towelling. Tufted fabrics, such as fabric fur or candlewick, have a pile inserted with needles into a base fabric.

Garments

Napped and pile fabrics are used for all garment types and also for lingerie, accessories and trims. Flannel and melton are traditionally made into outerwear. Velvet is often made into eveningwear and velour into suits, jackets, coats and dresses. Corduroy is a very durable pile fabric popular for casual wear. Frotte and towelling are looped pile fabrics with maximum moisture absorbency, ideal for casual clothing, bathrobes and towels. Fabric fur is suitable for outerwear, and fleece or polar fleece are often used for sportswear, outerwear and casual wear.

Weave, treatment and finish

The napping process – which can be applied to one or both fabric sides – brings fibre ends to the surface to be brushed flat, clipped or left raised. Pile fabrics may be woven with an extra warp or weft yarn taken over a rod or wire to form loops; when the rods or wires are removed the surface loops are cut to create pile or left for loop-back fabric. Another technique is to weave a double cloth with an extra warp yarn interchanging between layers; the connecting warp yarn is then cut between the layers creating a dense pile on both surfaces (some velvets are produced this way). Loops can also be created by floating an extra weft yarn on the fabric surface.

Velvet trousers with giant side pockets giving an unusual silhouette, and a waistband with fly zip construction. Jean Paul Gaultier Haute Couture, AW 2013.

VELVET

Velvet has been in and out of fashion but is always suitable for special garments because of its luxurious texture and soft hand. It is a fabric with life because it moves in the cutting and sewing process; use tissue paper beneath to secure it when cutting and hand-tack before stitching seams.

What to consider when buying

- Buy extra length to allow for one-way layout.
- Check quality – hold the fabric up to the light and examine for flaws.
- Keep the fabric on a roll or hang by the selvedge; do not fold because wear shows first at fold lines.

Napped fabric

- Loosely woven and knitted fabrics will mat and pill more than tightly woven types.
- Rub right sides together on a corner and then shake to see if fibres shed. Examine the surface for pilling.

Pile fabric

- Good-quality pile fabric is defined by fibre content, closeness of weave and density, lustre and evenness of pile.
- Pile fabrics including nylon are easier to manufacture and resist wrinkling.
- Rub right sides together on a corner and then shake to see if fibres shed. Examine for fraying or flaking.
- A W-shaped pile construction – instead of a V-shape – will be more durable because threads pass under-over-under interlacing yarns.

DUFFLE

Duffle is a heavyweight, woven wool fabric with a dense nap on both sides, originating from Duffle outside Antwerp in Belgium. It is hardwearing and waterproof and is traditionally made into a short 'duffle' coat that features a hood, a yoke over the shoulder from front to back, two patch pockets and a toggle fastening. The duffle coat was first worn by the British Royal Navy sailors in World War I.

Designer version of a classic duffle coat in pure felted wool. Burberry Prorsum, Fall 2011.

Single-breasted panne velvet jacket. Panne velvet is a type of crushed velvet with the pile pressed in one direction. Gucci, AW 2010.

Pattern Cutting

- Mark the direction of the grain line clearly on each pattern piece.

Napped fabric
- Use any design shape. With medium- to heavyweight fabrics simple designs with loose fit work best.

Pile fabric
- Designs with simple lines and loosely fitted shapes work best.
- Some beautiful evening dresses are tightly fitted on the bodice – underlay the fabric to support seams, avoiding seam slippage.

- Make a toile to refine the shape – too much handling can spoil the final fabric and holes cannot always be removed if seams are altered.
- Add generous seam allowances to the pattern; pile fabric can fray badly.

Cutting Out

Preparation

- Pre-shrink the fabric lightly before cutting; avoid over-pressing, use steam if appropriate. Take extra care not to crush pile fabric.
- Stroke with your hand parallel to the selvedge; it will feel smooth with the nap or pile, and rough stroking against it. Mark the direction onto the wrong side.
- Pile fabric looks lighter, with more shine, with the nap running down, and darker and richer the other way. Decide the nap direction for the finished design before cutting out pattern pieces.
- Velvet looks more luxurious with the nap running up; but with the nap running down less abrasion means longer-lasting pile.
- Use the lengthwise straight grain; avoid the crosswise grain or bias cutting.
- Avoid too much handling – some fabrics are marred by fingermarks and tend to fray.
- Always cut in the direction of the nap.
- Remove pins straight after cutting out to avoid leaving marks.

Layout

- Use a one-way pattern layout so all pattern pieces face one direction.
- Most napped fabrics can be cut on a double layer. Some, such as velvet, should be cut on a single layer to avoid slippage. Reverse pattern pieces when cutting the second piece.
- For more information on layout for napped and pile fabrics see page 50.

Marking

- On both pile and napped fabric mark on the wrong side with chalk.
- Mark placement points on napped fabric with chalk or thread, or transfer with tracing paper.
- Use notches, clips or pins on napped fabric to mark points on the pattern edge.
- Some pile fabrics are easily damaged by pins so use fine pins or weigh down the pattern pieces.
- Placement points on pile fabric can be chalk or thread marked but keep notches to a minimum on the edge to avoid fraying.
- Two-sided pile fabric is difficult to mark – if chalk marks do not show, use safety or pearl-head pins and thread marking for placement points, and notches on the fabric edge.

Shears

- For napped fabrics use medium or large shears matched to the fabric weight.
- Use serrated shears or a rotary cutter for pile fabrics, or sharp shears when cutting a single layer.

Pressing

- Press in the direction of the nap.
- Press and steam seams as you go but avoid handling damp fabric – only move once it has cooled down.
- Avoid ironing from the right side – lightly steam if necessary, without touching the fabric with the iron.
- Use only the tip of the iron along the seam, then press lightly with your fingertips to flatten the seam.
- Place a piece of self-fabric, right sides together, or a towel over or under napped fabric before pressing.
- Use a needle board – also called a velvet board – when pressing pile fabrics. Place the pile facing the needles so it sinks into the needle board, which stops the pile from crushing.
- Avoid impressions of construction elements showing on the right side by placing a piece of paper between them and the garment before pressing.

TIP

If pile has been crushed, use the steam from the iron directed lightly against the nap to lift the pile. To revive pile fabric, hang it in a steamy bathroom.

To restore a shiny surface caused by pressing, some napped fabrics can be lightly sprayed with water and brushed with a clothes brush. Alternatively, try lightly steaming from the right side of the fabric without the iron touching the garment.

 # Sewing

Hand-sewing needle

- Use a sharps needle for most hand-sewing tasks.
- For blanket stitching with yarn instead of thread use a chenille or embroidery needle.

Machine needles

- Use a universal sharp point needle, size 70/10 to 100/16 depending on fabric weight and texture.

Stitching size

- For napped fabric use a 2.5–3.5mm stitch.
- For most pile fabric use a 2–3mm stitch.
- When stitching thick pile fabric use a 3–3.5mm stitch.
- Topstitching on both nap and pile should be 3.5–5mm depending on design style, fabric weight and quality.

Avoiding stitching problems

- Always hand-tack seam layers before stitching to avoid shifting. Tack within the seam allowance to avoid marks.
- Reduce the pressure on the presser foot to avoid pile damage.
- Loosen the thread tension slightly.
- Do stitching tests first on a scrap of the garment fabric.
- Stitch with the nap direction.
- If the seam puckers or shifts, try reducing the pressure on the pressure foot and/or reduce the needle-thread tension. Alternatively, try an even (walking) or roller foot, which feed both layers of fabric through the machine at the same speed.
- When topstitching on the right side, check for presser-foot marks. To avoid marks place a layer of tissue paper between the fabric and the foot and remove after stitching.

Thread

- For most machine-sewing tasks use cotton-wrapped polyester or polyester thread, matched to the fabric weight.
- For fabrics with silk use mercerized cotton, or silk thread for hand sewing.
- Use thicker or topstitching thread for topstitching in a matching or contrasting colour.

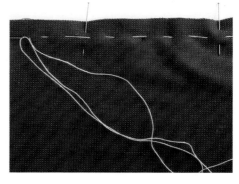

Pin and hand-tack the seam allowance on velvet, velveteen or corduroy before stitching.

Construction

Seams

The type of seam and seam finish depends on the fabric weight, structure and garment design. Some napped fabrics do not fray and can be cut with pinking shears or have a raw edge finish. All woven napped fabrics can be stitched with a plain seam; for knitted napped fabrics see Knitted and Stretch-Woven Fabrics, page 254. Depending on the design, you can also use a flat fell seam, welt seam or topstitching for a casual look.

Some pile fabrics fray badly because the short pile fibres are released from the surface after cutting, so clean up the cutting edge before stitching the pieces together. All woven pile fabrics can be stitched with a plain seam. For a quick finish use overlocking, which adds the least bulk to the seam edge or for a quality finish, use a bound edge. For a casual look on fabrics such as corduroy use a flat fell, topstitched or welt seam.

Some napped fabrics are non-fray so the slot, lapped or tucked seam (see both, below) and welt seam (see page 129) can be used for a decorative seam finish.

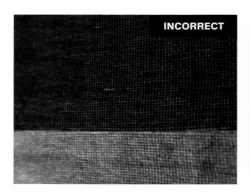

Take care of the nap/direction when sewing velvet seams.

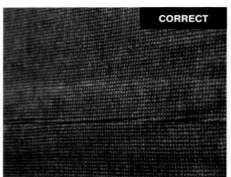

An overlocked plain seam on velvet.

Slot seam

1. Cut a 3cm (1⅛in) wide strip of fabric the length of your seam to use as an under layer.

2. Turn under the seam allowance on both sides of the garment pieces to be sewn together. Press.

3. Place the turned-under edges of both garment pieces, right side up, on the centre of the strip, also right side up. For a slot seam, place the edges against each other. For an open-slot seam, leave a gap between the edges, ensuring the gap is even along the length of the seam.

4. Topstitch each side of the garment pieces to the strip.

Lapped or tucked seam

1. Turn under the seam allowance on one of the garment pieces to be sewn together. Press.

2. Place the folded edge on the seam line of the other garment piece.

3. Topstitch down the folded edge.

Slot seam.

Open-slot seam.

Lapped or tucked seam.

Hemming

Test hem finishing ideas on a test garment before applying to the final garment. If the fabric is too heavy for a turned hem, use hem-tape or a lighter fabric alternative to face the hemline, both to avoid bulk and stop the hem from showing on the right side. Most napped fabrics can be topstitched or finished with a hand-sewn hem finish. Be generous when adding the hem allowance – small turn-ups look cheap. Hems on pile fabrics are best hand stitched with silk thread and a fine sharps needle.

Some pile fabrics benefit from adding a bias strip of sewn-in interfacing between the hemline and garment to reduce wrinkling, add body and prevent the hem from showing through on the right side. For more information see Hemlines, page 204.

Hand-sewn hemlines
When hemming a napped or pile fabric by hand, use an invisible hemming stitch for woven fabric and herringbone stitch for fabric with stretch (see pages 116–17).

Edge finish

Consider the garment design when choosing an edge finish; possible options include ribbing, tape or binding, or blanket stitching on woollen napped fabrics. Facings can be used but some napped and pile fabrics are bulky; try cutting the facing from a lighter-weight fabric. Alternatively, line the garment to the edge.

Interfacing, underlaying and lining

Interfacing on napped fabrics can be sew-in or fusible, while for most pile fabrics a sew-in type is best. For more information on interfacings see Supporting Materials, page 91.

Interfacing or underlaying napped and pile fabrics will support the garment shape and help stop construction elements showing on the right side. On a semi-fitted or fitted garment it is advisable to underlay pile fabrics, such as velvet or velveteen, both to support seams and add body and quality. Garments such as jackets and coats benefit from stabilizing the shoulder seam and neckline with iron-on or sew-in tape applied before sewing the seam. Jackets, coats, trousers, skirts and dresses are likely to be fully or half lined. Consider bagging certain parts, such as the underside of a collar, cuffs or pocket flaps, with lining to eliminate bulk.

Fastening

Use a loop fastening with decorative buttons on fine pile fabrics such as silk velvet, or a concealed zip finish for an invisible fastening option. Any casual fastening – zips, magnets, press-studs, buttonholes with button – works well on medium- to heavyweight napped and pile fabrics. Research traditional fastening options, such as the toggle button and loop fastening on the duffle coat.

TIP

For more stability on both napped and pile fabrics use a taped seam finish (see page 139).

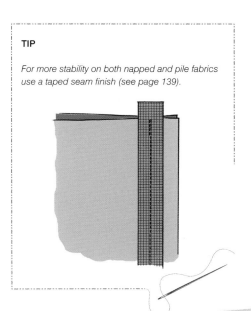

Leather and Fur

Leather is the natural skin of an animal, either hides from larger animals like the cow, or skins from smaller animals such as the sheep. Fur is animal skin with hair still attached. This section also covers imitation leather, suede and fur. Real fur has become widely unpopular due to concerns about animal welfare, but fake fur – also called fabric fur – is now so advanced that it can be mistaken for the real thing. The same is true of fake leather – also called leatherette or faux leather – which is less expensive, lighter in weight, often more flexible and comes by the metre. Faux suede became popular in the early seventies when American fashion designer Halston created his Ultrasuede® shirtdress.

Layered cropped jacket in a selection of bright-coloured real fur, teamed with a fur clutch bag. Fendi, AW 2013.

Garments

Leather is flexible, windproof, breathable and can be waterproofed, so it is ideal for outerwear as well as for other clothing and accessories. Suede is softer and thinner with better drape and is also used for garments and accessories, or it can be cut into strips and knitted. Real fur and fabric fur are used in garments for warmth, sometimes as a lining, or as a luxurious trim on collar and cuffs. Fur can be combined with leather or suede – for example the body of a jacket could be fur and the sleeves leather, or it could have alternate bands of leather or suede with fur. Outer garments may be constructed with the leather side on the outside and the fur facing the body – these garments are often reversible.

Treatment and finish

The skin of leather and fur is stabilized chemically to make it supple and to prevent decomposition; for leather this is called 'tanning' and for fur 'dressing'.

Leather

Leather comes from almost any animal or reptile – common sources are the cow, pig, goat, lamb, deer, horse, crocodile, snake and elk – and can also be taken from fish. Thick leather can be split into layers – the top grain or outer layer is leather and the inside layer becomes suede. Suede may be split cowhide or suede calfskin, lambskin or pigskin. Split cowhide is coarse and brushed and mostly used for accessories and casual wear. Suede calfskin, lambskin and pigskin are finer, thinner and napped and are used for luxurious items. Finishing techniques can be applied to leather to enhance the look and reflect current fashion trends – some designers work directly with leather suppliers to create their own techniques.

Embossing: A process where the skin is embossed with patterns using metal plates. A common pattern choice is to imitate the skin patterns of endangered animal skin, such as elephant and alligator. Decorative all-over patterns are also available.

Printing: Designs can imitate both fabric patterns and distressing for a vintage look.

Dyeing: Skins can be dyed in any colour.

Laser cutting: This can be used to create intricate lacy patterns.

Embroidery and *appliqué:* Applied techniques add texture – other such techniques include smocking, crocheting, painting, tie-dyeing, pleating, patchwork and lacing.

Moulding: Leather can be formed into a shape.

Foil overlays: These can be used to create metallic leather.

Patent leather: This has been varnished to a high gloss or treated with waterproof film on one surface.

Buffed: Nubuck is leather with the grain side buffed to look like suede.

Brushed: Suede can be brushed and napped for a softer texture.

Fur

Fur comes from animals such as the beaver, chinchilla, fox, goat, mink, otter and rabbit. Real fur can be bleached, sheared, stencilled, dyed or feathered in the dressing process to soften and preserve it. Fabric fur is a pile fabric with a long nap and pronounced nap direction; the pile is usually synthetic staple fibres secured in a backing fabric, which might be woven, knitted, tufted or stitch-bonded. The pile can vary in colour and length and the fabric can be dyed, printed or given a special textural finish to imitate animal fur.

What to consider when buying

- If possible, purchase in person and do your homework to be sure you get the skin you asked for – some traders might try to sell one skin as another.
- Shop around and compare prices; these materials can be expensive so it is worth going to suppliers instead of retail outlets.

- Leather, suede and fur are sold by the individual skin – the size of animal defines the skin size.
- Faux leather and suede and fabric fur come by the metre and will be consistent in colour, thickness and texture so less material is needed.

Leather, suede and faux leather

- Smell the skin – improperly tanned skin has a bad odour.
- Hold the skin up to the light and look for scars, holes, shading and discolouration.
- Select skins that weigh the same for one garment.
- Take all pattern pieces with you to be sure to buy enough skins.
- Leather and suede skins have imperfections that will influence pattern layout.
- If mixing colours rub a white cloth on the skins; if the colour transfers there will be a problem with colour bleeding.

Fur and fabric fur

- Consider recycling existing garments from family, friends or second-hand shops.

> **TIP**
>
> Matching issues can cause considerable waste, but keep scraps for future projects; leather scraps can be used as binding, pockets or a collar to enhance another garment and smaller scraps used for accessories, appliqué or trims.

Coloured leather dress with matching belt. The seams and hems are glued, rather than topstitched, for a clean look. Jean Paul Gaultier Couture Collection, AW 2013.

Pattern Cutting

Working in leather, suede or fur is labour-intensive; take your time and research material-specific finishing techniques. The pattern may need more seam lines than for woven fabric because seam placement will be determined by skin size, which should be considered in the garment design. Make a test garment in woven fabric the same weight as the final material – cut on the bias if the hide or skin has a lot of give – and draw or mark seam lines with style line tape to see if seams joining pieces together can be hidden or placed as part of the design.

- Avoid placing joining lines at stress points and consider aesthetic placement on the body.
- Choose seam, edge and hem finish and alter the pattern accordingly. Generally, seam allowances are 8–10mm (5⁄16–3⁄8in); for bagged out seams allow 5mm (3⁄16in).
- Reset marking points within the pattern piece so they will be hidden after construction.
- Avoid too much ease; for example, on a sleeve reduce to 2.5cm (15⁄16in) at most.
- Avoid designs with gathers.
- Copy paper patterns onto card for ease of marking and better cutting stability.

Leather, suede and faux leather
- Fabric fur and faux leather has a grain direction; mark the grain line on each pattern piece.
- Suede has a nap; mark the direction on each pattern piece.

Fur and fabric fur
- Avoid double-breasted or wrap-over designs, which add bulk at centre front.
- Some long-hair fur looks better when the hair falls against the grain, so decide which way the hair should fall on the garment before marking the grain/nap direction.

Cutting Out

Preparation

- Allow extra time when cutting out leather and fur. Faux leather and suede and fabric fur come by the metre, so are less time-consuming.
- Double-check all pattern pieces are correctly placed before cutting out.
- Leather, faux leather and suede do not need pre-shrinking or pressing. Fabric fur can be lightly pressed from the wrong side before cutting out.
- Straighten the material out to lie flat on the cutting surface.
- Small fur skins must be joined before pattern pieces are laid out.

Layout

- Cut out in a single layer. Duplicate all pattern pieces to be cut out twice.
- Place the pattern onto the right side or outside of the skin so flaws can be spotted and avoided.
- Suede, fabric fur and real fur have a nap, so cut out in a one-way layout.
- Faux leather has a grain direction but no nap. Pattern pieces can be placed both ways.
- Leather has no grain line, but place pattern pieces lengthwise; the width has more give. Some areas of the skin stretch more than others. Keep such areas away from garment stress points.

- On leather, faux leather and suede use weights or tape to hold pattern pieces in place; avoid pins, which will leave holes.
- On fur use weights to hold pattern pieces in place or tape them to the skin side.
- On fabric fur pin pattern pieces down using pearl-head or T-head pins.
- On leather and suede match colour, thickness and texture of related/duplicated pattern pieces – for example, sleeves must be the same weight/thickness.

TIP

When cutting out fur and fabric fur make sure you only cut the skin or backing fabric, not the hair. On real fur try sliding the blade of your cutting tool along the skin to push the hair out of the way. Take your time – there is not much you can do if hair has been cut accidentally.

Marking

- Use waterproof marking pen or chalk on the right side of leather, faux leather and suede and on the wrong side of fur and fabric fur. Do not use ink pen.
- Cut out inside the marking line to avoid adding extra width and length.
- Mark placement points within the pattern piece with chalk or an awl.
- If using an awl reset marking points to be hidden on the finished item: mark pocket positions 5mm (³⁄₁₆in) inside the pocket edge so the pocket covers the holes, move the end of a dart point 5mm (³⁄₁₆in) inwards so the marking is included within the stitching.
- Edge markings can be clipped or notched.

Shears

- For leather and suede use a short knife such as a craft, Stanley knife or scalpel so blades can be replaced easily when blunt. Alternatively, use heavyweight, sharp shears or a rotary cutter.
- Once all pieces are cut out, roll them up loosely and tie together or store lying flat on a surface until ready for construction. Do not store them folded, as the creases along the fold line may not come out.
- On faux leather and suede use sharp shears matched to the weight of the material, or a rotary cutter.
- Cut fur and fabric fur with a scalpel, Stanley knife or razor blade.

Pressing

- Leather and suede are extremely heat sensitive and should not be touched directly with an iron – always place heavy paper over the garment and use a low temperature. Do not steam or use a pressing cloth and do not rest the iron on one spot, which can create permanent markings. To flatten seams, darts and hems use topstitching and gluing.
- Faux leather and faux suede can be lightly pressed with paper or self-fabric between the iron and the material. Under-press or put a strip of paper under seams and darts to prevent an imprint showing on the right side.
- Real fur should not be pressed; seam allowances can be hand stitched down to flatten.
- Fur fabric can be lightly pressed from the wrong side at a low temperature. Test on a sample piece and avoid crushing the pile.

 # Sewing

Hand-sewing needle

- For leather, suede, faux leather and suede and fur use a leather glover needle size 2–8, matched to the material weight. Use size 2 for sewing on buttons.
- For fabric fur use a sharps needle, matching the size to the job at hand.
- Use a thimble.

Machine needles

- For leather, suede, faux leather and suede and fur use a leather needle matched to the material weight. The most common size is 16 or 18, with tri-point or diamond-point needles on industrial sewing machines.
- For fabric fur use a universal machine needle for woven backing fabrics and a ballpoint needle for knitted backing fabrics.

Stitching size

- Use a stitch size of 2.5–3mm; smaller stitches will cause tearing at the stitching line.

Thread

- On leather, suede and real fur use polyester thread – avoid silk, cotton or cotton-wrapped threads because chemical treatments on the skin rot them.
- Consider topstitching or three-cord thread for stitching seams on thick leather.
- Use topstitching thread for all topstitching.
- On faux leather and suede and fabric fur use either polyester thread or cotton-wrapped polyester thread.
- Wax the thread for hand sewing, such as for sewing on buttons.

Avoiding stitching problems

- Avoid backstitching; it cuts the leather. To secure stitching tie off the threads.
- If the presser foot leaves marks, reduce the pressure or change to a roller or Teflon foot for leather/suede or a roller or even feed (walking) foot for fur.
- To help the material glide smoothly, place tissue paper between garment and the machine while stitching.
- Change to a new machine needle to resolve skipped stitches.
- If stitches skip when sewing over a thick seam, place a piece of folded card or fabric under the end of the presser foot to level out with the seam and operate the sewing machine with the hand-wheel for better control.

Construction

Seams

For sample construction, choose a sewing machine that can stitch the weight and thickness of the material – it must be able to tackle several layers. An industrial flatbed machine or leather-sewing machine is best – a domestic sewing machine might not be up to the task. To hold seams together before sewing use paper clips or bulldog clips. It is essential to test stitching ideas on a scrap of the final material. Establish the stitching order and style – especially when sewing leather and faux leather, because stitching holes will be permanent. These materials do not fray so seam edges do not need finishing.

Leather and faux leather

For light- to medium-weight materials use a plain seam; on heavyweight material use a lapped seam to avoid bulk (see page 280). For a decorative seam finish choose a welt or slot seam (see pages 129 and 280). Compared to some leather, suede is thinner and easier to sew.

Some seams may need reinforcing with tape for extra stability (see page 139). Seams on leather and faux leather cannot be pressed so pound flat with a cloth-covered hammer, then either topstitch the seam allowance down or glue in place. Use leather glue or a latex-based rubber cement, which is more flexible – apply with a brush and use a roller tool to flatten the seam.

Turned-back sleeve cuff on a shearling coat. The cuff can also be turned down for a simple raw edge finish.

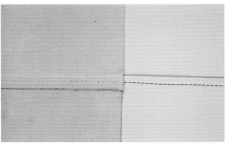

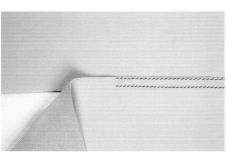

Top: Leather/non-woven flat fell seam.
Above: Non-woven lapped seam.

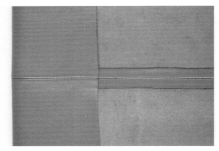

Top: Non-woven taped seam with edge stitching.
Above: A plain seam with a glued seam allowance.

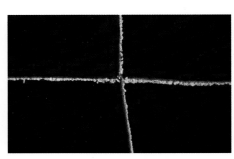

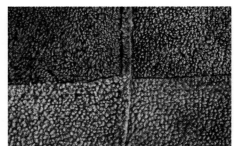

Top: Seam on a shearling leather coat showing the leather side with a raw edge lapped seam finish.
Above: The fur side of the raw edge lapped seam finish.

Darts

Darts are stitched, cut open and topstitched or glued down to reduce bulk.

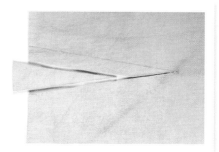

For a **Lapped Dart** finish, cut out allowance on one side of the dart leg and leave 1cm (⅜in) allowance on the other side to overlap.

Overlap the dart legs and edge stitch from the right side of the garment.

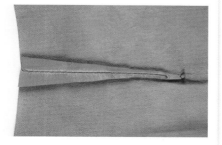

Alternatively, you can close up the dart, sew it on the wrong side, cut it open and glue the allowance down.

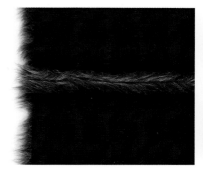

Plain seam.

Trapped hair pulled out with a pin.

FUR AND FABRIC FUR

Real fur should not be pressed; seams and darts are hand stitched down to flatten them. Use a plain seam but first push the hair towards the garment to avoid it being caught in the stitching. Stitch the seam with the pile on the wrong side and then turn to the right side and use a pin to carefully pull trapped hair out of the seam. Trim away hair on the seam allowance to avoid bulk.

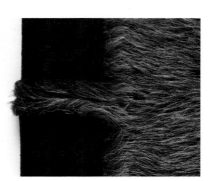

Plain seam, wrong and right side.

Fabric fur seam with zigzag stitch.

Hemming

Leather and faux leather

Hemlines can be topstitched or glued into place; first pound the hemline to establish a fold line. If the garment is lined, only glue along the fold so the hem edge is free to stitch the lining onto – if applying topstitching attach the lining first and then topstitch. If the leather is very heavy use a raw edge finish and for a decorative finish consider a wrong-side-out hem or a contrast facing, tape or ribbing. On a curved hemline use a facing or turn up the hem, then snip small wedges from full areas and bring the cut edges together. Faux leather and faux suede can also be turned up and hand stitched.

Fur and fabric fur

Use a facing or tape to hem fur and fabric fur, because most fur materials are too bulky to turn up. The facing can be cut from leather or any other fabric that complements the fur material. Attach the hemline on fur with a hand stitched blind-hemstitch. For fabric fur use blind-hemstitch for a woven backing and a herringbone stitch for a knitted backing.

Applying tape as hem or edge finish

1 Move the hair out of the way and pin the tape right to the edge.

2 With the hair pushed away, hand stitch with an invisible stitch both sides of the tape onto the fur.

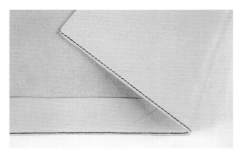

Edge stitching with topstitching thread stabilizes a raw edge. This finish can be used as a facing.

Edge finish

For leather, faux leather and suede, finish the edges with either a raw edge or contrast facing, tape, binding or ribbing. On fur and fabric fur avoid adding bulk by using edge-to-edge lining, binding, contrast facings, tape or ribbing. Do not cut off the fur hair along edges and hemline, let it finish naturally.

Front row, left to right: roller to flatten seams, skiver knife to reduce bulk, Stanley knife and craft knife for cutting. Back row, left: adhesive to glue seams and hem allowances down; right, hammer device to flatten seams.

> **TIP**
>
> To reduce seam bulk on heavyweight leather use a skiver knife, but practise on a scrap piece first. Place the leather seam onto a flat surface. Hold the knife parallel to the surface on top of the seam allowance and apply even pressure to peel away wedge-shaped layers.

Patent leather biker jacket with a large plastic zip as a front fastener, by Julien Macdonald.

Lining, interfacing and interlining

Leather, suede and fur garments are usually lined or half lined for comfort, durability, to hide the inside and to prevent the garment from stretching out of shape. Consider bagging parts such as the underside of collars, cuffs or pocket flaps with a lighter-weight fabric, and lining hidden sections such as underneath the top yoke, because this will save money and make the garment lighter and less bulky. On outerwear interlinings can be added between garment and lining for additional warmth; consider ice-wool, wadding or thermal insulation materials. For more information see Lining fabrics, page 76. Reinforce shoulder seams, edges, necklines and fastening areas with tape to prevent stretching.

Leather, faux leather and suede
Interfacing is added to areas that stretch or are under stress, such as armholes, necklines, pocket openings, fastening areas, hemlines and edges. Also apply interfacing to collars, pocket welts/flaps/jets, lapels, vents, cuffs, tabs, waistbands and belts. Match the interfacing, which can be iron-on, to the weight, drape and type of skin – for example, on suede or soft leather use a tricot or knitted interfacing, which is soft and lightweight, adding body and support without restricting the drape of the material. Choose an iron-on interfacing with a low melting point.

Fur and fabric fur
Use a sew-in interfacing to support stress areas and apply stabilizer to collars, pocket welts/flaps/jets, lapels, vents, cuffs, tabs and belts.

Fastening

Thick and heavyweight materials should be matched with a sturdy fastening option; research iconic garments for inspiration.

Leather and faux leather
Jackets, coats and waistcoats can be fastened with a button with bound, in-seam or slash-stitched buttonholes or leather loop fastenings. Also popular are press-studs and zips, while lacing or a hook-and-eye fastening can work for some garment styles. For a concealed fastening consider Velcro or magnets. Attached belts may have a buckle, clasp or tab fastening.

Fur and fabric fur
Consider the length of the hair and match the fastening to the garment style. For long hair fur use a large, covered hook-and-eye or big leather buttons and loops – zips should not be used because the hair gets caught up in the teeth. For short hair fur most button and buttonhole options are possible and a zip can be tried. Magnetic and press-studs are also an option, and large hooks-and-eyes or frogging. For more information refer to Haberdashery, page 80.

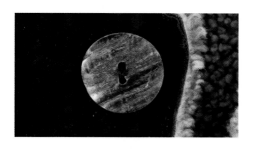

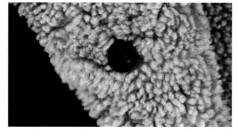

Left: Shearling fur coat by Bradley Snowden with horn toggles and leather pocket welts and toggle fastenings.

Right: When sewing a button fastening onto a heavy leather or fur, use a backing button: a horn button fastener (above) and the inside of the garment showing the backing button (below).

Felted and Non-Woven Fabrics

Felting is the oldest known method of producing a non-woven fabric. Felt can be made of different fibres; the best quality is wool. Felt has no grain direction and the denser it is the stiffer it will be. It does not fray, but is easily damaged because it has no stretch or recovery. Felted woven or knitted fabrics are given a special treatment to produce a matt surface with a nap. Traditionally made of wool and animal hair, they drape better than felt and are more resistant to abrasion. These fabrics are worn for warmth and are generally medium- to heavyweight.

Garments

Felt is used mostly for one-off items and can inspire experimental shapes; because of its ability to mould, it is also a favourite material for hats and other accessories. Other uses include theatrical costumes, appliqué and as interlining or padding. Faux suede and spunlace are also produced using fibre-massing techniques and have the same qualities and usage as felt. However, felted fabric has a woven or knitted fabric base and therefore has the character of a structured fabric. This makes it suitable for most garments. Its insulating properties create beautifully warm garments. Felted fabrics, such as boiled wool, duffle, loden and melton, are also water-resistant and therefore perfect for outerwear.

Felt fabric lends itself to sculptural showpieces. Comme des Garçons, AW 2012.

Treatment and finish

Wool fibre or animal hair is used for traditional felting, in which the application of heat, moisture and friction is used to compress and shrink fibres into an interlocking mass. Another technique is needle-felting, in which loose fibres are interlocked mechanically using barbed needles – this method can also be used on man-made fibres, cotton, rayon or waste fibres. Felted woven or knitted fabrics are fulled while immersed in a soap solution – heat, moisture and mechanical compressing causes the fibres to interlock together to create a felted surface. The original fabric, which can be made of animal fibre, wool or blends, shrinks by 20–50% in the process, which obscures the weave/knit construction and produces a dense surface and thicker fabric.

 ## Pattern Cutting

Designs with simple lines and loosely fitted shapes work best. Delete seam allowances if the edge will be left raw or bound.

Felt

- Use minimal seams; felt tears easily.
- To add volume use gathers and pleats.
- One-off garments do not require lining, interfacing or facing patterns.
- Felt has no grain; mark the lengthwise grain on pattern pieces for information.

Felted fabric

- For heavyweight fabrics avoid designs with gathers or pleats – use darts or seams for shaping to eliminate bulk.
- Some felted fabrics have a nap; mark the nap direction onto the pattern.

Hooded cape in melton wool, a water-resistant, felted wool with good insulation. Christopher Raeburn, AW 2011.

Cutting Out

Preparation

- These fabrics can shrink badly if not treated, so pre-shrink.
- Iron and steam consistently so all areas shrink equally.

Layout

- Place the pattern onto the wrong side.
- Pattern pieces can be laid in any direction on felt without affecting the garment hang, so place for most economical usage.
- For felted fabric with a nap use a one-way pattern layout, either single or double layer depending on fabric weight.

Marking

- It is difficult to identify right and wrong sides on these fabrics so mark each piece on the wrong side with chalk or on the right side with a safety pin – decide on one method and stick to it.
- Mark with chalk.
- Placement points can be thread or chalk marked on the wrong side.

Shears

- Use sharp, medium to large shears, to suit the fabric weight.

Pressing

- These fabrics react well to heat and steam and are easily moulded. This means they are also easily deformed, so press with care using as little moisture/ steam as possible.
- Test temperature on a sample piece and avoid heavy pressing.
- Avoid moving the fabric immediately after pressing – allow it to cool first.
- When pressing from the right side, use a pressing cloth to protect the surface.
- Some felted fabrics have a nap – use self-fabric or a towel to protect the nap, and iron in the direction of the nap. See Napped and Pile Fabrics, page 276, for more information.

Sewing

Hand-sewing needle

- For most tasks use a sharps needle.
- For blanket stitching, or when using yarn instead of thread, use a chenille or embroidery needle.

Machine needles

- On felt and woven felt fabrics use a universal sharp point needle, size 70/10 to 100/16, matching the size to fabric weight and structure.
- On boiled wool or fleece knitted fabrics use a ballpoint needle, sizes 70/10 to 90/14.

Stitching size

- For medium-weight fabric use a stitch size of 2.5–3mm.
- For heavyweight fabric use a stitch size of 3–3.5mm.
- Topstitching on felt or felted fabric should be 3.5–5mm, depending on design and fabric quality.

Avoiding stitching problems

- Loosen the thread tension slightly.
- Reduce the pressure on the presser foot for thick fabrics.
- If the fabric shows a nap, stitch with the nap direction.
- Test stitching on a fabric scrap first; mistakes cannot be mended.
- Some felted fabrics, such as fleece or boiled wool, have a stretch; use a 4- or 5-thread overlocker or a cover

stitch machine. On a domestic sewing machine, use a slight zigzag stitch or stretch the fabric slightly when stitching the seam.
- Use super fine pins in the seam allowance to secure seams on felt before stitching or use clips – felt tears easily.
- On thick felted fabric use extra long pins.

Thread

- Use all-purpose cotton, cotton-wrapped polyester or polyester thread, matched to the fabric weight. For topstitching use machine embroidery or topstitching thread, or experiment with metallic or silk threads.

Construction

Seams

Felt and felted fabrics do not fray and hardly ever need an edge finish, which makes them easy to sew and allows for interesting and decorative seam finishes. Use a plain seam for a quick finish or any tricky areas. For a decorative edge finish use a pinked seam, any type of topstitching or construct the seams wrong-side-out – let your imagination take over and design a seam finish to suit your garment. Always experiment on a sample of the final fabric before cutting out pattern pieces, because seam finishes require different seam allowances.

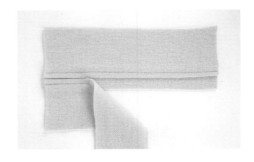

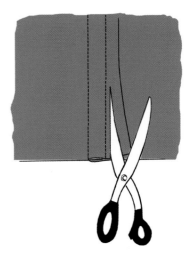

Above: Abutted seams are a good choice for a decorative finish, and similar to a slot seam (see page 280). The garment pieces have no seam allowance and the raw edges are aligned over the centre of the backing strip.

Above right: Avoid bulky seams such as the flat fell; use a non-woven flat fell, welt or lapped seam instead, which are suitable for unlined outerwear or casual wear. On a non-woven flat fell seam, instead of turning the uncut seam edge under, to enclose the trimmed edge, topstitch in place to cover the trimmed seam allowance and then trim the raw edge close to the topstitching.

Darts

Darts can be bulky in felt and felted fabrics. For a flatter finish, slash and press the dart open or cut the dart contents down to a centimetre each side and overlap and secure with a topstitch.

1 If the fabric is very heavy, cut all allowance out of the dart and bring the dart edge-to-edge. **2** Then place a tape behind the dart on the wrong side of the garment. **3** Either topstitch or zigzag stitch the dart onto the tape.

To secure seams on felt before stitching use super fine pins only in the seam allowance or clips, as felt tears easily. Always do stitching samples, as felt cannot be mended.

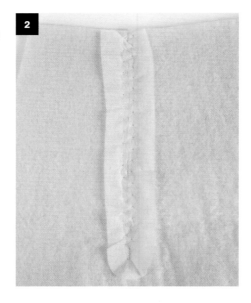

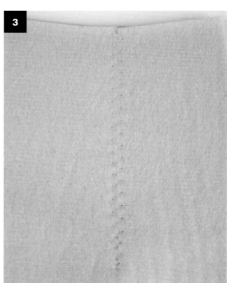

Hemming

The hem can be left raw with a clean cut edge or turned under and topstitched, hand sewn or fused in place. When choosing a hem finish consider fabric weight and garment design – avoid double-turned hems on heavyweight fabrics, only turn once to reduce the bulk. To finish the edge on a single-turn hem, add a binding and secure with hand sewing or topstitching. Be generous when considering the hemline – deep hems work best on heavyweight fabrics. Use a raw edge finish on shaped hemlines, or a facing. To avoid adding bulk with a self-fabric, consider using a lighter contrast fabric. For a different look try a wrong-side-out hem finish, blanket stitching or a contrast trim.

Edge finish

Since these fabrics do not fray, edges can be left unfinished, although it is advisable to strengthen edges subject to stress, such as necklines, armholes and pocket openings. Choose an edge finish to suit the garment design and fabric structure. If the fabric is not too thick a self-fabric facing gives a clean finish; on a heavier fabric use a lightweight fabric facing. Try different facing options such as an outside or decorative facing. For a decorative edge finish consider binding, ribbon or braid; try using a contrast colour or texture, such as leather or suede binding. A blanket-stitch finish is popular on woollen wrap skirts or blanket-style jackets and coats – use wool yarn to add extra stability and try a contrast colour to highlight the garment edge. For a clean cut or raw edge finish delete the seam allowance but consider topstitching for extra stability.

Linings and interfacings

Felt garments are mostly one-offs and do not require lining or interfacing, but felted fabric garments are likely to be fully lined or half-lined. Consider bagging out the underside of collar, cuffs or pocket flaps with a lighter fabric to reduce bulk. Garments such as jackets and coats benefit from stabilizing on the shoulder seam and neckline – use iron-on or sew-in tape applied before sewing the seam. Interfacing is added to areas that stretch, are under stress or which need extra structure. Interfacing felted fabric will support the garment shape and help to prevent seams, darts and hemlines from showing on the right side.

Fastening

Research iconic garments and analyse fastening ideas. The fastenings on felted knits or fleece fabrics are best applied to a firmer trim, tape or braid. Most blazer-style garments fasten with buttons and machine or bound buttonholes; metallic buttons give a military feel and wooden or horn buttons a rustic look. A more casual alternative would be a press-stud or zip – or for a concealed fastening try sew-in magnets or Velcro. For a different look consider tab and buckle closures or a duffle coat toggle and loop – particularly for garments with hoods. Capes and big wrap-around jackets and coats sometimes fasten with a belt only; add belt loops to the garment to keep the belt in place. To fasten the belt, choose from a variety of D-rings, buckles and clasps or bag out a strip of self-fabric for a tie-belt.

Latex, Neoprene and Plastic Materials

Fashion designers such as Thierry Mugler, Atsuko Kudo and Gareth Pugh are well known for their love of coated and rubber materials. Such materials invite creative development in cut and construction and most fashion students feel drawn to them. Latex, neoprene and PVC materials are tricky to cut and sew and require a range of specialist tools. Before attempting the challenge, research and purchase the equipment and be prepared to practise techniques.

Latex coat with a two-colour latex layover. The layers and seams are glued together. Designed by Itziar Vaquer.

Garments

Latex or rubber sheeting creates attention-grabbing garments. It can be used for everything from outerwear to lingerie and for everyday items – use talcum powder inside a garment to make it easier to put on. Neoprene is popular for winter and water-sport garments, as well as protective or orthopaedic clothing. It is also a great material for experimenting with shapes and silhouettes. PVC-coated fabrics can be worked into many designs; corsets, jeans, off-the-hip trousers, skirts, dresses and bomber jackets all look great in shiny material. For garments that require some stretch, 2-way stretch PVC is appropriate, while 4-way stretch PVC is good for swimsuits, lingerie and fitted and semi-fitted garments in general. PVC-coated fabrics are also used for protective wear.

Material construction, treatment and finish

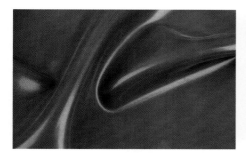

Latex

Latex, the trademark name for a natural rubber made from milky white plant juice, is a very stretchy waterproof material. The sheets come in different thicknesses and colours and with a flat or textured surface. Rubber fibres are used with other fibres to make stretchy woven or knitted fabrics and for elastic sewing tape. Rubber can also be applied in liquid form to fabrics as a protective coating, creating waterproof and durable surfaces, or produced as lightweight foam that is laminated to other materials as an insulator. Latex sheets have a layer of talcum powder applied on both sides to stop sheets from sticking to each other and silicone-based polish can be used to bring the surface to a shine.

Neoprene

Neoprene is a synthetic rubber material that is flexible, waterproof and durable with insulating properties. Neoprene sheet comes in different thicknesses and can be smooth or textured; it is laminated between two backing fabrics, usually warp-knitted tricot. Neoprene can also be applied in liquid form to woven, knitted or non-woven materials as a protective coating on one or both sides of the fabric.

Plastic materials

PVC stands for polyvinyl chloride, also called vinyl, a protective and water-resistant plastic. It is produced as a fine polymer sheet, as fibres or as a liquid to coat other fabrics. PVC-coated fabric is shiny and plastic on one side with a woven, knitted or non-woven backing fabric and may be non-stretch, 2-way stretch or 4-way stretch. The 2-way stretch is most common; it stretches more horizontally than vertically. The 4-way stretch version stretches equally in both directions.

What to consider when buying

- Creases cannot be ironed out since these materials are heat sensitive. Do not purchase them if folded.
- Do not store the materials folded; spread out on a flat surface or roll up onto a cardboard tube.

Neoprene coat by Meagan Wellman. The seams are sewn with a flat-lock finish and all edge finishes, such as the hemline, are turned under and glued.

Pattern Cutting

Latex
- Simple design shapes without darts work best.
- Any pattern for stretch material can be used.
- Make the seam allowance 4–5mm (⁵⁄₃₂–³⁄₁₆in) for glued seams and 1cm (³⁄₈in) for a plain seam.
- Eliminate fastenings and turn into a 'pull-on' garment if possible.
- If the design requires pockets, change inserted pockets into patch pockets or create faux pockets – pocket bags will not look good.
- If darts are required, cut excess material within the dart down to 2mm (³⁄₃₂in) at the dart point and 4mm (⁵⁄₃₂in) at the widest part.

Neoprene
- Any garment shape works with light- to medium-weight neoprene.
- Medium- to heavyweight neoprene can be used to create sculptural fashion pieces.
- Use simple shapes for heavyweight neoprene.
- Choose seam, edge and hem finishes and adjust the pattern pieces.

PVC
- Consider the stretch direction and degree when choosing the pattern – for semi-fitted and fitted garments use a stretch pattern.
- Determine which grain line has the most stretch. In general the greatest stretch goes across the body.
- Avoid any design element that needs pressing, such as pleats.
- Avoid darts as they will stand out, especially diagonal darts near the bust line. Try changing the dart direction to vertical or make the dart into a seam.
- Avoid garment designs with gathers and reduce ease from sleeve heads.
- Add an ease allowance when using a non-stretch PVC.
- Consider seam, edge and hem finishes and adjust the pattern pieces.

Cutting Out

Preparation

- It is not necessary to pre-shrink coated and rubber materials.
- When working with stretch PVC, ideally allow the material to lie flat on the cutting surface for 24 hours.

Layout

Latex
- Latex has no grain line and stretches in all directions so pattern pieces can be laid for economy.
- Cut in a single layer, wrong side up.
- When cutting out, cut in one continuous line.

Neoprene
- Consider the stretch direction; place pattern pieces for stretch in the right places such as at bust/chest, waist, knee and elbow.
- On a non-stretch neoprene pattern pieces can be laid in any direction.
- Pattern pieces can be pinned or weighed down.
- Cut in a single layer, right or wrong side up.

PVC
- Consider the stretch direction; place pattern pieces for stretch in the right places such as at bust/chest, waist, knee and elbow.
- On non-woven coated PVC, pattern pieces can be laid in any direction.
- The fusion of the PVC to the backing fabric can be less secure near the edge of the selvedge; if so lay pattern pieces a couple of centimetres away.
- Weigh down pattern pieces or tape with masking tape. Do not use pins, as pinholes are permanent.
- Cut in a single layer, right or wrong side up.

Marking

- On coated and rubber fabric reset marking points within the garment part so they will be hidden after garment construction.

- Cut out on the inside of the marking line to avoid adding extra width and length.

Latex
- Use a water-based marker on the wrong side.
- Do not clip edge marking points; mark notch positions with a water-based marker or biro.

Neoprene
- Use chalk or a disappearing marking pen.
- Edge marking points can be clipped with short cuts. Do not notch any edges to have a raw edge finish.

PVC
- Use chalk on the wrong side or a disappearing marking pen or water-soluble pen on the right side.
- Edge marking points can be clipped with short cuts. Do not notch any edges to have a raw edge finish.

Shears

- Cut latex with a rotary cutter. Small pieces can be cut with sharp shears and insertion cuts with a scalpel.
- For neoprene use sharp shears or a rotary cutter.

- Cut PVC with bent-handled, sharp shears or a rotary cutter. Stop regularly to allow the material to settle back into place.

Pressing

- Avoid pressing if possible.
- Latex, PVC and neoprene are very heat sensitive; do not touch with an iron.
- Set the iron on a low temperature and protect the material with paper between it and the iron.

Sewing

Hand-sewing needles

- For neoprene use a sharps needle, matching the size to material weight.
- For PVC use a sharps needle or leather hand-sewing needle with a thimble.

Machine needles

- Always start with a new needle. Change the needle every four hours for coated and rubber materials.
- It is not advisable to sew latex, but if necessary use a universal needle.
- Neoprene varies in thickness from 1.5–7mm (¹⁄₁₆–⁹⁄₃₂in) and larger needles work best. Try a size 100 denim/jeans needle for 2mm (³⁄₃₂in) thick neoprene.
- For PVC use a sharp machine needle or a leather machine needle, matching the size to the fabric weight.
- Do not use a ballpoint needle on PVC fabrics with a knitted backing fabric – it will tear holes in the coating.

Stitching size

- Latex is weakened by stitching holes so use a larger stitch size of 3.5–4mm.
- On neoprene a 3mm stitch length works best and for topstitching use 4–5mm. For zigzag stitching use the largest setting on the machine.
- For PVC use 2–3mm for seam construction and 3.5–4.5mm for topstitching.

Avoiding stitching problems

- Stitch with tissue paper over the material or decrease the pressure if the presser foot leaves marks.
- If the fabric sticks to the presser foot, change to a roller, even feed (walking) or Teflon foot; use talcum powder or stitch with tissue paper over the material. Also try silicone spray or needle lubricant.
- Clean the needle regularly with alcohol when sewing coated fabric.

- Avoid ripping and re-stitching and backstitching, because it cuts into the material. Tie off the thread after stitching to secure.
- Jackets and coats in these materials often have eyelets at the top of the underarm seam for ventilation. When applying eyelets or grommets to latex, back the area with fabric or tape first.
- PVC breaks thread very easily so check regularly to make sure you are still stitching with thread.

Thread

- On latex use polyester thread.
- For neoprene use heavy-duty nylon thread or polyester thread.
- On PVC use polyester thread to construct the garment, but try topstitching with rayon thread or embroidery thread, which have a shine that complements the material's shiny surface.

Construction

Seams

Seam finishing options for these unconventional fabrics should be tested on your own equipment to find what works best, because they are unforgiving of stitching mistakes. Keep the end use in mind when choosing a seam. Some seams may need taping to become waterproof.

Latex

Latex can be glued or sewn, but stitching holes weaken the material so sewing is not advisable. If sewing is necessary follow the tips on page 297 and place a tape or woven fabric strip under the latex seam for support.

Gluing latex successfully takes practice so try on scraps first. For a glued seam the seam allowance can vary: 8–10mm (⁵⁄₁₆–³⁄₈in) is the standard. Clean the seam area only, using solvent on a piece of cloth, then apply a thin layer of solvent or water-based glue using a broad-edged spatula or cotton bud. Let the glue dry for about 5 minutes, then overlap the seam allowance. It will take a while for the adhesive to dry. The edges will curl slightly once the glue has been applied; run a roller over the seam to flatten and seal it.

Neoprene

An industrial sewing machine is recommended to stitch neoprene. Change the presser foot on the sewing machine to an even feed (walking) foot and match the seam finish to the material thickness. Seams can be held in place with pins or glued together before sewing – gluing will increase seam durability. For light- to medium-weight neoprene use a plain or overlocked seam. The overlocked seam is durable but the ridges left inside might be uncomfortable, so cover the seam with a Lycra or elasticated tape or topstitch the seam allowance down. For medium- to heavyweight (4mm/⁵⁄₃₂in and thicker) neoprene use a butted or flat-lock seam finish.

PVC

Use paper clips or basting tape to hold pieces together before stitching – pin holes are permanent. For 2-way stretch PVC use a straight-stitch plain seam and try not to stretch the seam while sewing. This material does not fray so seam edges do not need finishing. PVC should not be pressed and needs to be under stitched, topstitched or glued. Use edge stitching on facings to prevent them from rolling to the right side and topstitch or glue all seam allowances down, using either a textile glue or latex-based rubber cement. For a decorative seam finish consider a non-woven flat fell (page 292), welt (page 129), slot or lapped seam (both page 280).

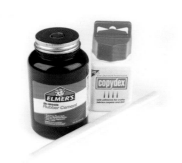

TIP

Make sure the gluing area is free from dust and grease and cover the work surface with plastic or pattern paper, shiny side up, so you can peel the glued pieces away easily. Wash your hands and do not use hand cream before gluing latex.

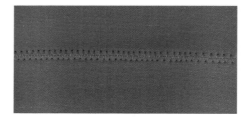

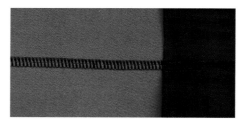

Top: On a butted seam the seam allowance is cut off and the edges brought together. The seam line is covered with tape on the wrong side for extra stability and sewn in place with a wide zigzag stitch from the right side. It can also be sewn without a backing tape.
Above: A flat-lock seam is decorative with stitching showing on the right side. It is also a durable and comfortable way of binding two pieces of fabric together. Usually sewn on an overlocker with the cutting blade removed.

TIP

The industry uses specialist machinery to heat-seal seams on plastic fabrics. Design studios and home sewers are not able to construct a heat-sealed seam but seam sealing tape, which is applied with an iron, can be used to waterproof seam lines. Follow the manufacturer's instructions and experiment on a scrap of material to get temperature/time/pressure right.

Hemming

Latex

Latex does not fray and could be left as a raw edge finish, but a turned up and glued hemline adds a quality finish and strengthens and seals the end of each seam. For a straight hem use a 1–5cm (⅜–2in) turning, but reduce to 5mm (³⁄₁₆in) on curved hemlines – generally, the sharper the curve the smaller the hem allowance.

Neoprene

On stretch neoprene either bind the hem with Lycra or elasticated tape, topstitch with zigzag stitching or turn the hemline up and cover stitch. On non-stretch neoprene apply topstitching or face the hem with tape or a contrast fabric. Alternatively, leave as a raw edge finish.

PVC

To ensure an even hemline on stretch PVC let the garment hang for 24 hours. PVC hemlines look best with single or double topstitching but can also be glued. Occasionally a hemline is turned up and hand sewn with a blind hemstitch, or may be bound, finished with ribbon or left as a raw edge finish.

Edge finish

Latex does not require an edge finish. Bind edges on stretch neoprene with Lycra or elasticated tape to add body and stability; if working with non-stretch material use any kind of binding, trim or tape that suits the garment design. Edges can also be left unfinished, as neoprene fabrics do not fray. On PVC, bindings, ribbon, bias tape, trims, elasticated trims and bands can be matched to the garment design. Facings can be applied to necklines and arms, including shaped, decorative or bias facings.

Interfacing and lining

On latex, reinforce fastening areas; apply cotton tape or woven fabric between two layers of latex to create a non-stretch area. Interfacing is rarely used on neoprene, but sew-in or iron-on interfacing with a low melting point can be applied. Neoprene may be lined for comfort or to neaten the inside: match lining weight and fabric structure to the neoprene. On PVC use sew-in interfacing only. PVC garments can be lined for aesthetics and durability; use stretch lining for stretch PVC and woven for non-stretch. Always stitch the lining in from the lining side.

Fastening

The most common fastening option on latex is a zip with plastic teeth and cotton backing, which is good for gluing. Other fastening options include press-studs, lacing and tie-fastenings – use plastic or rubber trims, because metal can discolour latex. Zips and press-studs work well on neoprene; use a waterproof zip for watertight garments. Other options include casing with drawstring, eyelets with cord or string fastening, Velcro or a magnetic fastening. PVC outer garments can be fastened with a zip, Velcro, sew-in magnets, press-studs, or buttons with any type of buttonhole. For dresses, trousers and skirts use zips, press-studs and buttons. On stretch PVC consider an elasticated waistband.

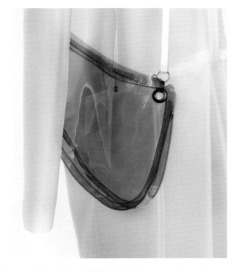

A coat design by Iryna Mikhailovich in transparent plastic materials with neoprene shoulder yoke detail. The seam finish, edge and hem finish needs to be carefully considered when constructing a garment from transparent plastic material – topstitched seams, welt or lapped seams work best. Cutting out the pattern pieces must be done in one, showing clean-cut edges. Fastening options should match the design of the garment and transparency of the material.

> **TIP**
>
> When sewing a seam allowance with tissue paper, cut strips 6–10cm (2⅜–3⅞in) wide and long enough to cover the seam length. If the material is sticking to the feed teeth, place the tissue strip underneath the garment between machine and material. If the material is sticking to the presser foot and it cannot be replaced with a Teflon, even feed (walking) or roller foot, place the tissue paper between the foot and the garment – use transparent paper so you can still see where you are sewing. If necessary, tissue paper can be placed on both sides of the material. Gently tear away the tissue paper when stitching is complete, making sure not to stretch the seam.

Patterned Fabrics

Patterned fabrics have an instant impact no matter how simple the garment shape. They are time-consuming but fun to work with. Patterns might be woven or knitted into a fabric, or printed onto the surface of a woven, knitted or non-woven material. They can also be created by embroidery techniques or through special dyeing methods. Patterned fabrics can be produced from natural, man-made or synthetic materials and in any weight.

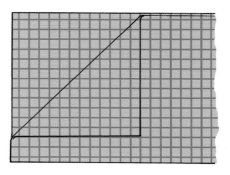

Uneven check (top) and even check (above).

Checks

Check fabrics can have a regular or irregular pattern. Beginners should start with a regular check because they are the easiest to match – irregular checks are more difficult although the basic idea is the same. Garments made in a regular check look the same on both sides of the centre, whereas irregular check patterns continue in one direction around the body. There is a great variety of check patterns to choose from; here are a few options to start with.

Gingham is a lightweight cotton fabric with alternating bands of white and coloured yarns and a regular check.

Houndstooth, also known as dogstooth check, is a woollen twill-weave fabric with a distinctive pattern of small-scale pointed checks in alternating light and dark colours.

Madras is a lightweight cotton fabric with bold irregular woven checks or stripes in multiple bright colours.

Tartan has an elaborate check pattern woven in cotton, wool or silk taffeta. It is the fabric used for Scottish kilts.

Stripes

Stripes are easier to handle than checks, since the pattern only runs in one direction, either vertical or horizontal to the selvedge. The stripes can be any size from pinstripe to block-stripe and may be equal in size or vary in width. Stripes may be regular or irregular; an irregular stripe pattern has a different arrangement of stripe width or colour to either side of the dominant stripe. Examples of stripe fabrics are dimity, ottoman, seersucker and pinstripe.

Jacket and skirt in striped fabric by Ulyana Danyleyko. The large box pockets on the jacket are mitred to create a pattern, while the skirt is cut to create a geometrical feature at the waist.

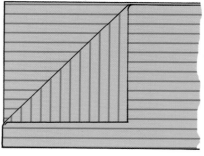

Irregular stripe (top) and regular stripe (above).

All-over/repeat pattern

Any all-over-pattern fabric has a repeated design; the size of the repeat will vary depending on the motif size and arrangement. Small-scale repeats can look like a plain colour from a distance. Small-scale patterns are easier to work with, because large-scale patterns require careful placing of the motifs.

Border pattern designs

Bordered fabrics have a decorative design along or instead of the selvedge. The pattern can be printed, embroidered or scalloped, or a combination of all three. This fabric design is unique, creating a quality finish to a garment that cannot be recreated by combining fabrics.

T-shirt vest with large graphic all-over pattern and chiffon sunray-pleated skirt with all-over printed graffiti pattern. Celine, SS 2014.

Full skirt featuring a repeat face-pattern border, teamed with an all-over floral print top. Dolce & Gabbana, SS 2013.

Placement design

A placement design is a single motif located on specific areas, created either through weaving or knitting, or printed or embellished onto an uncut material. It is important to place the pattern pieces carefully so that the motif is balanced.

Diagonal patterns

Diagonal patterns can be woven, knitted or printed in a diagonal arrangement. Woven diagonals have ridges formed by a twill weave, which can be inconspicuous or distinctive. Diagonals can be at varying angles; some are at 45 degrees – the true bias – which makes the cutting out and making of the garment easier. Diagonal patterned fabric can have a regular or irregular pattern.

On this dress the placement design has been carefully positioned at centre front, with the bust strap appearing as a 'headband' on the printed image. Prada, SS 2014.

Distinctive checks and diagonal lines on the fabric are used to break up the shape of a suit and coat into a series of monochrome blocks. Issey Miyake, AW 2014.

Pattern Cutting and Layout

When working with patterned fabrics always buy extra fabric to match the design.

Match the pressing requirements, marking technique, equipment, seam finish and fastening options to the fabric weight, texture and garment design. Refer to individual fabric-specific techniques elsewhere in this chapter for further information.

Checks

The placement of the check pattern should be carefully considered for a professional-looking garment. Select a check in a suitable scale for your garment design. Allow plenty of time to prep and cut check materials.

- Examine a printed check fabric carefully to make sure it is printed on grain – avoid those printed off grain.
- To see if the check is regular, fold the fabric in half and line up the dominant stripe. Turn back the top corner at a right angle. If stripes match across the diagonal fold in both colour and width the check is regular. If the design does not match, the checks are irregular (see illustration on page 300).
- Plan the layout before buying the fabric.
- Analyse the check to identify dominant stripes or squares and consider where they will be positioned on the garment.
- You will have to make some compromises; not every seam can be matched. Try and match visual focal points on garments, such as centre front and back, at side seams and the front part of set-in sleeves. Match the back of the collar to the centre back.

- Either match the check across pockets, collar, flaps, yokes, cuffs and facings, or cut in the opposite direction or bias. Sometimes the size of these small pieces must be slightly altered to fit the check design, or consider cutting them in a plain contrast fabric.
- Avoid placing dominant stripes at points you do not want to draw attention to, such as at the hip or bust line.
- Consider the check pattern on trousers with pleats or crease lines. Carefully place any dominant stripes around the front and back crotch.
- Take extra care on a two-piece outfit: use the same check pattern and match at waist and hip, and at centre front and back, of both garments to make sure the check will not be broken where the garments meet.

- Finish hemline and sleeve edges with the dominant check or stripe.
- Ideally, cut check materials as a one-way layout in a single layer. Duplicate pattern pieces that must be cut twice.
- If cutting out as a double layer, fold the fabric in half and line up at the selvedge. Pin layers together along a stripe or bar so they match exactly in both layers. Place pins every 5–10cm (2–3⅞in) horizontally and vertically so pieces such as sleeves will look identical on either side of the garment.
- Mark the check pattern onto adjoining pattern pieces and match up on the seam line, not the cutting line.
- Place adjoining pattern pieces next to each other.

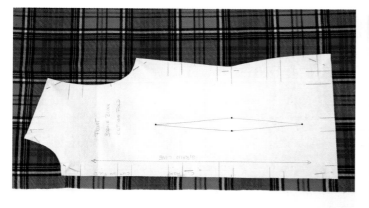

Place the pattern on the fabric and mark the position of the stripes onto the pattern.

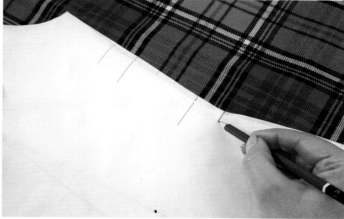

The pattern piece marked with stripe positions can then be matched to adjoining pattern pieces on the seam line.

Stripes

Put all your effort into matching stripes – the seams and centre lines must match.

- Examine a printed stripe pattern carefully; avoid any printed off grain.
- To check if the stripe is regular fold the fabric in half, lining up the dominant stripe. Turn back the top corner at a right angle. If stripes match across the diagonal fold in both colour and width the pattern is regular. If not, the stripes are irregular (see page 300).
- Plan the layout before buying fabric.
- Establish the stripe direction for each pattern piece and mark as a grain line. Stripes can be used horizontally, vertically or diagonally; make sure the grain direction works with the garment area and fabric structure. Mixing directions in one garment can look interesting.
- Mark the stripes onto adjoining pattern pieces at seam line, not cutting line.

- Match visual focal points on the garment: at centre front and back, at side seams and the front part of set-in sleeves. The stripes might not match on shoulder seam, back sleeve and dart.
- If stripes run horizontally, finish the hemline and sleeve edges with the dominant stripe
- Either match stripes across pockets, collar, flaps, yokes, cuffs and facings, or cut in the opposite direction or bias. Sometimes the size of these small pieces must be slightly altered to fit the stripes, or consider cutting them in a plain contrast fabric.
- For a two-piece, make sure stripes will match where the garments meet.
- When using stripes vertically, place a dominant stripe in centre front and back and/or at any other focal points on garment sections.
- Align buttonholes with the stripe

direction and match the colour of the buttonhole to the colour of the stripe.

- For an irregular stripe design decide whether the stripes will repeat around the garment in one direction or to the right and left of centre front and back. For a mirror image result, you need a centre front and back seam or opening.
- Use a one-way layout and cut as a single layer. If the print does not show on the wrong side, place pattern pieces on the right side to match the stripes.
- Avoid placing dominant stripes on the bust, waist or hipline.
- If cutting out as a double layer, fold the fabric in half and line up at the selvedge. Pin layers together along stripe lines so stripes in both layers match exactly. Place pins every 5–10cm (2–3⅞in) horizontally and vertically so pieces such as sleeves will look identical on both sides.

All-over/repeat pattern

The key point here is to consider pattern repeats when placing pattern pieces. Select a pattern size that is suitable for your garment design.

- For large-scale fabric patterns select a simple garment design with minimum seams, darts and fussy details.
- When purchasing a small-scale pattern unroll the fabric and look at a couple of metres, not just a small sample.
- Consider the placement of dominating motifs on large-scale patterns. Avoid placing large motifs onto the bust area.
- Consider mixing small-scale patterns with other fabrics, patterned or plain. Some garment designs also work with collar, cuffs, waistband, pockets and flaps or yokes in a contrast fabric.
- For large motifs use a one-way layout and cut as a single layer.
- Some patterned fabrics have no dominant design to match, so pattern pieces can be placed lengthwise and crosswise on a double layer, right side together.
- Small-scale patterns with a direction must be cut as a one-way layout on a double or single layer.

Border pattern design

Border designs can be incorporated into the hemline, waistline, collar, patch pockets, yoke and cuffs. Try different options, such as placing the border at the top of a garment instead of the hemline.

- Let the border inspire your design.
- Simple shapes work best to showcase the fabric.
- Avoid A-line designs and circular hems.
- Plan the layout before buying fabric.
- The length of a garment might be restricted by the fabric width if the border pattern is used on the hemline. To avoid this use patterns with seams towards the top, such as at the yoke or under-bust, to lengthen the garment.
- Delete the hem allowance if using a finished edge border as the hem.
- Border fabric designs are cut on the cross grain in a one-way layout, single layer and right side up.
- Try to lay all pattern pieces in one direction. Occasionally, the patterns can be placed both crosswise and lengthwise – check the fabric works together either way.
- Do not over-use the border design; less is more.

Diagonal patterns

Select a simple garment shape with as few seams as possible. Bias-cut pieces do not look good unless the material has a true bias pattern.

- Avoid bias darts, shaped and curved seams, kimono, dolman or raglan sleeves, turned-back lapels and V-necklines. Set-in sleeves, round or square necklines, horizontal seam lines and straight edge finishing work best.
- If unsure about the stripe direction and design, draw the stripe pattern onto the pattern pieces before cutting.
- Do not cut the collar with a fold at centre back. Add a seam at centre back and cut half on the lengthwise grain and the other on the crosswise grain.
- Use a one-way layout and cut as a single layer.
- Duplicate pattern pieces that need to be cut twice, place the adjoining pieces together on the fabric and draw on the stripes to make sure they continue across seams. Match at centre front and back and, if possible, at the sleeve head, side seams at the most visible point, pockets and any adjoining seam within the garment.

Construction

Cutting, construction methods, finishing and fastening options must be tailored to the individual material. This section is about a range of patterned materials so after selecting fabric combinations refer to specific techniques for each individual fabric elsewhere in this chapter.

Sewing check and striped fabrics

Choose a seam finish that matches the weight, texture and design of the garment – if possible use a plain seam to make design matching easier.

- Select the machine needle and thread to match fabric quality.
- Match thread colour to blend with the fabric design.
- Place adjoining seams right sides together.
- Insert the pin directly at the sewing point and match up every line or small pattern at 2cm (¾in) intervals.
- Stitch the seam, removing pins as you go – try not to stitch over pins. Alternatively, hand-tack the seam on the sewing line, then machine stitch.
- Check the seam from the right side; do not press until you are happy with the result.

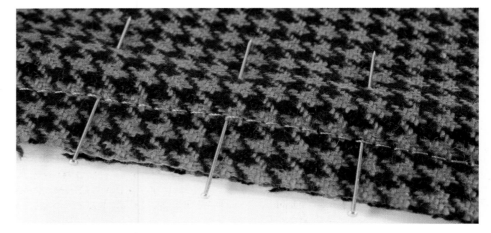

Top right: Pinning check fabric.

Centre: The pieces sewn together.

Right: The seam stitched and pressed, seen from the right side of the fabric.

Pleating stripes and checked fabrics

Purchase plenty of fabric for pleating. The stripe will determine the pleat size; a wider stripe creates a bigger pleat. Pleating a striped fabric so only one colour shows on the outside of a garment can create a stunning effect.

- If pleating a two-colour stripe use the darker stripe on the outside to avoid it showing through the lighter one.

- It is easier to pleat the fabric before cutting out the pattern piece.
- Fold the fabric on one edge of the stripe and press.
- Bring the fold over to the start of the next same-colour stripe.
- Press and repeat.
- Hold the pleats in place with pins and hand-tack before cutting out.

Dress with a pleated skirt by Ulyana Danyleyko made of fabric with irregular stripes. The use of deep pleats softens the stripes.

Contrast fabric areas

Parts such as collars, cuffs, yokes, waistbands and pockets can be cut in different material. If so, small parts, such as belt loops, epaulettes, tabs and bound buttonholes, should also be cut in the different material to match, but they are rarely the only contrast part.

Contrasting collar and cuffs can create an identity, such as for uniforms. There are classic combinations to study when choosing contrast fabrics for an original design, such as the heavyweight tweed Chesterfield coat with a velvet collar.

Dress influenced by Picasso and Cubism, with fabric patchwork using a combination of felt, felt covered with heat-transferred film and leather. Helmut Lang, AW 2013.

Mixing Fabrics

Designers often add visual and textural interest to garments by mixing different fabric qualities, creating new materials through embellishment or providing focal points with appliqué. Fashion students come up with the most weird and wonderful combinations, perhaps because their creativity is not limited by knowledge of what works technically. Do not shy away from opportunities to find new methods of combining unusual materials – often, breaking the rules leads to innovative fashion items.

Fabric combinations

Colour

Applying different tones of colour in one garment creates an immediate visual impact. Contrast colour can be used to highlight sections or to enhance body shape – for example, using a darker colour on side panels of a fitted item will make the wearer look slimmer. Test the fabric for colourfastness, because darker colours may bleed into lighter colours when wearing or washing the garment. Make sure colours complement each other and do not clash.

Texture

Mixing different fabric textures in one garment is a longstanding tradition – one of the obvious examples is the dinner jacket or tuxedo, in which a jacket in matt wool has a shiny silk satin lapel and covered buttons. Other common combinations are woollen fabrics with fur, velvet or leather trims. Watch out for different shrinkage rates or care requirements, colour bleeding issues and abrasion resistance. In some cases the contrast fabric can be constructed separately for ease of care – for example, a wool coat can have a detachable fur collar.

This dress not only features vibrant complementary colours, but also a mixture of sparkly and matt fabrics for an interesting contrast in textures. Diane von Furstenberg, SS 2013.

Weight

Mixing different fabric weights in one garment can be tricky – in general, try to match fabric weights as closely as possible to avoid an ill-fitting garment. A lightweight material sewn to a heavyweight one can lead to pulling or a stretched seam. Cut the adjoining seam of the lightweight fabric slightly longer and ease the extra length onto the seam of the heavyweight fabric; the thinner fabric will then lie smooth.

Stretch and non-stretch

This combination has become fashionable – for example sweatshirt tops are constructed with collar and pocket fastening in woven cotton fabric. Non-stretch materials are also used to stabilize specific areas on stretch garments, such as the neckline or armhole. Stretch materials can be used to enhance comfort and flexibility at the bust/chest, waist, elbow or knee, while the rest of the garment is constructed with a non-stretch material for stability. Mixing stretch with non-stretch can result in interesting garment shapes, for instance using the drape of jersey with the structure of a woven fabric as a foundation to anchor the drape.

Care requirements

Try to match care requirements, although the most interesting material combinations are probably the least compatible in terms of care. Obvious problems include colour bleeding and different shrinkage rates; check colourfastness and pre-shrink all fabrics before cutting out. If care instructions for different fabric qualities in a garment are not the same, use the care requirement of the fabric with the lowest option. For example, there might be a difference in heat resistance so use the lowest heat setting specified when washing and pressing to avoid damage.

What to consider when buying

Begin with fabric research. Visit different kinds of fabric shop to collect samples, then lay out swatches next to your garment design. Play around with different fabric and colour combinations until you find the most suitable.

Colour mood board. Collecting imagery and fabric swatches can inspire interesting colour stories.

Appliqué

An appliqué is an applied decorative design in one or many materials. Appliqués can be constructed from any material and there are no limits to the imagination, but some combinations work better than others.

- When using a lightweight base fabric consider the weight of the final appliqué – heavy appliqué can pull the garment out of shape. Back the base fabric under the appliqué to add stability and stop it ripping.
- On a knitted fabric the appliqué area should be supported to stop the knit from stretching. Some loosely woven fabrics also need backing.
- Analyse the weave and texture of the base fabric before choosing the appliqué materials; in general, choose a smooth/flat material to appliqué onto a textured surface and a dimensional/textured appliqué material for a flat/non-textured surface.
- The appliqué can be attached to the base fabric by hand or machine stitching, fusing, gluing, embroidery or a combination of techniques. The method may depend on the texture and weight of the fabrics used – and heat sensitive fabrics cannot be fused.
- Consider care requirements for the base and appliqué materials; test for shrinkage, colourfastness and abrasion resistance.

Edge finish and hem finish

Simple design shapes and plain fabrics can be made interesting by applying contrast facings, bindings, tapes, trims and ribbon. Consider the quality, care requirements, durability and end use when choosing the edge or hem finish and keep the overall design in mind because contrast finishing will have a strong visual impact.

Facings cut in contrast fabric may be used for visual impact or to add stability and support.

Bindings create decorative outlines to finish off edges and hemlines. Bindings are usually bias-cut strips, which can be folded in different ways. A single-folded strip has raw edges sewn into the seam, and is used as piping – with or without a round cord filler – to define an edge or outline the garment shape. A double-folded strip encases the raw fabric edge with binding and is topstitched in place.

Tapes add detail and texture, or support and strengthen garment areas. There are several tapes to choose from; see Tapes and bindings, page 88.

Decorative ribbons are available in different widths and materials such as velvet, satin, taffeta, grosgrain, Jacquard and dobby ribbon.

Other options are available including more opulent items such as braid, fringe, tassels and novelty trims.

Silk satin duchesse kimono-style top with Pop Art daisy appliqué, embroidered with papery origami flower patterns. Prada, SS 2013.

Bonding different fabric qualities

Two fabrics can be combined by bonding them together with fusible webbing, either before the fabric is cut or after the individual pieces have been cut out – but always before garment construction. Fusible webbing is available by the metre and comes with a paper backing.

- Place a sheet of fusible webbing onto the wrong side of one fabric with the paper side facing up.
- Following the manufacturer's instructions, iron the fusible webbing onto the fabric.
- Let the fabric and fusible webbing cool down and then carefully peel off the paper backing.
- Place the fusible webbing side onto the wrong side of the second fabric and iron until the two materials stick together.
- Let the fabric cool down before continuing the construction process.

Bonded materials have more structure and are ideal for sculptural pieces. They are also suitable for reversible designs since they are equally attractive on both sides. Seams can be constructed as a plain seam, either topstitched or bound, or as a welt, lapped, flat fell, wrong-side-out or French seam. Reversible garments are not interfaced or lined. Use patch pockets, or if using inserted pockets make sure the pocket bag is self-finished. Edges can be left as a raw edge finish or bound. Use simple garment designs and consider how to showcase both fabric sides of the fabric – for example add fold-back cuffs. Consider fastening options: lacing, tie closing, reversible zips and wrapped designs with a belt work best; buttons and buttonholes can be used, but consider the positioning for both sides. A bound or in-seam buttonhole looks particularly attractive.

A dress by Iryna Mikhailovich using a bonded satin and wool fabric. The fabric was bonded before cutting and constructing the garment. The wool forms the outer layer. The garment is slashed to reveal the satin layer.

Bias-Cut Fabrics

Garments cut on the bias drape beautifully. Choose a fabric that is light- to medium-weight or loosely woven such as satin crepe, georgette, chiffon or crêpe de Chine. For a good-quality finish on bias-cut garments, specific cutting and sewing techniques are required.

Pattern Cutting

- Avoid set-in pocket designs such as the jet pocket. Use an applied pocket design instead, for example the patch pocket.
- Adjust all grain lines on the pattern pieces by drawing a line at a 45-degree angle to the original straight grain line. It is best to use a 'true' bias, as the fabric will hang better.
- Add a generous 2.5cm (¹⁵⁄₁₆in) seam allowance to the pattern pieces.
- Add notches to align bias-cut seams.

Cutting Out

Preparation

- Place a layer of tissue paper under the fabric. Pin the pattern pieces on top and cut out the fabric while it is still attached to the paper to stop the fabric from moving around.

Layout

- Use a single layout and place the pattern pieces onto the fabric at a 45-degree angle to the selvedge.

Shears

- Use a rotary cutter or sharp shears to cut the fabric as fabric cut on the bias moves easily.

Spiral-cut silk dress cut on the bias, with a pinhem finish and bound armhole and neck edges. Gareth Pugh, SS 2014.

Sewing

Avoiding stitching problems

- Stretch the fabric slightly when sewing a plain seam on the bias. The ripples in the seam will iron out. This will prevent the thread from snapping.
- Bias seams stretch. Test out stitching ideas to find the right machine and seam type. Sewing with a 4-thread overlocker works well, as this type of seam allows the fabric to stretch.

 ## Construction

Seams

- Most bias-cut garments will have fit problems. When you fit the garment you may need to reduce excess fabric. Sew the centre seams first and adjust the fit at the side seams.
- Tape armholes, necklines and shoulders to avoid stretching.
- When sewing two pattern pieces together where one is cut on the straight grain and one on the bias, stitch the seam with the bias side facing up. Do not stretch the bias seam; ease it slightly onto the straight grain seam.

Hemming

- The hems of some bias-cut garments hang longer on one side than the other. This is because the yarn used in the straight grain is twisted tighter than the yarn in the crosswise grain. Let the garment hang for a day before hemming. Correct the lower edge if necessary by cutting it straight along the shortest point.
- Use a pin hem finish or a narrow double-turned hem, a bound hem or add a decorative trimming. A baby-locked hem also works well. You can also use a raw edge finish.

Edge finish

- If you are using a facing, cutting it on the straight grain will prevent stretching.
- Use a narrow straight grain tape to finish necklines and armholes to stop them from stretching.

Fastening

- The best fastening option for bias-cut garments is a zip. Hand-tack the zip in place or add a tape to the seam allowance before sewing the zip to prevent the seam from stretching. Ease the fabric onto the zip.
- Tape or interface button-fastening options with a straight grain tape to avoid stretching.
- Use rouleau loops for an elegant finish.

Glossary

abutted seam On this seam the pieces have no seam allowance and the raw edges are aligned and stitched over the centre of a backing strip (see page 292).

all-over pattern A pattern that covers the entire fabric surface, usually in small repeats.

applied pocket Also known as a patch pocket, a pocket that is sewn onto the outside of a garment.

appliqué An applied decorative design in one or many materials.

backing see Underlining.

backstitch tack A small backstitch made at the beginning or end of a line of hand sewing to secure the thread end.

bagging out A method of cleaning up garment edges at neckline, hemline or around sleeveless armholes using a tape or a facing.

balance points Marks or lines on a pattern piece that should be kept in the same relation to each other when a pattern is adjusted for size if the garment is to fit as it should.

bar-tack A tight, narrow line of zigzag machine stitching run back and forth, used to reinforce weak stress points.

basque A type of corset that shapes the upper body down to the hip and has added suspenders.

bellows pocket A type of applied pocket with a pleat along the sides and bottom so it is roomier inside.

bias grain A 'true' bias grain line runs at a 45-degree angle to the selvedge. See also Straight grain.

binding Decorative edging to finish off edges and hemlines by enclosing the raw edge.

block see Pattern block.

block fusing Fusing the interfacing to the wrong side of the fabric before cutting out the pattern pieces.

bodkin A heavy needle-type tool with a blunt end and a large eye, used to thread tape, elastic, ribbon or cord through a casing.

body The amount of natural stiffness that a fabric has, which will allow it to stand away from a supporting shape rather than cling to it. See also Drape and Hang.

body-conscious clothing Clothing that clings to and reveals the underlying shape of the body.

boll The seedpod of the cotton plant.

bonded fabric Layers of fabric that are permanently attached together across their entire surface so they work as one fabric.

boning Strips of metal or plastic used to stiffen and support a corset, enabling it to shape the body.

box pleat Two pleats the same width turned towards each other, either folded outwards or inverted.

break line The line where the collar stand breaks into the collar fall.

break point The point at which the lapel/revers begins to fold back from the edge.

breathable Quality of a fabric that stops liquid water from passing through from outside but allows moisture vapour to escape from inside.

busk fastener A pair of flexible strips containing loops on one side and pegs on the other, commonly used to fasten corsets.

bustier Also called a brassiere, this shapes the bust area to the waistline and can be worn with or without shoulder straps.

butted seam On this seam the pieces have no seam allowance and the raw edges are aligned and stitched with a wide zigzag stitch from the right side. The join can be covered with a backing tape on the wrong side (see page 298).

casing A tube of fabric along the edge of a garment piece, through which elastic, cord or ribbon is threaded.

centre back/front An imaginary line that runs vertically down the centre of the back or front of a garment.

clipping Making small snips into the seam allowance on an inward curve to open up so the seam will lie flat around the curved area.

closed lining A lining that is attached to the hemline so seams and hem allowance are encased completely. See also Open lining.

collar fall The visible part of the collar that turns down from the break line.

collar style line The outside edge of a collar, which defines its extent.

corset A closely fitted bodice, stiffened with boning to reshape the torso.

corsolette/corselet A tubular corset with shoulder straps and suspenders that gives support to the bust, waist and hip.

courses The horizontal rows on a knitted fabric that correspond with the crosswise grain on a woven fabric.

crisp Quality of stiffness in a fabric, or the sharpness of a crease.

crosswise grain This runs at a 90-degree angle to the selvedge, in the direction of the weft threads on a woven fabric.

couture dart Also known as a double-pointed dart. This is a wedge-shaped dart at the centre that narrows to a dart point at each end.

dart A wedge-shaped pleat with two equal length dart legs ending in a dart point.

deconstructed A minimalist design style without much traditional structure that has a soft hang. It may also feature exterior seams or deliberately frayed edges as decorative features. See also Distressed.

design placement Placing the motifs in a large pattern so that they fall in the best way on the finished garment.

directional design Also known as a one-way design, this is a printed or woven design that has motifs with a definite top and bottom that all run in the same direction.

distressed Deliberately frayed edges or surfaces as a decorative feature of the design. See also Deconstructed.

double jersey A knitted fabric that looks the same on both sides and can be double the weight of single jersey.

double layout Laying out the pattern pieces on fabric that is folded on the lengthwise grain so you can cut pairs of pieces at the same time.

double-pointed dart see Couture dart.

drape The way a fabric flows naturally over a supporting shape. See also Body and Hang.

ease stitching A type of subtle gathering, without visible puckering or pleating, used to enable a long edge to be stitched to a slightly shorter one.

edge stitching A single row of topstitching, stitched very close to the seam line to highlight and flatten a seam, and/or keep the seam allowance in place.

elasticity The ability of a fabric to stretch.

enclosed seam A type of seam in which the raw edge of the seam allowance is hidden within the seam construction.

even feed foot An even feed foot, also known as a walking foot, is a foot for a sewing machine that has its own set of feed dogs that work in conjunction with the machine's feed dogs to improve the flow of the fabric through the machine. A rotary even foot is similar but has caterpillar tracks on each side, which independently grip the fabric to allow different height fabrics to feed evenly through the machine.

even stripe/check see Regular stripe/check.

fabric structure The way a fabric is created, by weaving, knitting, matting the fibres or bonding.

facing A piece of fabric applied to a garment edge at openings that may be functional, decorative or both. An extended facing is cut as part of the garment. An all-in-one facing is used to finish both the neckline and armhole edges on garments without sleeves.

feed dogs The moving parts under the throat plate of a sewing machine that come up after the needle has completed a stitch to move the fabric along ready for the next stitch.

felt A non-woven fabric made from wool fibres matted together using heat, moisture and friction, or from wool and other fibres by stabbing with a felting needle.

filament fibres Yarn fibre in a long continuous strand.

finger press Pressing a crease into the fabric with your fingers rather than an iron.

fitted A garment that is structured to follow the shape of the body.

frogging A type of ornamental braiding that incorporates loops and buttons or braid knots to fasten a garment.

fulling A finishing process on woollen fabrics using water, friction and pressure to create controlled felting of the fabric surface.

fusible The ability to be attached to another fabric, usually by the application of heat and pressure.

gathers Small irregular pleats that regulate fullness for fit or decorative effect.

girdle A type of corset that supports from the waist down to the lower hip and which often has added suspenders.

gorge line The seam that joins the collar and lapel/revers.

grading see Layering.

grain The direction of the yarn on a piece of woven fabric.

gusset A piece of fabric sewn into a slash to provide extra space for movement.

hang The way a fabric flows from a supporting point. See also Drape and Body.

hanger A strip of stiffening across the back neckline of a jacket or coat.

heat-sealed seam A seam that is welded together with heat rather than being sewn.

insertion cut A cut made into flat fabric into which another piece will be sewn.

interfacing A type of stiffening that can be applied to the whole garment to support the fabric or only to parts that need more structure, such as collars and cuffs.

interlining A layer between the fabric and the lining, usually to add insulation or to improve the hang.

irregular stripe/check A stripe or check that can only be matched in one direction.

Jacquard weave A type of fabric weaving in which the warp and weft threads are programmed independently to rise and lower, to create quite complex textural patterns.

jersey Any type of knitted fabric.

jet pocket A type of set-in pocket in which the slash opening has a narrow binding, or jet, along each edge.

keyhole buttonhole/opening An opening with a rounded shape at one end.

kimono/batwing sleeve A sleeve cut as part of the garment front and back, which can have shoulder and side seams or be cut with no shoulder seam.

knife pleats A series of pleats folded in the same direction, either overlapping regularly or at spaced intervals, and right round the garment or in grouped sections.

lapels Also known as revers. The turned-back facings on the front of a garment.

lapped zip A zip in which the teeth are covered with one flap of fabric, with only one line of stitching showing.

layering Also known as grading, this is a technique in which one seam allowance is trimmed more than another before pressing both to one side, to avoid bulk showing on the right side.

lengthwise grain This runs parallel to the selvedge, in the direction of the warp threads on a woven fabric.

linen weave see Plain weave.

loft The thickness of a fabric, usually one that can be compressed.

man-made fibres Fibres made by regenerating a natural material, such as cellulose.

manufactured fibres Artificial fibres, which can be man-made or synthetic.

mercerized A treatment for cotton yarn or fabric that gives it a lustrous appearance and added strength.

mitre A 45-degree angle diagonal join between two strips at a corner.

mounting see Underlining.

nap A one-directional surface on a fabric created by bringing the thread ends up; it reflects light differently depending on which way it is viewed. See also Pile weave.

needle board Also known as a velvet board. A board covered with wire needles; pile fabric is placed face down for pressing to prevent the pile from matting and crushing.

needle-ready A fabric that is ready for immediate cutting and sewing, because it has been treated and will not shrink after washing or dry-cleaning.

non-woven A fabric that has been created by bonding the fibres together using mechanical, chemical or heat treatments.

notching Cutting V-shaped wedges from the seam allowance on an outward curve to reduce bulk for a flat and smooth finished shape.

one-way design see Directional design.

one-way pattern layout Laying all the pattern pieces onto the fabric for cutting so they all run in the same direction. See also Two-way pattern layout.

open lining A lining open at the bottom so the seams and hem allowance are partly exposed and need to be finished. See also Closed lining.

patch pocket see Applied pocket.

pattern block The set of basic pattern pieces required when designing a garment.

pattern repeat The way in which the individual motifs are repeated to make up the overall pattern on a fabric.

picot A type of edging with small loops or bobbles of thread.

pile weave A three-dimensional weave constructed over rods to insert an extra set of weft or warp yarn in loops, which can be left as loops or cut to create a pile surface. See also Nap.

pilling Damage to the fabric caused by abrasion in which loose fibres form small fuzzy balls on the surface.

pinking Cutting fabric with pinking shears so it has a zigzag edge.

pin tuck see Tucks.

pitch Of a sleeve, the way a set-in sleeve hangs in relation to the garment.

placement design A single motif located on specific areas, created either through weaving or knitting, or printed or embellished onto an uncut material.

placement points The marking points that indicate where to place other elements of a garment, such as a pocket.

placket An opening with over- and under-lapping flaps of fabric, which allows a garment to be put on easily and often incorporates a fastening.

plain weave Also known as linen weave. A basic weave in which the weft thread is taken over and under alternating warp threads at right angles to each other.

pleats A way of controlling fullness by making even folds in the fabric.

pocket bag The bag of fabric behind an inset pocket.

power-net A stretch mesh fabric that provides support and controls shape in body-conforming garments.

pre-shrinking Shrinking the fabric before cutting and making up into a garment.

presser foot The foot on a sewing machine that presses the fabric against the feed dogs so they move the fabric at the right speed.

pressing cloth A cotton or woollen loose-woven fabric that is placed between the fabric and the iron to prevent shine and protect the surface.

quilting A technique where fabric and wadding are stitched together for insulation and decorative effect.

raglan sleeve A sleeve with a diagonal seam running from underarm into the neckline at front and back of the garment. It can be cut with a shoulder seam or shoulder dart or, on knitted fabric, may have neither.

raschel knit A type of warp knitting that allows interesting textures and designs to be created.

recovery The ability of a fabric to return to its original shape after having been stretched.

regular stripe/check A stripe or check that can be matched in either direction.

resilience The ability of a fabric to retain its properties during wear.

retain stitching Also called under stitching, this is a row of stitching close to the seam line onto a facing, lining or under layer to prevent them from rolling to the right side of the garment and give a crisp edge.

revers see Lapels.

rigilene Woven nylon rods used as boning.

roller foot A foot for the sewing machine that incorporates textured rollers, which help sticky or slippery fabrics move through the machine at an even rate.

rotary even foot see Even feed foot.

rouleau loop A small loop of fabric extending from the opening edge to hook over a button.

sample To try out a technique or a material to see how well it will work in a given application.

scalloping An edging that is made up of a series of small convex curves.

seam allowance The width of fabric between the stitching of a seam and the edge of the fabric.

seam slippage When two layers of a slippery fabric slide apart when being stitched so the seam no longer lines up at each end.

self-fabric Using the main fabric of a garment to make up construction parts that are often made in a different fabric, such as facings.

selvedge The finished edge on each side of a length of woven fabric, which may be more closely woven and contain information from the manufacturer, such as the fabric composition or the pattern/colour code.

separating zip A zip that opens at both ends for a two-way opening.

set-in pocket A pocket set into a seam line or slash.

set-in sleeve A sleeve that is completed and then sewn into the armhole with ease around the sleeve head.

sheer A fabric that is lightweight and finely woven so it is translucent.

shirtsleeve A sleeve attached into a dropped shoulder armhole, with very little to no ease in the sleeve head.

shirring Parallel rows of gathering.

single jersey A knitted fabric with plain knit on one side and purl knit on the other.

single layout Laying out the pattern pieces on a single layer of fabric so you cut only one piece at a time.

sink stitch Also known as stitching in the ditch, a line of stitching made into a seam line so it is not visible on the right side of the garment.

size chart A list of standard sizes with their actual measurements.

sleeve board A firmly padded, cylindrical-shaped cushion, used to press hard-to-reach areas such as seams in sleeves.

smocking A way of controlling fullness by using rows of stitching to gather the fabric into a decorative panel.

stabilizer A fabric used to add body or weight to another fabric.

stand The part of a collar that rises from the neckline and helps the collar to stand up, or the band of fabric that holds the buttons on a garment.

staple fibres Yarn fibres in short lengths.

stay-stitching A row of stitching on a single layer of fabric using a long stitch, made to reinforce notched or clipped seams and to prevent seams from stretching out of shape during the sewing process.

stitching in the ditch see Sink stitch.

stonewashing A finish most often used on denim, in which an industrial tumble-washer with pumice stone is used to abrade the surface for a worn appearance and to soften the fabric.

straight grain The grain that runs in the direction of the warp threads, parallel to the selvedge, or in the direction of the weft threads at a 90-degree angle to the selvedge. See also Bias grain.

structured A garment that is made with very defined shapes with a sharp silhouette.

S-twist Yarn spun with a left-hand twist.

sunray pleats Knife pleats that are narrower at the top than at the bottom, so radiate out to produce a flared shape. They are often made on fabric cut on the bias.

synthetic fibres Fibres made entirely from chemical compounds.

tab A small flap of fabric extending over an opening that may hold a button or a buttonhole. A tab loop is made from a flattened loop of fabric.

tailor's ham A small, firmly padded, oval-shaped cushion, with a cotton fabric on one side and wool on the other, used for shaping collars, lapels, darts and sleeve cups, to shrink fullness and to press rounded areas.

tailor's tacks Loose stitch loops made between layers of fabric; the layers are then separated and the threads cut between them, leaving matching thread marks in each layer.

thread marking see Tailor's tacks.

throat plate The metal plate on a sewing machine that the needle passes through. It is often engraved with measurement lines to keep seam allowances consistent.

toile A garment made up in a cheaper fabric to check the construction and fit before it is made in the final fabric.

top collar The outer or upper layer of the collar.

topstitching A single or multiple line of stitching on the right side of a garment to support and strengthen a seam and/or enhance the design. It can be done in thread to match the fabric or in a contrast colour to highlight the seam or as a design feature.

trapezoid pleats A pleating combination of parallel and radial pleating patterns in which the parallel folds reverse direction at regular intervals, creating radial folds across at top and bottom, to form a series of three-dimensional trapezoid shapes.

tricot A type of warp knitting with fine lengthwise ribs on the surface and little crosswise stretch.

tucks Rows of small pleats partly or entirely stitched down, which are used decoratively or to control fullness at both ends but which release it in the centre. Pin tucks are very narrow.

twill weave A method of weaving that creates diagonal lines or ridges on the fabric surface.

two-way pattern layout Laying the pattern pieces onto the fabric for cutting in both directions. See also One-way pattern layout.

under collar The facing on the underside of the collar.

under stitching see Retain stitching.

underlining Also called a backing or mounting, this covers an entire fabric piece to add stability, structure or insulation.

under-pressing Pressing from the wrong side to prevent construction elements marking the right side of the garment.

underskirt One or more layers of fabric under a skirt to support the outer layer.

under-structuring Making a structured layer underneath a garment to hold it in place on the body.

uneven stripe/check see Irregular stripe/check.

velvet board see Needle board.

vent An opening placed where a garment needs to open for comfort when walking, sitting or stretching, such as at garment or sleeve hemlines.

wadding A non-woven material that is added behind the fabric to add insulation or to pad areas to create shaping.

waist stay A strip of fabric cut to fit the waist and sewn inside a garment to keep it in place at the waistline.

wales The vertical rows on a knitted fabric that correspond with the lengthwise grain on a woven fabric.

walking foot see Even feed foot.

warp The threads that run lengthwise in a woven fabric.

warp knitting Warp knit is formed by looping stitches in the lengthwise grain, utilizing many yarns. See also Tricot and Raschel.

waste knot A temporary knot that is used at the start but clipped away after the stitching is complete.

weave Creating a fabric by taking weft threads over and under warp threads on a loom.

weft The threads that run crosswise in a woven fabric.

weft knitting Weft knitting uses one continuous yarn looping stitches in the crosswise grain, producing two main knitting types, single knit and double knit.

welt pocket A type of set-in pocket in which the slash opening has a wide band, or welt, that defines the opening of the pocket.

yoke A shaped pattern piece that fits closely around the neck and shoulders of a garment to support looser parts below, or occasionally around the hips just below the waist to support a skirt.

zip guard A facing that covers the teeth underneath a zip so they do not touch the body.

Z-twist Yarn spun with a right-hand twist.

Further Reading

Amaden-Crawford, Connie. *A Guide to Fashion Sewing*, 5th edition. Fairchild, New York (2011)

Bressler, Karen, Newman K., and Gillian Proctor. *A Century of Lingerie: Revealing the Secrets and Allure of 20th-Century Lingerie.* Chartwell Books, New Jersey (2000)

Cabrera, Roberto and Patricia Flaherty Meyers. *Classic Tailoring Techniques: A Construction Guide for Men's Wear.* Fairchild, New York (1996)

——. *Classic Tailoring Techniques: A Construction Guide for Women's Wear.* Fairchild, New York (1998)

Chunman Lo, Dennic. *Pattern Cutting.* Laurence King Publishing, London (2011)

Cole, Julie, and Sharon Czachor. *Professional Sewing Techniques for Designers*, 2nd edition. Fairchild, New York (2014)

The Complete Book of Sewing. Dorling Kindersley, London (2006)

Di Lorenzo, Milva Fiorella. *Tailoring Techniques for Fashion.* Fairchild, New York (2009)

Fischer, Anette. *Basics Fashion Design: Construction.* AVA Publishing, Lausanne (2009)

Gioello, Debbie Ann and Beverly Berke. *Fashion Production Terms*, 2nd edition. Fairchild, New York (2001)

Gioello, Debbie Ann. *Understanding Fabrics from Fibre to Finished Cloth.* Fairchild, New York (1982)

Hallett, Clive and Amanda Johnston, *Fabric for Fashion: The Swatch Book*, 2nd edition. Laurence King Publishing, London (2014)

Humphries, Mary. *Fabric Reference*, 2nd edition. Pearson, New Jersey (2013)

Kiisel, Karolyn. *Draping: The Complete Course.* Laurence King Publishing, London (2013)

Knight, Lorna. *The Dressmaker's Technique Bible: A Complete Guide to Fashion Sewing.* Krause Publications, Cincinnati (2008)

Long, Connie. *Easy Guide to Sewing Linings.* The Taunton Press, Connecticut (1998)

Maynard, Lynda. *The Dressmaker's Handbook of Couture Sewing Techniques.* A&C Black, London (2010)

Mooney, Sian-Kate. *Making Latex Clothes.* B.T. Batsford, London (2004)

Moyes, Patricia. *Just Pockets: Sewing Techniques and Design Ideas.* The Taunton Press, Connecticut (1997)

Page Coffin, David. *Shirtmaking: Developing Skills for Fine Sewing.* The Taunton Press, Connecticut (1998)

Shaeffer, Claire. *Claire Shaeffer's Fabric Sewing Guide*, 2nd edition. Krause Publications, Cincinnati (2009)

——. *Couture Sewing Techniques*, 2nd edition. The Taunton Press, Connecticut (2011)

——. *High-Fashion Sewing Secrets from the World's Best Designers.* Rodale Press, Pennsylvania (2001)

——. *Sewing for the Apparel Industry*, 2nd edition. Prentice Hall, New Jersey (2013)

Sterlacci, Francesca. *Leather Fashion Design.* Laurence King Publishing, London (2010)

Tailoring: A Step-By-Step Guide to Creating Beautiful Customized Garments. Apple Press, London (2005)

Wilson, Janet. *Classic and Modern Fabrics: The Complete Illustrated Sourcebook.* Thames & Hudson, London (2010)

Wolff, Colette. *The Art of Manipulating Fabric,* Krause Publications, Cincinnati (1996)

Websites

www.catwalking.com
www.fashion.about.com
www.fashion-era.com
www.fashionoffice.org
www.hintmag.com
www.infomat.com
www.londonfashionweek.co.uk
http://makinglatexclothing.com/
www.costumes.org
www.mjtrends.com
www.premierevision.fr
www.promostyl.com
www.rockywoods.com

www.shaunartcosplay.wordpress.com
www.showstudio.com
www.style.com
www.wgsn-edu.com

Fashion Forecasting
www.edelkoort.com
www.itbd.co.uk
www.londonapparel.com
www.modeinfo.com
www.peclersparis.com
www.wgsn-edu.com

Fashion Trade Shows
www.indigosalon.com
www.magiconline.com
www.pittimmagine.com
www.premierevision.fr
www.purewomenswear.co.uk

Index

abutted seam 124, 292
adapting a block 35
all-over/repeat, pattern cutting layout for 303
applied pockets 178–180
appliqué 308
appliqué seam 274–275
applying binding 123
applying fusible interfacing 95
applying sew-in interfacing 96
applying sew-in tape 140
applying underlining 97
awl marking 53

baby-locked hem 208
backstitch 115
backstitch tack 113
bagging out 135, 138
bar-tacks 253
basic corset, constructing 107–108
beaded fabric, working with 270–275
bellows pocket 180
belt loops 167–168
bias binding
    applying 123
    making 122
bias-cut fabrics, working with 310–311
bias grain 44
bindings 88, 90
blanket stitch 118
blind-stitch machine 24
block fusing 96
blocks
    adapting 35
    measurements for 30
bobbins 23
body measurements, taking 30–33
border pattern, pattern cutting layout for 303
bound finish 122–123
bound hem 208
box pleat 148
buckles and clasps 85
butted seam 298
button sewing machine 25
buttonhole and keyhole machine 24
buttonhole stitch 118
buttonholes 224, 230–233
    bound 231–232
    hand-sewn 230
    in-seam 233
buttons 80–81
    sewing on 229

carbon paper marking 54
chain stitch 23
chalk marking 52, 53
checks, pattern cutting layout for 51, 302
clean-finished seam allowance 124
clipping 135
coat lining 212
collars 156–160
    attaching 157

corner seams, sewing 137
corners
    bagged out 138
    French seam for 127
corsetry 103–109
    construction 107–108
    supporting materials for 104–105
    types 103
    variations 109
cotton fabric 62–63
cover stitch 23
cover stitch machine 24
crosswise grain 44
    finding the crosswise grain 45
cuffs
    closed 202
    open 201
    trouser 200, 207
curved seam 136
cutting equipment 14–15
cutting out 55
cutting plans *see pattern cutting layouts*

darts 53, 151–154, 287, 292
    double pointed 154
    single pointed 152–153
    marking 53, 151
    on felted/non-woven fabrics 292
    on leather 287
    pressing 153
    securing the point 152
deconstructed finish 134
denim, working with 248–253
diagonal patterns, pattern cutting layout for 303
drawstring waistband 174
dress lining 213

ease, allowing for 33
ease stitching 131
edge finishing
    binding 122–123
    for felted and non-woven fabrics 293
    for knitted and stretch-woven fabrics 259
    for lace, sequined and beaded fabrics 275
    for latex, neoprene and plastics 299
    for leather and fur 288
    for napped and pile fabrics 281
    for transparent and semi-transparent fabrics 267
    hemline 204–211, 251, 259, 267, 275, 281, 288,
        293, 299, 308, 311
    neckline 156–164
    on bias-cut fabrics 311
    ribbing 260
    seam allowance finishes 119, 122–124
    waistline 165–176
    when mixing fabrics 308
edge stitch 132
elastic 89
elasticated waistband 169
embroidery machine 25

fabric 42–55, 59
    beaded, working with 270–275
    bias-cut, working with 310–311
    bonding different 309
    buying 248, 255, 263, 271, 277, 283, 295, 307
    composition 59
    construction 60–61
    cotton 62–63
    cutting out 55, *see also pattern cutting layouts*
    denim, working with 248–253
    duffle 277
    felt and non-woven, working with 290–293
    finishes 249, 255, 263, 270, 276, 282, 290, 295
    grain line 44
    knitted and jersey 74–75
        working with 254–261
    lace 78–79
        working with 270–275
    linen 68–69
    lining 76–77
    man-made 70–71
    marking the pattern 52–54
    napped and pile, working with 276–281
    pattern cutting layouts 48–51
    patterned, working with 300–305
    preparing 46–47
    pre-shrinking 46
    right and wrong side 43
    sequined, working with 270–275
    silk 66–67
    smart 59
    straightening 47
    structure 42–43
    supporting 91–102, 104–105
    synthetic 70–71
    textured 72–73
    transparent and semi-transparent, working with
        262–269
    using contrast elements 305
    weave on specific fabrics 248, 255, 263, 270, 276
    wool 64–65
        mixing fabrics 306–307
        working with 247–311
facings 142–143
    hem 206
    neckline 163–164
    waistline 175
fastenings 80–85, 224–244
    button stands 225–228
    buttons and buttonholes 224–225, 229, 230–233
    corsetry 106
    for denim 252
    for felted and non-woven fabrics 293
    for knitted and stretch-woven fabrics 261
    for lace, sequined and beaded fabrics 275
    for latex, neoprene and plastics 299
    for leather and fur 289
    for napped and pile fabrics 281
    for transparent and semi-transparent fabrics
        268–269
    hooks-and-eyes 237

magnetic fastenings 236
   on bias-cut fabrics 311
   rouleau loops 233–234
   snap fasteners 236
   tabs 235
   thread loops 269
   ties 269
   Velcro fastening 237
   waistline 176
   zips 238–244
felt fabrics, working with 290–293
figure-eight knot 113
finishing 245
flat fell seam 128
French curves 18
French seam 126–127
fur, working with 282–289
fused hem 211

garment construction 145
gathers 146
grain lines 44
   knitted fabric 44
   laying out pattern pieces on 48

haberdashery 80–90
hand-sewing techniques 111–118, 208
   figure-eight knot 113
   backstitch 115
   backstitch tack 113
   blanket stitch 118
   buttonhole stitch 118
   hemming stitch 116
   herringbone stitch 117
   overcast stitch 117
   prick stitch 115
   rolled hem 208
   running stitch 114
   slipstitch 116
   starting and finishing 112–113
   tacking stitch 114
   tailor's knot 113
   turned-up hem 208
   waste knot 112
hem allowances 40–41
hemlines 204–211
   baby-locked 208, 267
   bound 208, 267
   faced 206
   for denim 251
   for felted and non-woven fabrics 293
   for knitted and stretch-woven fabrics 259
   for lace, sequined and beaded fabrics 275
   for latex, neoprene and plastics 299
   for leather and fur 288
   for napped and pile fabrics 281
   for transparent and semi-transparent fabrics 267
   fused 211
   hand-sewn rolled 208, 267
   hand-sewn turned-up 208
   mitred 209
   on bias-cut fabric 311
   pin hem 206
   shirt hem 210
   topstitched hem 205
   turned-under hem 204
   when mixing fabrics 308

hemming stitch 116
herringbone stitch 117
hooks-and-eyes 84, 237
horizontal grain *see crosswise grain*

industry production 56–57
interfacing 92–93, 94–96, 98–99
   applying 94, 95, 96
   block fusing 96
   for felted and non-woven fabrics 293
   for knitted and stretch-woven fabrics 260
   for lace, sequined and beaded fabrics 275
   for latex, neoprene and plastics 299
   for leather and fur 289
   for napped and pile fabrics 281
   for transparent and semi-transparent fabrics 268
   fusing plan for a jacket 99
   sampling 95
   where to apply 98
interlining 289

jacket fusing plan 99
jacket lining 212, 217–219
jersey fabric 74–75
jet pocket 180–184
   with flap 184

knife pleat 149
knitted fabric 74–75
   working with 254–261

lace fabric 78–79
   types 271
   working with 270–275
lapel collar 158–160
latex, working with 294–299
layering 135
layout plans *see pattern cutting layouts*
leather sewing machine 24
leather, working with 282–289
lengthwise grain 44
linen 68–69
lining 212–223
   for felted and non-woven fabrics 293
   for knitted and stretch-woven fabrics 260
   for lace, sequined and beaded fabrics 275
   for latex, neoprene and plastics 299
   for leather and fur 289
   for napped and pile fabrics 281
   full 214–216
   jackets and coats 212, 217–219
   partial 222–223
   patterns 212
   skirts and dresses 213
   trousers 213
   vents 220–221
lining fabric 76–77
lockstitch 23

machine seams 26–27, 125–130
   basic seam 120
   choosing 125
   flat fell seam 128
   French seam 126–127
   intersecting seams 131
   matching up seams 130
   plain seam 125

problem solving 26–27, 257, 265, 273, 279, 285,
   291, 297, 311
   welt seam 129
machine stitching 119–120, 131–133
   ease stitching 131
   edge stitch
   preparing to stitch 119
   retain stitch 133
   sink stitch 133
   stitch length 121
   topstitch 132
magnetic fastenings 84, 236
man-made fabric 70–71
marking the fabric 52–54
marking tools 16–17
measuring tapes 18
mitred hem 209
mixing fabrics, 306–309

napped fabric, working with 276–281
neckline 156–164
   collars 156–160
   facing 163–164
   stretch 161–162
needle threader 13
needles 12–13, 21, 250, 257, 265, 273, 279, 285, 291, 297
   hand-sewing needles 12–13
      for felted and non-woven fabrics 291
      for knitted and stretch-woven fabrics 257
      for lace, sequined and beaded fabrics 273
      for latex, neoprene and plastics 297
      for leather and fur 285
      for napped and pile fabrics 279
      for transparent and semi-transparent
         fabrics 265
   sewing machine needles 21
      for denim 250
      for felted and non-woven fabrics 291
      for knitted and stretch-woven fabrics 257
      for lace, sequined and beaded fabrics 273
      for latex, neoprene and plastics 297
      for leather and fur 285
      for napped and pile fabrics 279
      for transparent and semi-transparent fabrics 265
neoprene, working with 294–299
netting 100
non-woven fabrics, working with 290–293
notches, marking 53
notching 135

organza and organdie 100
overcast finish 124
overcast stitch 117
overlock stitch 23
overlocked finish 122

padding 101, 102
patch pockets 178–179
pattern cutting layouts 48–51, 302–303
   for all-over/repeat pattern 303
   for bias-cut fabrics 310
   for border pattern 303
   for checks 51, 302
   for denim 250
   for diagonal patterns 303
   for felted and non-woven fabrics 290–291
   for knitted and stretch-woven fabrics 256–257

for lace, sequined and beaded fabrics 272–273
for latex, neoprene and plastics 296–297
for leather and fur 284–285
for napped and pile fabrics 278
for placement design 51
for stripes 51, 303
for transparent and semi-transparent fabrics
    264–265
pattern master 18
pattern types 300–301
patterned fabrics, working with 300–305
patterns, working with 34–35
    adapting a block 35
    symbols 36–38
pile fabric, working with 276–281
pin hem 206
pin marking 53
pinked seam allowance finish 123
pinning
    ease 131
    to match pieces 130
    seams 121
pins 11
placement design, pattern cutting layout for 51
placement points, marking 53
placket shirt, sewn on 227
plain seam 125
plain weave 60
plastic materials, working with 294–299
pleats 147–150
    striped and check fabric 305
pockets 177–191, 253
    applied pockets 178–180
    bellows pocket 180
    jet pocket 180–184
    on denim 253
    patch pockets 178–179
    pocket bag 177
    set-in pocket 181–191
    side seam pocket 190–191
    slant pocket 188–190
    welt pocket 185–187
preparing fabric 46
pressing equipment 28–29
pressing tips 29
prick stitch 115
purl merrow machine 24

quilting 101, 102

raw edge finish 124, 134
reducing bulk 135
retain stitch 133
ribbing 260
rivets 253
rouleau loops 233–234
rulers 18–19
running stitch 114

sampling 26, 34, 45, 72, 95
satin weave 60
seam allowance finishes 119, 122–124
seam allowances 39
seam types
    abutted 124, 292
    appliqué 274–275
    baby lock 266

basic 120
butted 298
flat fell 128, 266
French seam 126–127
lapped 280
plain seam 125
slot 280
welt seam 129
seams
    choosing 125
    corner 137
    curved 136
    on bias-cut fabrics 311
    on check and striped fabrics 304
    on denim 251
    on felted and non-woven fabrics 292
    on knitted and stretch-woven fabrics 258
    on lace, sequined and beaded fabrics 274–275
    on latex, neoprene and plastics 298
    on leather and fur 286
    on napped and pile fabric 280
    on transparent and semi-transparent fabrics 266
    pinning 121
    preparation 119
    problem-solving 26–27, 257, 265, 273, 279, 285,
        291, 297, 311
    semi-circular, inserting 136
    shaped 136–137
    stay-stitching 141
    taped 139–141
    trimming and reducing bulk 135
self-enclosed seams
    flat fell 128, 266
    French seam 126–127
    welt seam 129
semi-transparent fabric, working with 262–269
sequined fabric, working with 270–275
set-in pocket 181–191
sewing machine 20
    bobbins 23
    feet 22
    needles 21
        for denim 250
        for felted and non-woven fabrics 291
        for knitted and stretch-woven fabrics 257
        for lace, sequined and beaded fabrics 273
        for latex, neoprene and plastics 297
        for leather and fur 285
        for napped and pile fabrics 279
        for transparent and semi-transparent fabrics 265
    setting up 119
    stitches 23
sewing machines, specialist 24–25
    blind-stitch machine 24
    button sewing machine 25
    buttonhole and keyhole machine 24
    cover stitch machine 24
    embroidery machine 25
    leather machine 24
    purl merrow 24
    superlock 24
    twin-needle lockstitch machine 25
sewing on buttons 229
shaping techniques 155
shirring 155
shirt collar 158
shirt hem 210

side seam pocket 190–191
silk 66–67
sink stitch 133
skirt lining 213
skirt marker 19
slant pocket 188–190
sleeves 192–203
    cuffs 200–202
    kimono/batwing 192, 193
    placket and sleeve openings 196–199
    raglan 192, 193
    set-in sleeve 192, 194–195
    shirtsleeve 192
    underarm gusset 203
slipstitch 116
smocking 155
snap fasteners 83, 236
stablizing tape 93
stay-stitching 141
stitch length 121
    for denim 250
    for felted and non-woven fabrics 291
    for knitted and stretch-woven fabrics 257
    for lace, sequined and beaded fabrics 273
    for latex, neoprene and plastic 297
    for leather and fur 285
    for napped and pile fabrics 279
    for transparent and semi-transparent fabrics 265
stitch problem solving 26–27, 257, 265, 273, 279, 285,
    291, 297, 311
straight grain 44
straight waistband 165–166
stretch neckline 161–162
stretch-woven fabric, working with 254–261
stripes, pattern cutting layout for 51, 303
studio 10
superlock machine 24
supporting fabrics 91–102, 104–105
    for corsetry 104–105
    using 91, 94–99
synthetic fabric 70–71

tabs 235
tacking stitch 114
tailored waistband with zip guard 170–173
tailor's knot 113
taking body measurements 30–33
taped seams 139–141
tapes 88
textured fabric 72–73
thimble 13
thread loops 269
thread marking 54
threads 86–87
    colour matching 87
    for denim 250
    for felted and non-woven fabrics 291
    for knitted and stretch-woven fabrics 257
    for lace, sequined and beaded fabrics 273
    for latex, neoprene and plastic 297
    for leather and fur 285
    for napped and pile fabrics 279
    for transparent and semi-transparent fabrics 265
topstitching 132
    hems 205
    on denim 251
transparent fabric, working with 262–269

trimming 135
trims 90
trouser cuffs 200, 207
trouser lining 213
tucks 150
tulle 100
turned-under hem 204
twill weave 60
twin-needle lockstitch machine 25

underarm gusset 203
undergarments, supporting 103
underlining 97
    for lace, sequined and beaded fabrics 275
    for napped and pile fabrics 281
    for transparent and semi-transparent fabrics 268
underpinnings 103–109
under-pressing 245

Velcro 83, 237

waistline 165–176
    belt loops 167–168
    drawstring waistband 174
    elasticated waistband 169
    facings 175
    fastenings 176
    on denim 253
    on stretch fabric 260
    straight waistband 165–166
    tailored waistband with zip guard 170–173
waste knot 112
web bonding 93
welt pocket 185–187
welt seam 129
wool 64–65

zigzag finish 124
zips 82, 238–244
    centred 239
    concealed 244
    exposed 242–243
    fly zip 240–241, 253
    lapped 242
    open-ended 244
    shortening 238

Picture Credits

The author and publisher thank the following for images used in this book. Every effort has been made to trace copyright holders but should there be any errors or omissions, the publisher would be happy to insert corrections in any subsequent editions of this book.

Akris, St.Gallen, Switzerland: p156 middle. **Alamy:** p57 top. **Bernina International AG:** p20 bottom, 24 top left. **catwalking.com:** p62 right, p64 main pic, p66 right, p70, p72 right, p76, p78 top, p91, p100 centre, p101 right, p142, p146 top, p147 left, p148 bottom right, p149 bottom right, p155 left, p156 left and right, p157, p160, p162 right, p174, p178 left, p184 left, p193 both, p197, p208 bottom right, p238 top right, p248, p262, p263, p269 right, p272 bottom, p276, p277 both, p294, p301 top left, bottom left and right, p306. **Chang Dae Machine Tech:** p74 left. **Courtesy of Baby Lock:** p24 top middle. **Fotolia.com:** p62 left, p64 top right and bottom left, p66 left. **Franklins Juki UK. Tel 01206 563955:** p20 right, p24 top right and bottom middle, p25 left and middle. **Gamma-Rapho via Getty Images:** p74 right, p100 left, p147 middle and right, p234 bottom right, p235, p301 top right, p305 bottom, p308, p310. **Getty Images:** p68 right, p103, p155 right, p207 bottom right, p254, p261 right, p270 top, p282, p283, p290 both. **Hashima:** p29 top right. **Hengye:** p72 left. **iStock:** p56, p68 left. **Museum de Kantfabriek www.museumdekantfabriek.nl:** p78 bottom. **Purl Merrow:** p24 bottom right. **Shima Seiki Mfg., Ltd:** p74 centre. **Shutterstock:** p29 bottom, p64 top left, p64 bottom right, p249 centre left. **Singer:** p25 right. **Superstock:** p57 bottom.

The following are reproduced by kind permission of www.simonarmstrong.com. Pages 90 bottom right / design by Christina Ruby Walton; 93 bottom right / design by Iryna Mikhailovich; 101 centre / design by Nadine El-Oun, BA (Hons) Fashion; 150 right / design by Ulyana Danyleyko; 270 bottom / design by Christina Ruby Walton; 289 left / design by Bradley Snowden; 295 bottom / Meagan Wellman, Graduate Collection; 300 left and 305 top / design by Ulyana Danyleyko; 309 / design by Iryna Mikhailovich.

Photographs on the following pages by James Stevens: 6–19, 20 top, 21–23, 24 inset pictures, 25 inset pictures top centre and right, 25 bottom, 27, 28 top left, 29 top left and middle row, 30, 34, 35 step 5, 43, 45, 47, 48 bottom, 52–55, 58, 61, 63, 65, 67, 69, 71, 73, 75, 77, 79, 81–89, 90 all except bottom right, 92, 93 top and bottom left, 94, 99, 100 right, 101 left, 102, 104–112, 119–124, 127, 130–131, 133–135 (page 134, Vania P. Gouveia, designer and maker), 138–141, 144, 146 bottom row, 147 top row, 148–149 step by steps, 150 all except bottom right, 151 bottom left, 152–154, 155 top centre and bottom right (Vania P. Gouveia, designer and maker), 158–159, 160 all except bottom right, 161, 162 all except right, 163–168, 170–173, 176–177, 178 all except bottom left, 179–183, 184 all except left, 185–187, 190, 194–195, 198–201, 204–206, 207 all except bottom right, 208 all except bottom right, 209–211, 214–223, 226–233, 234 all except bottom right, 236–237, 238 top left, 239–246, 249 all except centre left, 250–253, 255, 258–260, 261 left and centre, 264, 266–268, 269 left, 271, 272 top, 275, 279–280, 284, 286–288, 289 right top and bottom, 292, 295 top row, 298–299, 302, 304, 307.

Line drawings: p60 by Lily Tennant; all other illustrations by Gary Kaye.

Front cover: Photographs by James Stevens, needle illustration Shutterstock. **Back cover:** catwalking.com.

Acknowledgements

I would like to thank the following people who have made this book possible.

To the photographer, James Stevens, and the illustrator, Gary Kaye a massive thank you for your focus and hard work. They have supplied this book with beautiful images and been a steady support throughout the writing process.

A warm thank you to Valentina Elizabeth and Sue Turoff for making the beautiful sewing samples, for their dedication and support as well as patience with me.

To Anne Townley, Clare Double and Helen Rochester a big thank you for sharing my passion for this book and your support along the way. To Marie Clayton for making sense of my writing. To Evi Peroulaki thank you for your picture research and a thank you to the graphic designer Vanessa Green.

To Poppy Gooderick and Brooke Grindlay for sourcing the fabric samples.

To Simon Armstrong who kindly gave me permission to use his images of the UCA catwalk show.

To Gemma Ainsworth, Head of Design for Licensing & Atelier at Julien Macdonald for supplying me with images and garments by Julien Macdonald.

A long overdue thank you to Maria Gmuend who taught me how to sew over 28 years ago.

A special thank you goes to my dear Sam for his unconditional support, his understanding, love and encouragement, which kept me going.

A genuine thank you to the students, colleagues and friends who have supported and inspired the writing of this book through their contributions and design work. Thank you to the following individuals for giving me your time and sharing your experience with me:
Kelly Bromfield
Lavinia Cadar
Ulyana Danyleyko
Aaron Davison
Steven Dell
Nadin El-Oun
Vania Gouveia
Slavina Georgieva Kalendzhieva
Ann Leighs
John MacLachlan
Kiran Mahmood
Iryna Mikhailovich
Moira Owusu
Bradley Snowden
Toni Tester
Christina Ruby Walton
Meagan Wellman